臺灣第一領事館
洋人、打狗、英國領事館

The Story of
the British Consulate
at Takow, Formosa

David Charles Oakley / 著

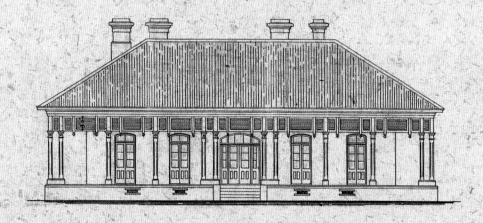

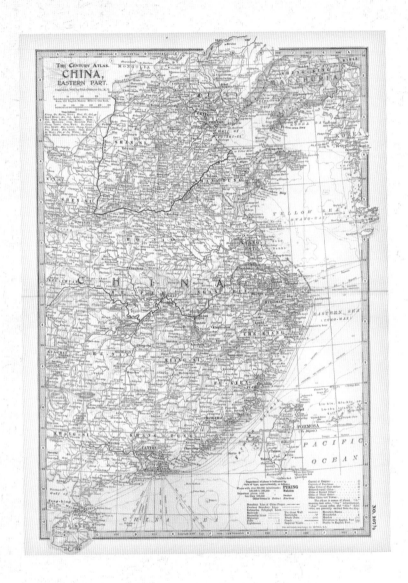

中國東部地圖：
1898年中國東部地圖，顯示中國省份與城市舊名，包含通商口岸，臺灣與日本之一部分。
（取自作者個人收藏之世紀地圖集，版權所有，翻印必究）

China, Eastern Part :
1898 Map of the eastern part of China, showing the old names of the Chinese provinces and cities, including the Treaty Ports, with Formosa then part of Japan.

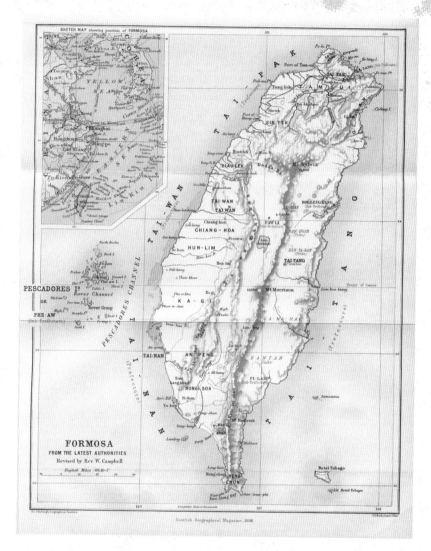

福爾摩沙地圖：
1896年福爾摩沙地圖被雷・威廉・坎培爾〔Rev. William Campbell〕定名爲「福爾摩沙島：她的過去與未來」，
本圖出現於蘇格蘭地理誌 12 期。
（來自皇家蘇格蘭地理學會之慷慨授權，版權所有，翻印必究）

Formosa Map：
1896 Map of Formosa that accompanied the article entitled The island of Formosa: Its past and future by Rev. William Campbell,
that appeared in The Scottish Geographical Magazine, Volume 12, Issue 8, 1896, facing page 398.
(By kind permission of the Royal Scottish Geographical Society. All rights reserved)

目錄
Contents

Chapter One 第1章	**打狗英國領事館在旗後設立的經過** *Setting up of British Consulate at Takow and on Chihou*

Chapter
Six

第**6**章

日本統治臺灣時期的打狗領事館
The Takow Consulate under the Japanese Rule of Formosa

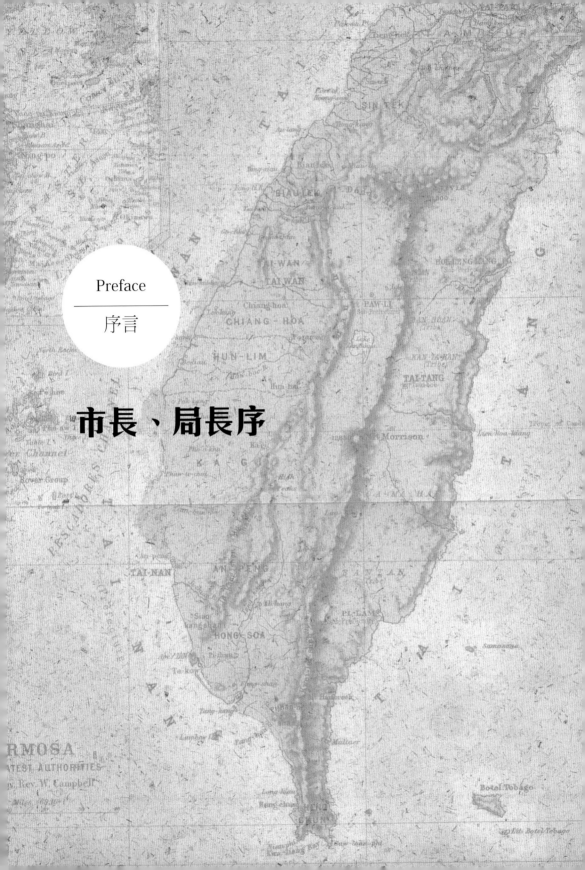

市長、局長序

市長序

追尋海洋城市的出發點——打狗英國領事館

每個精采的城市必定會有一個動人的身世，不論是古文明裡匯聚了權力與富裕的首善之都，或是在大航海時代中崛起，充滿了多元異族氛圍的殖民港口，甚或是鄉野平疇間慵懶閒適的小村鎮，細心去挖掘，我們會看到一個個都是在時間的魔法裡，將無機質的空間轉化成獨具特色的、有機的人文地景。縣市合併後，高雄迎來了一個快速蛻變發展的時代。到處都有新的建設，新的氣象，在新的經貿擘畫與城市美學中，我們並沒有忘記舊日的高雄，歷史的高雄。

打狗英國領事館文化園區，就是在探索高雄的歷史、省思新與舊的交替，與體驗全球在地文化的思維下，本市所推動的嘗試之一。因爲清朝末年打狗開港，洋商嗅到商貿契機而紛至沓來，於是英國外交部與工部決定在打狗設立並建造領事館與官邸以維護商業利益，正是因爲現代化早期商人在全球走透透競逐利益，打狗哨船頭山上與水邊才出現這兩棟迴廊紅磚相映怡人的英式印度殖民地風格洋樓。然而時移勢轉，打狗港的成長因內港淤積與臺灣發展重心北移而頓挫，於是領事館與官邸因之荒廢傾頹，日本接手後轉爲其他用途，它的歷史身世不只沒於荒煙蔓草，更爲世人記憶所遺忘。

現在，文化局選擇在領事辦公處修復完成之際出版《臺灣第一領事館》這本書，可說具有歷史里程碑的意義。在本市放眼全球進行海洋布局，積極建設高雄成爲東亞新灣區的當下，本書呈顯的打狗英國領事館來龍去脈，不啻是高雄市本身所具備的全球歷史之在地根源：從打狗到高雄，從糖貿易到重工業、加工出口區，以至於今日的文化觀光及數位、美學產業，這本書爲我們大家驕傲自豪的城市提供了一種歷史向度，爲未來的航圖提供了參考座標。藉由建築的修復再生，再加上歷史的爬梳與建構，遊人訪客得以親炙領事館過去的輝煌、困頓以及種種風華，在溫潤潮濕的南風吹拂中，聽它喃喃述說著這個城市的過往與未來。

歡迎所有來到高雄的訪客都能親自到哨船頭來看看由登山步道連結山上山下的這兩棟洋樓，拜訪在海風中新生的打狗英國領事館文化園區。也推薦每位喜愛高雄海洋氣息與文化的朋友，都能親自一讀此書，探究打狗英國領事館的身世秘密。

高雄市市長

陳　菊

局長序
你所不知道的打狗英國領事館

曾經，哨船頭山上佇立著一棟「英國領事館」，由英商天利洋行興建，經歷歲月的摧殘與風雨的肆虐而凋敝，於1986年完成修復，今天它已經成為遊人如織的重要觀光景點。

但是，如今藉由《臺灣第一領事館——洋人、打狗、英國領事館》這本書的出版，我們要告訴大家，上面的歷史敘述其實是一段美麗的錯誤。

本書作者David Charles Oakley為旅居高雄的英國人，多年以前就開始對居高臨下俯視高雄港、被訛傳為打狗英國領事館的洋樓建築感到興趣。他利用閒暇之虞以私人身分進行調查研究，從英國國家檔案局、大英圖書館，以及世界各地許多私人收藏家手中蒐集到不少珍貴的第一手史料，抽絲剝繭後所得的結論居然推翻了一直以來的常識，宛如推理小說中的安樂椅名偵探（armchair detectives）一般，還原了「真假打狗英國領事館事件」的真相。

在本書問世之前，無論是專家亦或是一般人士，咸認為山上的建築是1865年由英商天利洋行所興建的，並於1867年租與英國為領事館。其實，英國首任駐臺領事郇

和確實曾在1866年向天利洋行租下一棟洋房，以作為領事辦公處及官邸，但它的位置在旗後（今旗津），而非哨船頭山上。山上領事館建築真正的身分是官邸，是領事官員跟家眷的住所，並非辦公室；當我們確認這是英國官員與他的夫人、子女的起居空間後，我們應該就能了解山上建築底層絕不會設有犯人牢房。

那麼，真正的領事辦公處到底在哪？如果你/妳順著今天的鼓山區哨船街一路往西子灣方向前行，來到哨船街7號，望右手邊就可見到日治時期的高雄州水產試驗場，也就是驗明正身、剛剛修復完成的打狗英國領事館辦公處。有關1879年前後打狗領事館的興沒沿革，本書透過珍貴的檔案文件及私人收藏的老照片，詳盡而清楚的交代了這段滄海桑田、物換星移的歷史。

除了釐清領事館本身的身世之外，本書更難得之處在於讓讀者一窺打狗的盛衰更迭與全球歷史的潮流趨向是如何息息相關。打狗，也就是今天的高雄，很早之前就已經呈現了一種全球性格與多元風貌。在清末開港前後，打狗就已經緊密地鑲嵌在資本主義世界體系的全球網絡之中，外商、水手、買辦、領事官員、傳教士（通常也是醫生）、

非亞洲來的僕役、在地的漢族與原住民等形形色色的族群在此匯聚，交換著商品、技術、知識、信仰，甚至是血緣。透過這本書，我們可以更清晰地掌握旗後、哨船頭地區作爲西方文化傳入打狗之門戶，當中的歷史細節，不只有各家洋行的宅院、倉庫、碼頭，跟著作者David的指引，你還可以發現打狗英國領事館文化園區裡有一條花崗岩砌成的唐納森步道，以及隱身於今日臺灣港務公司後方、登山街60巷山坡民宅群內外國人墓園的蛛絲馬跡。讀完此書，讀者們何不找個晴朗午後，來一場哨船頭歷史街道漫步，順道拜訪新成立的打狗領事館文化園區，享受穿越過去與現在的樂趣。

本書能夠付梓，除了得歸功於作者David Charles Oakley十幾年來埋首檔案文獻寫成此書之外，更要感謝高雄漢王洲際飯店董事長林富男先生。若非他獨具慧眼私費印製了David的書稿，讓世人初次了解打狗領事館背後的歷史謎團，文化局也不會有機會與作者接洽，邀請作者重新修訂校正原稿，以嶄新的面目出版這本《臺灣第一領事館》，林富男先生的夫人史育女女士也慷慨應允讓本局使用她的中文譯稿來進行修改；本人藉此機會對兩位玉成本書的義舉衷心致謝。

高雄市文化局局長

Preface

序言

推薦序

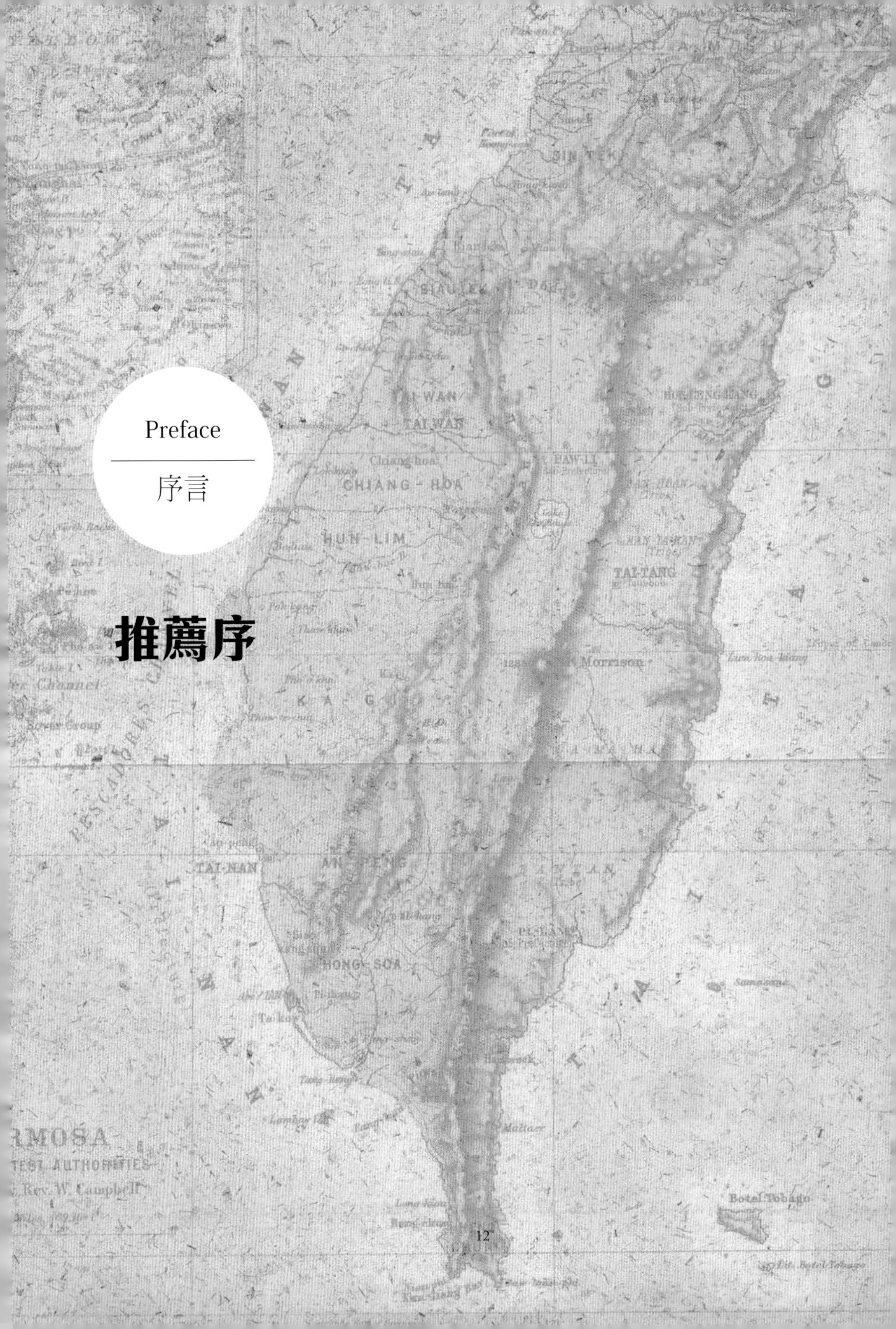

推薦序　吳密察

　　高雄西子灣國立中山大學校門口左方小山丘上的英國領事官邸及山腳下的英國領事館，經過整修之後，現在每天都吸引爲數眾多的遊客前來參觀。但是來到此地參觀的遊客，相信鮮少有人對於這兩棟建築之歷史，及曾經在此活動之西洋人的過往，和這兩棟建築所承載之十九世紀末年、二十世紀初年之當年歷史，有比較深刻的認識與理解。

　　如今英國人David Charles Oakley充分利用英國國家檔案館的史料和私人照片，爲我們重建了這兩棟建築的歷史，和在此生活、辦公之歷任英國領事的生平。這是一本既有堅實的史料基礎，文筆又平實流暢易讀的好作品。

國立臺灣大學歷史系兼任教授

吳密察

2013年9月

推薦序　翁佳音

　　好書。作者利用罕見的英國檔案文獻，在釐清長久被誤解的打狗英國領事館、領事官邸正確位置與產權移轉外，又向讀者述說這些建築物所收容的大時代外交和商業公司鬥爭往事，以及港市外國人小社會百年來之歷史影像，十分精彩。

中央研究院 臺灣史研究所

翁佳音

2013年9月

推薦序　林會承

　　在世紀交替之際，透過清末洋人古地圖及日清移交清冊圖文，部分臺灣史學界及文化界的學者專家對於高雄哨船頭山腳下的英國領事館及山頭上的英國領事官邸有初步的理解，高雄市政府並於2005年將長久被忽視的山腳下館舍指定爲市定古蹟。龔李夢哲先生以一己之力，窮數年功夫，蒐集整理保存於英國各處的打狗英國領事館相關檔案、圖面與老照片，用以重建館舍遷移、土地租賃、營建歷程、以及使用後至出售爲止的詳細事蹟，書中許多史料與圖像均爲首次披露，對於瞭解臺灣早期外交關係及高雄早期歷史演變有顯著的幫助。

國立臺北藝術大學 文化資源學院院長
建築與文化資產研究所教授兼所長

2013年9月

推薦序　　李乾朗

　　十九世紀的臺灣在世界地圖上突然明亮起來，當時隨著中國開放五口貿易的商業機會，臺灣的茶葉、蔗糖與樟腦引起西洋人的興趣，其中英國商人與傳教士來臺較多，分別在北部的基隆、滬尾與南部的安平、打狗設立據點。外人與清廷訂立條約，獲准可在岸上租地建屋。位於打狗港口哨船頭山丘上的洋樓即是英國人所建，連同山丘下的領事館建物至今猶存，可謂是臺灣保存年代最早的洋樓，在臺灣與西洋關係史上具有很高的歷史文化意義。

　　我在1985年曾有機會對哨船頭山丘上的領事館官邸作過測繪調查，當時建築物因受颱風侵襲而大部分牆體倒塌，後來由內政部、文化建設委員會（今文化部）及高雄市政府合作編列經費修復，除了無法復原的北段建築外，其餘大多復原了。近幾年來，又有幾次修葺，朝活化再利用方向發展，並且成為高雄市最具吸引力的景點之一。可是對其始建的來龍去脈，卻始終眾說紛紜，只知其為臺灣年代最早英式洋樓，但正確年代與變革卻撲朔迷離。

　　閱讀David Charles Oakley先生近日所出版的《臺灣第一領事館》，我覺得這是一本考證極為深入，論述詳細，且內容很吸引人的書，具有極高的學術研究水準。作者龔李夢哲為英國人，他本著好奇的動機，耗費多年時間努力蒐集史料考證，終於確定山丘上的英國領事館住宅初建於1878年前後，其紅磚、木材的來源與建築設計師也明朗化了。紅磚來自福建廈門一帶，木材來自南洋、設計者為上海的英國工部辦公室。並且原始構想與後來實現的成果有一些差異，顯示建築設計經過臺灣與上海兩方面的多次討論才定案，在建造過程中也遇到承包商失信的困境。落成之後，又經過幾度修改，才成為今天我們所見的形貌。這些曲折的真實故事，透過龔李夢哲先生的詳細考證，並由相關人物的後代提供照片，使人讀起來如置身於百年前的打狗碼頭邊。過去有人誤以為由洋行轉變為領事館用途，此書提出許多論證，有正本清源之貢獻！

　　這本書除了詳細的年代考證之外，相關人士書信來往的內容也很重要，也釐清了一

些歷史的真相，並且還附上許多珍貴的圖片
與人物照片，對研究百年前臺灣與英國關係
史而言，是很有份量的著作。我覺得這是很
新鮮而生動的一種歷史研究法，更是值得關
心臺灣古建築的人士仔細閱讀的好書。

國立臺灣藝術大學
藝術管理與文化政策研究所教授

李乾朗

2013年9月

作者序
Author's Preface

多年以前，我初至高雄，有人告訴我這個英國人，市內有一座老英國洋樓喔！當我好奇詢問它的坐落處，人們回答它就在港口景致最佳的所在。不用多久，我就發現在哨船頭的山丘上，俯視著港口的那棟老舊的英國領事館建築。

有兩件事讓我覺得驚訝與不解。首先，我覺得把領事館設置在一座山丘上這件事相當奇怪，這麼做豈不是要所有的訪客與洽公者都得在熱帶惱人的氣候中爬上這段陡峭的步道才能一訪領事館。其次，在1866年一處臺灣西岸的小村落中，這棟建築似乎蓋得非常巨大壯觀，頗不協調。

於是，我開始利用閒暇之餘，自己負擔所需的研究開銷，逐漸地調查隱藏在這棟屹立在高雄港入口山丘上，於落日餘暉中閃閃發亮，壯麗的紅磚建築身後那段被湮沒的曲折故事。

到了2004年，我終於能以山丘上這棟建築為主題，在臺灣文獻這本期刊上發表一篇小論文。我的這篇文章解釋了山丘上這棟建築事實上是1878年時，蓋來給高雄（打狗）此地的領事官員做為官邸的。更重要的是，我發現更早之前，英國領事辦公處首先是設立在高雄港南邊的旗後，一直到1879年才搬遷到對岸的哨船頭山丘旁，正好位於領事官邸之下。

我的這篇文章沒有在高雄文史圈裡激起任何的漣漪與討論的興趣。事實上，當時文史圈的共識已經形成，咸認為山丘上的建築最初的建造者是天利洋行，建於1865年，並在1867年之後設立為英國領事館。尤有甚者，許多人聲稱這棟哨船頭山上的建築裡，就在領事腳下以及他的家庭使用的餐廳底下，設有一間牢房。

夠了，是時候做一次更加嚴謹的全面性調查了。

於是，再一次從頭開始，每一件證據都清楚地顯示了哨船頭山丘上的英國領事官邸乃是建於1878/79年這段期間，而山下的英國領事辦公處也在同一時間建造。更重要的是，我發現英國領事辦公處（也就是山下的館舍）才設有所謂的牢房，也就是說山上的官邸從不曾有過囚禁犯人的地方。

　　身為此書作者，我之所以將這個有關高雄英國領事館舍的嚴謹研究公諸於世，乃是希望遊人訪客能藉此認識到舊時英國領事館物業的真正歷史。

　　在此，我要特別感謝林富男先生他對此書出版的協助，此外，更要由衷謝謝史育女女士，她負責我英文原稿的中譯，在過程中非常地辛勞並保持耐心；謝謝兩位的支持。

龔李夢哲，2007年於高雄

§

Many years ago, when I first came to Kaohsiung, I was told of an old British building that stood in the city. When I asked where it was, I was told to look for the finest site in the port. It did not take long to find the the old British consular building overlooking the harbour from its site upon the hill at Shao-chuan-tou.

At that time the old consular building had just been restored, and in front of building stood a stone stele. This stele eloquently expressed China's shame over the Opium Wars and proclaimed that the building had been constructed in 1866. Moreover, the stele announced, this was the first Western-style building (洋樓) on Taiwan and the first foreign consulate built on Taiwan.

Two things had struck me then. Firstly, it seemed strange to build a consulate on top of a hill, thereby obliging all visitors to climb up the steep steps in such a tropical clime. Secondly, it seemed a very grand building to have constucted in what was, in 1866, little more than a village upon the West coast of Taiwan.

Using my own time and spending my own money, I gradually began to investigate the story behind the splendid red-bricked building that shone on the hill above the entrance to Kaohsiung Harbour as the sun set.

By 2004, I was able to publish an article in Taiwan Historica upon the subject of the building on the hill. My article showed how the building on the hill had, in fact, been built as a Residence for the Consular Officer at Kaohsiung in 1878. Furthermore, I found that the British Consular Offices had earlier been on the southern side of the Kaohsiung Harbour, at Chihou, until they had been moved across to sit at the base of the Shao-chuan-tou hill, below the Consular Residence, in 1879.

My article caused scarcely a ripple of interest on the surface of Kaohsiung history. Indeed, by now the consensus was that the building on the hill had originally been built by McPhail & Co in 1865, and occupied by the British Consulate in 1867.

Moreover, claims were being made that there had been a gaol beneath the very feet of the Consul and his family as they sat in their dining room upon the hill at Shao-chuan-tou.

The time had come to make an even more thorough investigation.

Once again, every piece of evidence showed that the British Consular Residence on the hill at Shao-chuan-tou was built in 1878/79 and that the British Consular Offices below were also built in 1878/79. Furthermore, it was discovered that the British Consular Offices contained the Gaol, and there was never any prison up at the Residence.

The author offers this meticulous research to show the history of the British consular buildings at Kaohsiung, in the hope that visitors will learn the factual history of the old British Consular properties.

Especial thanks are due to Frank Lin for his support on the publication of this work, and, above all, to Annie Shih for her diligence and patience in translating my English text.

David Oakley, Kaohsiung, 2007.

打狗英國領事館
在旗後設立的經過

Setting up of British Consulate
at Takow and on Kiau

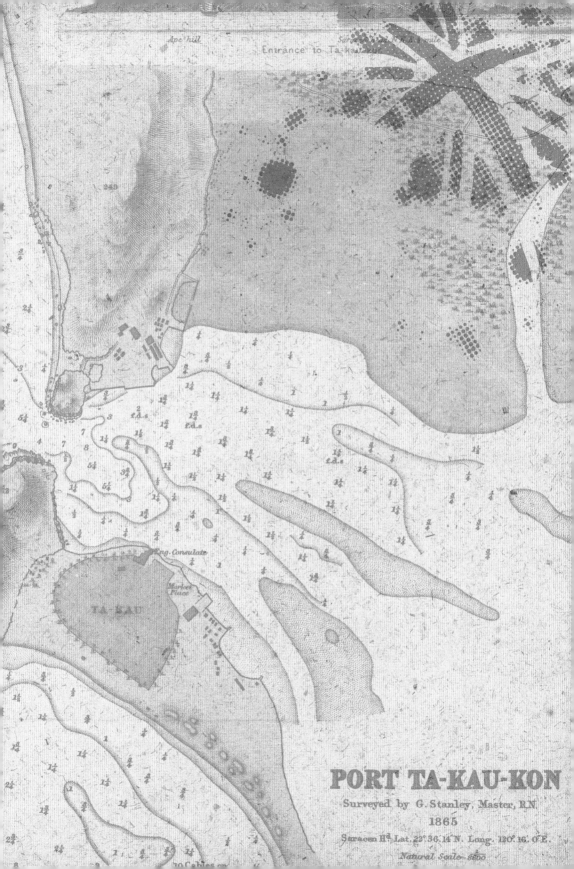

Ape hill

Entrance to Ta-kau-kon

Eng. Consulate

Market Place

TA-KAU

PORT TA-KAU-KON

Surveyed by G. Stanley, Master, R.N.

1865

Saracen Hd. Lat. 22°.36′.14″ N. Long. 120°.16′.0″ E.

Natural Scale 8600

Introduction
緒論

　　本書述說的是有關1878年英國領事館在打狗（如今我們稱之爲高雄）設立的故事；關於那些設計、建造它，以及1925年它被賣出之前曾經居住於內的人們，所交織成的點點滴滴。英國領事館包含了兩棟建築，由花崗岩及磚塊所築成的步道串連在一起。在哨船頭山上，俯瞰著臺灣海峽，矗立著的是領事官邸，或是稱作領事公館。沿階而下，建於哨船頭街上大清皇家海關（臺灣關）旁的是英國領事處，這個地點相當方便，因爲領事館每天需要透過船務辦公室與海關公務往返。除了船務辦公室外，領事館並設有領事辦公室、領事法庭，以及領事牢房。

§

This is the story of the 1878 construction of the British Consulate [英國領事館] at Takow (now known as Kaohsiung); those who planned and built it; and those who lived there until its sale in 1925. The British Consulate consists of two buildings linked by a flight of granite and brick steps. On the hill at Shao-chuan-tou [哨船頭], overlooking the Taiwan Strait, stands the Consular Residence [領事官邸], or Consul's house. Down the steps are built the Consular Offices [領事處] conveniently situated beside the Custom House of the Imperial Maritime Customs [臺灣關] at Shao-chuan-tou with whom the Consulate needed to transact on a daily basis through the Consular Shipping Office [領事船務辦公室]. The Consular Offices also housed the Consul's Office [領事辦公室], the Consular Court [領事法庭] and the Consular Gaol [領事牢房].

Early Days
打狗英國領事館設立之前

　　西元1861年7月，新上任的英國駐臺灣（福建省治下）副領事官〔British Vice Consul〕郇和〔Robert Swinhoe，如圖1-1，又譯羅伯・史溫侯，生態文獻譯斯文豪氏〕乘著的皇家庫克號〔Cockchafer〕軍艦，因受西南季風的影響，無法在臺灣府〔Taiwan-foo，今臺南〕上岸，轉而在打狗港〔Takow Harbour〕登陸。他奉命在臺灣設置一個領事館，雖然我們從文獻上無法釐清此"臺灣"指的是臺灣府〔當時臺灣的首府，今臺南〕或臺灣島，即外國人稱之為福爾摩沙之地。登陸後，郇和接著乘轎由打狗北上臺灣府，於1861年7月29日在那兒設立了第一個英國駐福爾摩沙領事辦公處。當時，這個辦公處在體制上是一個英國副領事館，名義上隸屬於福建省福州〔Foochow〕的英國領事館，公事上郇和必須直接對福州領事負責。[1]

　　郇和很快就發現臺灣府城的外國貿易數量很少，主要是因為在缺乏屏障的安平港裝卸船貨並不方便，外國船隻偏好有礁岩屏障的打狗港。然而當時滿清官方尚未開放打狗港進行對外貿易，郇和旋即在1861年12月遷至更北方的淡水，他相信那裡有更大量的國際貿易聚集。1862年5月，郇和的健康狀況因不適應當時淡水與福爾摩沙嚴酷的生活環境而明顯地惡化，使得他必須倉促返回英國，把他的領事助理〔Consular Assistant〕布老雲〔George Compigné Parker Braune：又譯喬治・布勞・康皮內・帕克：柏卓技〕單獨留在淡水接管領事館業務。郇和歸國養病近二年，遲至1864年1月才回到淡水述職，當時孤獨無助的布老雲健康幾乎已完全崩潰；事實上，1864年5月16日，布老雲在赴江蘇鎮江〔Chinkiang〕就任代理領事官〔Acting Consul〕新職的旅程途中，因心臟病再次復發而病死於北京。同年8月，郇和被召回臺灣南部重新設一個副領事館，但這次地點在打狗而非臺灣府（譯注：即臺南），因為此時官方已正式開放打狗港進行對外貿易，就在大清皇家海關在該地設立分關不久之後。[2]

MR. ROBERT SWINHOE.

圖 1-1：郇和
郇和（1836-1877），英國副領事，1865年之後升為領事，於1861年至1873年任職福爾摩沙。
（來自哈佛大學比較動物學博物館之恩尼斯特圖書館收藏，由恩尼斯特圖書館授權使用。版權所有，翻印必究）

Image 1-1：Robert Swinhoe
Robert Swinhoe (1836-1877), British Vice-Consul, promoted to Consul after 1865, to Formosa from 1861 until 1873. Ibis, Vol. II, 1908, Jubilee Supplement, Ninth Series.

§

In July 1861 the newly appointed British Vice-Consul [副領事官] for the Fuchien [福建] prefecture of Taiwan, Robert Swinhoe [郇和], arrived aboard H.M.S. Cockchafer at Takow [打狗] after the south-west monsoon had prevented him from landing at Taiwan-foo [臺灣府]. He was under instructions to set up a 'Taiwan' Consulate, though it was never clear whether 'Taiwan' meant Taiwan-foo (the capital, now Tainan [臺南]) or the island of Taiwan [臺灣], known to foreigners as Formosa. Swinhoe then proceeded by palanquin up from Takow to Taiwan-foo where he established the first British Consular office on Formosa on 29 July 1861. At this time the office was a British Vice-Consulate [英國副領事館] nominally under the British Consulate [英國領事館] at Foochow [福州] to whom Swinhoe should report in the first instance.[1]

Swinhoe soon discovered that little foreign trade was conducted at the prefectural capital of Taiwan-foo due to the difficulties of unloading and loading ships anchored in the unprotected roadstead at its port of Anping [安平], and that foreign ships preferred Takow, with its sheltered lagoon, as a port. At this time Takow was not officially open to foreign trade, so in December 1861 Swinhoe moved further north to Tamsui [淡水] where he believed more foreign trade was transacted. In May 1862, with his health apparently so weakened by the conditions at Tamsui and the rigours of living on Formosa, Swinhoe returned precipitately to England, leaving his Consular Assistant [副繙譯官], George Compigné Parker Braune [布老雲], alone ailing, and in charge. Swinhoe delayed his return to Tamsui for nearly two full years until January 1864, by which time the marooned Braune's health had collapsed almost completely; indeed, though reassigned away from his wretched housing conditions at Tamsui, Braune was to die of a second heart attack at Peking on 16 May 1864 without proceeding to his new post as Acting Consul at Chinkiang [鎮江]. In August 1864, Swinhoe was ordered back to the south of Taiwan to re-establish the British Vice-Consulate, but this time it would be not at Taiwan-foo but at Takow which had now been officially opened to foreign trade following the establishment of a branch of the Imperial Maritime Customs [大清皇家海關].[2]

Ternate
三葉號收容船

郇和在1864年末返回打狗,很快地在11月7日就把副領事館旗掛在英政府向寶順洋行〔Dent & Co's;或譯甸地洋行〕租賃的三葉號〔Ternate〕收容船上,該船是長期停靠在打狗潟湖(或稱內港)的除役船隻,英國副領事館在此船辦公約有六個月之久。[3]

1865年2月4日,郇和被升任駐臺總領事,如此一來,他的地位才能和地方道臺〔Tao-t'ai〕或巡撫〔Circuit Intendant〕平等對話,巡撫是清朝派臺高階官員,必須向福建省的長官負責,因爲臺灣當時仍屬福建省轄下。因爲郇和的升官,打狗的外交館舍從(他升職)那一天起成爲英國駐臺灣的第一個正式領事館,正式對英國派駐北京大臣〔the British Minister〕直接負責,儘管實質上郇和自1861年上任後就一直如此。[4]英國駐京大臣的官職全銜是大英欽差駐劄中華便宜行事大臣,但在書信與對話中,稱呼他英國駐京大臣就足夠了。

在三葉號上度過六個月顚簸不適的船上公務生活後,1865年5月,郇和在旗後的潟湖岸邊租了一棟兩層樓的中式房子。我們或可揣測他此時正準備在對岸打水灣〔Freshwater Creek〕哨船頭〔Shao-chuan-tou〕剛租來的土地上,建造一個適合居住作息的領事館官邸。[5]

§

Swinhoe arrived back in Takow in late 1864 and promptly hoisted his flag on 7 November to set up the British Vice-Consulate in quarters chartered for 6 months by the British government on board Dent & Co's [寶順洋行] receiving ship the Ternate which was moored in the Lagoon, or Inner Harbour. [3]

On 4 February 1865 Swinhoe was appointed as full Consul [領事官] to Taiwan, principally so that he could converse on an equal footing with the local Tao-t'ai [道臺], or Circuit Intendant [巡撫], who was the senior Ching official reporting from the Prefecture of Taiwan to the Governor of Fuchien Province [福建省] of which Taiwan was then a part. As a result of Swinhoe's promotion, the diplomatic establishment at Takow became the first British Consulate [英國領事館] on Formosa at that date of 4 February 1865 and now officially reported to the British Minister [駐京大臣] at Peking, although in practice Swinhoe had done so since his original appointment in 1861. The British Minister's full title was Envoy Extraordinary and Minister Plenipotentiary to Imperial China [大英欽差駐劄中華 便宜行事大臣], but in correspondence and conversation the title British Minister sufficed. [4]

In May 1865, after enduring six uncomfortable months on the Ternate, Swinhoe rented a two-storey Chinese house on the Lagoon shore. One can surmise that this was in preparation for the construction of a fitting Consular residence on the recently-leased site at Freshwater Creek [打水灣], Shao-chuan-tou [哨船頭]. [5]

Freshwater Creek
打水灣

　　早在1864年11月郇和剛返回打狗時，就透過當地一位名叫孫可觀〔Sun Kho-kwan〕的仲介，取得一塊哨船頭土地的永久租賃權〔permanent lease〕。在權狀的原件上，這塊土地被描述爲「位於打水灣哨船頭」，其南邊面對著潟湖。在1864年時，土地是以郇和個人的名字承租的，後來上任的領事有雅芝 [Archer Rotch Hewlett]注意到這件事，於是在1878年5月31日（光緒4年4月30日），以英國工部主任委員的名義重新簽訂了一份永久租賃權合約，並於1878年10月25日正式向工部登記在案。時至今日，因潟湖北岸長期的泥沙淤積與填海造地，這塊土地目前已經離海岸很遠，隱退到目前臨海二路〔Lin-hai 2nd Road〕高雄港務局〔Kaohsiung Harbour Bureau〕建築的後方。[6]

　　大英駐中國公使拉塞福·阿禮國爵士〔Sir Rutherford Alcock〕曾在1867年來到打狗視察，他呈給倫敦外交部的報告裡曾描述打水灣的土地「非常適合做爲墓地來使用，但一點也不適合做其他用途。」同行的威廉·克里斯曼少校〔Major William Crossman〕也在他自己1867年的報告中提及此地「離（打狗的）小型商業聚落太遠了。」因爲如此，在打水灣一地建造領事館的官方許可就被擱置下來。在他呈給外交部的報告中，阿禮國另外提到他已經「授權⋯⋯給代理領事官（賈祿）可以將這塊土地送給打狗的外國人小社群，當作是英國政府爲在當地設立外國人墓園所盡的一點心意，不過前提是他們願意自己支付墓園設立的其他花費開銷，並負起後續管理維護之責。」在阿禮國視察完畢離開打狗之後，代理領事官賈祿更明白地向打狗的外國人說明：「在向公使大人（阿禮國）陳述了我們覺得這個港口迫切需要一個像樣且適合的墓園後，我被命令來轉告我們這個群體，拉塞福·阿禮國爵士已經準備好要向女王陛下的政府建議，將在打狗這裡被稱作領事館預定地的土地當作贈禮送給他們，前提是這個地方必須被妥善維護，並在墓園內蓋一座小的追思禮拜堂。」[7]

　　由此可知，雖然打水灣這塊地在英國外交部文件中一直被稱爲「領事館區」

〔Consular plot〕，但實際上從沒用來建過任何的領事館或居所。而且，在這個時期，在潟湖北岸或哨船頭也沒有任何其他土地被購買來做為領事館使用的記錄。

曾經有好幾年，打水灣這塊地是住在旗後〔Kiau〕的領事館人員日常清潔用水的來源地，因為在旗後當地的飲用水不僅含鹽分過高，也被污染了，這正是因為那裡的墳地與住家混雜在一起。在1871年後，另一個諷刺的事實發生了，恰恰應了阿禮國爵士對打水灣這塊土地的預言，有一部份打水灣土地真的成了打狗的外國人墓園。現今，這個墓園仍在那裡，就位於現在的高雄市鼓山區登山街60巷，雖幾乎已全部荒廢，被人們所遺忘，但不可抹滅的是，這裡曾是福爾摩沙最古早的英國領事館預定地。[8]

雖然在打水灣建館的計畫胎死腹中，不過位於潟湖南面，當時打狗主要貿易集散地的旗後，倒是有兩個地點相繼成為領事館設立的場所。

§

Upon his arrival at Takow in November 1864, Swinhoe, acting through an agent named Sun Kho-kwan [孫可觀], had obtained the permanent lease [永久租賃權] of a plot of land at Shao-chuan-tou. This land is described in the original Deed as being 'situated at Freshwater Creek [打水灣], Shaou-chuen-tow' with the Lagoon to the south, in otherwords, the land lay on the northern side of Takow Lagoon. In 1864 the site had been leased in Swinhoe's own name, a fact that did not escape Consul Archer Rotch Hewlett [有雅芝], who obtained a new Deed of Lease in Perpetuity in the name of H.M. First Commissioner of Works on 31 May 1878 [光緒4年4月30日], which he registered on 25 October 1878 . Today, the site lies far from the shore, being hidden behind the Kaohsiung Harbour Bureau building on Lin-hai 2nd Road [臨海二路], due to silting and land reclamation on the north shore of the Lagoon. [6]

The British Minister to China, Sir Rutherford Alcock [阿禮國], reporting on a subsequent inspection trip to Takow in 1867, was to describe the Freshwater Creek site to the Foreign Office [外交部] in London as being suitable 'for a convenient cemetery but fit for little else'. The site was further referred to by the accompanying Major William Crossman [克里斯曼] in his own 1867 report as being 'far removed from the quarter where the small business [at Takow] is carried on'. Official permission for the construction of a Consulate at the Freshwater Creek site was withheld. Alcock added in his Foreign Office report that he had 'authorised ⋯ the Acting Consul [Charles Carroll] to offer it to the small community as the Government's contribution to a cemetery if they chose to undertake all farther expenses to make it fit for the purpose and maintain it in good order'. After the departure of Alcock, Acting Consul Carroll elucidated further to the foreign community that 'having pointed out to H. M. Minister [Alcock] the want experienced at this port of a proper and fitting burial ground, has been directed to inform the Community that Sir Rutherford Alcock is prepared to recommend Her Majesty's Government to cede as a gift to them the piece of ground known as the Consular Site on the Takao side, on condition that the place shall be kept in decent order and a small mortuary chapel built therein'. [7]

Thus the Freshwater Creek site, though often referred to as the 'Consular plot' in British Foreign Office documents, was never used to build a Consulate or Consular residence. Nor was any other Consular site purchased at this time on the North, or Shao-chuan-tou, side of the Lagoon.

he Freshwater Creek site did at least serve for some years as the source of clean water for the Consular community at Chihou, or, in Hokkien, Kîau, [旗後], where the water was not only brackish but also polluted, not least as a result of the graves being intermingled with the dwellings. Thus another irony exists in the fact that after 1871, in line with Alcock's prophetic words, a part of the Freshwater Creek site became the Foreign Cemetery at Takow. The Cemetery is still there in Lane 60, Teng-shan Street, Ku-shan District, Kaohsiung City [高雄市鼓山區登山街60巷] and, though vastly ruined and neglected, has the distinction of being the oldest British Consular site on Formosa.[8]

There are, however, two other Consular sites that have come to light at Chihou, on the South side of the Lagoon where the main trade at Takow was then carried out.

Swinhoe's House
郇和的房子

　　第一個旗後領事館設立的場所，就是在1865年5月三葉號收容船租約期滿後，郇和在旗後陸地入住的第一個房子。

　　在一份1880年的土地權狀中，記錄了李察〔Li Chai〕這個人在「1865或1866年」曾釋出旗後一塊土地的永久租賃權，「在這塊土地上爲大英臣民郇和建造房子，地點就在潟湖岸邊的旗後村莊內」。唯恐這塊土地被誤認不在旗後，權狀上還詳述了該地點東接德記洋行〔Tait & Co's〕的倉庫，西鄰（福建）海關〔Haikuan〕的土地邊界，……北邊臨接潟湖。」郇和於1877年不幸早逝，到了1880年，應他的遺孀克莉絲汀娜‧郇和〔Christina Swinhoe〕的要求，這塊土地的永久租賃權才轉讓給怡記洋行〔Elles & Co〕的傑美笙‧艾理士〔Jamieson Elles〕。到了1883年，由於怡記洋行面臨財務困境，又把永久租賃權讓給德記洋行。[9]

　　入住後不久，郇和馬上就對當地稠密的住宅環境與擁擠的居住空間不甚滿意，就在1865年8月30日，窘迫不安的郇和曾寫信給當時駐北京代理公使威妥瑪〔Thomas Wade，又譯爲湯瑪斯‧威妥瑪〕反應此事。因爲郇和已經不再是一個單身漢住在打狗，他有一個新組成的家庭，包括他將近臨盆的妻子克莉絲汀娜，正期待著他們的第三個孩子出世；除此之外，還有在1865年7月22日上任加入領事館人員行列的助理領事官倭妥瑪〔Thomas Watters，又譯湯瑪斯‧倭妥瑪〕。況且房東李察在建物中還保留約四分之一的空間給自己使用，郇和得以使用的空間相當地擁擠。就在這樣窘迫的環境中，他「以欣賞的心情注意到一棟新建築的完工」，就位於他住處的附近，由天利洋行〔McPhail & Co〕雇用廈門〔Amoy〕的工匠，使用廈門建材所蓋的，他在信中說這棟房子是「這裡第一棟堅固且蓋得很好的房子。」[10]

　　英國皇家海軍在1865年初夏曾經對福爾摩沙海岸進行測繪，其中有一艘皇家多佛號〔HMS Dove〕測量艦，繪製了一份很詳細的打狗港地圖〔海事圖2376號，如圖1-2所示〕。皇家多佛號的艦長史坦利〔G Stanley〕曾經送過一份打狗港地圖副本給打狗領事館。這張地圖不僅把上面提到的天利洋行新房子的地理位置標示得很精確,也把旗後領事館兼郇和家的位置清楚地顯示出來。[11]

在書信中,郇和急切地懇求威妥瑪公使,如果不能永久租賃,至少也准許他租下天利洋行的新房子。

1866年5月初,當郇和的住所還權充領事館時,有位庫斯伯特‧柯林伍德〔Cuthbert Collingwood〕先生來訪,在他的記錄中曾記載有一位「副領事官」—據推測可能是倭妥瑪—住在領事館裡。在1866年5月6日到10日這段期間,柯林伍德,繪了一幅水彩畫,描繪了「由領事館眺望打狗港(位於福爾摩沙西南方)入口」的景觀〔Entrance to Harbour Ta-kau (S W Formosa) from the Consulate〕(這段說明寫在畫的左下角),因為他英文姓名的縮寫出現在畫的右下角,所以我們推測他是此畫作者。這幅美麗的圖畫,如圖1-3所示,現今收藏於臺南的臺灣歷史博物館,它是在領事館(譯注:指郇和位於旗後的住處)的陽台上取景畫成的,畫中可以很明顯地看到陽台的一小部份結構,以及朝西北方向望去的景觀,可看到(打狗)港灣入口與老碉堡。我們可以由剛提到過的打狗港地圖來對照,要看到這個景觀,只能從郇和房子的陽臺望出去,而不是從天利洋行的新房子。因此,雖然天利洋行的房子在1866年5月1日已經租出去了,但是我們可以知道領事館並未馬上遷移到那裡。[12]

根據皇家多佛號的測量圖,加上柯林伍德水彩畫中描繪出的地形細節來判斷,郇和的房子非常可能矗立在目前高雄市旗津區海岸路19巷的西邊。

§

The first Consular site at Chihou is the house that Swinhoe lived in after his charter on the Ternate finished in May 1865.

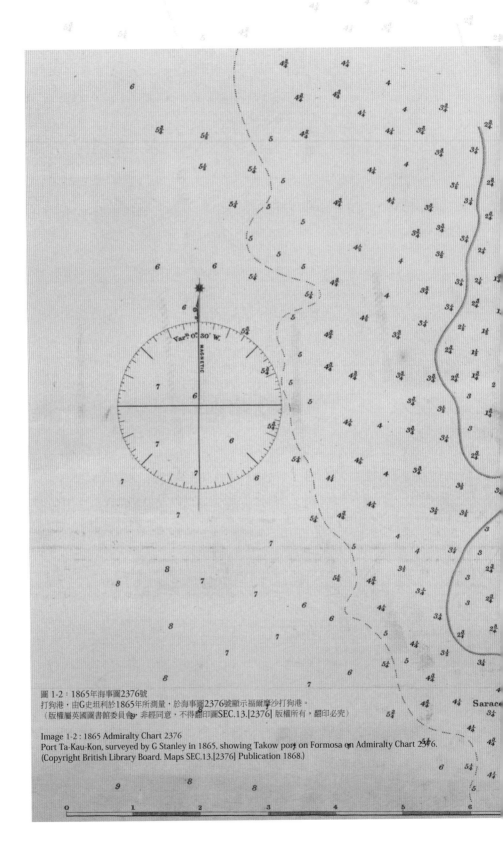

圖 1-2：1865年海事圖2376號
打狗港，由G史坦利於1865年所測量，於海事圖2376號顯示福爾摩沙打狗港。
（版權屬英國圖書館委員會，非經同意，不得翻印圖SEC.13.[2376] 版權所有，翻印必究）

Image 1-2 : 1865 Admiralty Chart 2376
Port Ta-Kau-Kon, surveyed by G Stanley in 1865, showing Takow port on Formosa on Admiralty Chart 2376.
(Copyright British Library Board. Maps SEC.13.[2376] Publication 1868.)

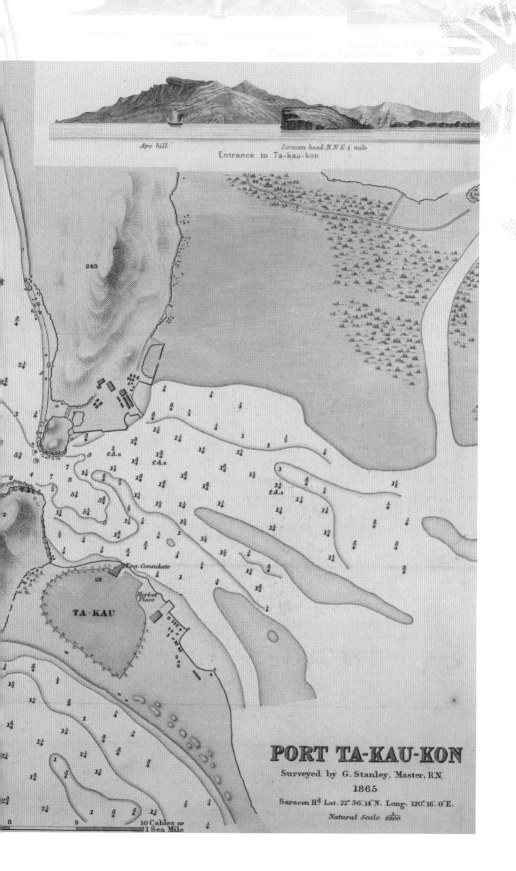

Ape hill

Saracen head N.N.E. ¼ mile

Entrance to Ta-kau-kon

Eng. Consulate

Market Place

TA-KAU

PORT TA-KAU-KON

Surveyed by G. Stanley, Master, R.N.

1865

Saracen H⁴ Lat. 22°.36′.14″N. Long. 120°.16′. 0″E.

Natural Scale ⅟₅₈₀₀

10 Cables or
1 Sea Mile

圖 1-3：1866柯林伍德水彩畫
水彩標題為〈由領事館望向（福爾摩沙西南）打狗港入口〉，來自庫斯伯特‧柯林伍德（Cuthbert Collingwood與其他人在皇家海軍巨蛇座軍艦上所繪水彩系列之一，當時軍艦自1866年5月6日起拜訪打狗 "3或4天"。
（來自臺灣歷史博物館之慷慨授權，版權所有，翻印必究）

Image 1-3 : 1866 Collingwood Watercolour
Watercolour Painting captioned 'Entrance to Harbour Takau (S W Formosa) from the Consulate'. One of a series of watercolours painted by Cuthbert Collingwood and others aboard H.M.S. Serpent, which visited Takow from 6 May 1866 for 'three or four days'.
(By permission of the National Museum of Taiwan History, Tainan. All rights reserved)

An 1880 land deed records the permanent leasing of a plot at Chihou in '1865 or 1866' by Li Chai [李察], who 'built thereon for the British subject Swinhoe, the said site being situated in the village of Chi-how on the shore of the lagoon'. Lest there be any mistake that this was not at Chihou, the deed also states that the site was bounded 'East by Tait & Co's [德記洋行] godown lot, West by the [Fuchien] Haikuan's [福建海關] boundaries, ... and North by the Lagoon'. Clearly, when the Inner Harbour, or Lagoon, is to the north the location must be at Chihou. It was not until 1880, following the early death of Swinhoe in 1877 and at the request of his widow Christina, that this permanent lease was transferred to Jamieson Elles of Elles & Co [怡記洋行]. In 1883, as Elles & Co ran into financial difficulties, the permanent lease was again transferred on to Tait & Co. [9]

Soon dissatisfied with both the crowded location and cramped condition of his Chihou house, the restless Swinhoe had written on 30 August 1865 to Thomas Francis Wade [湯瑪斯 · 法蘭西斯 · 威妥瑪], the Chargé d'Affaires [署欽差大臣], or acting British Minister, at Peking. Swinhoe was no longer alone at Takow: he had been joined by his young family including his heavily pregnant wife, Christina, who was expecting their third child; moreover, he had also recently been joined by Thomas Watters [倭妥瑪], his Consular Assistant, on 22 July 1865. As the landlord, Li Chai, had retained a quarter of the building for his own use, Swinhoe was sorely cramped for space. He had therefore "watched with satisfaction the completion of a new house" on a nearby site by McPhail & Co [天利行], using materials and workmen from Amoy [廈門], which he goes on to describe as "the first strong well-built house here". [10]

In the early summer of 1865, the British Royal Navy had made a survey of the coast of Formosa and one surveying vessel, H.M.S. Dove, had made a detailed chart of Takow harbour, which is shown as 1865 Admiralty Chart 2376 (Image 1-2). The commander of H.M.S. Dove, G. Stanley, had given a copy of the Takow Chart to the Consulate Office, and this Chart helps not only to identify the precise location of the McPhail building, but also clearly marks the location of the 'English Consulate', which was Swinhoe's house.[11]

Swinhoe earnestly implored Thomas Wade for permission to rent, if not permanently lease, the new McPhail building.

Swinhoe's house, when still the Consulate, was visited in early May 1866 by Cuthbert Collingwood, who records a 'vice consul', presumably Thomas Watters, as being in residence. Between the sixth and tenth of May 1866 Cuthbert Collingwood, whose initials appear on the bottom right border of the painting, painted a watercolour showing the 'Entrance to Harbour Ta-kau (S W Formosa) from the Consulate', as written on the left of the bottom border. This beautiful picture, shown as Image 1-3 and now in the National Museum of Taiwan History in Tainan, was painted from the Consulate verandah and shows part of a substantial structure, as well as the view towards the north-west showing the harbour entrance and old fort. It can be seen from the Takow Chart that this view could only be depicted from the Swinhoe house and not from the McPhail building. Thus, although the McPhail building was apparently leased on 1 May 1866, the Consulate was not transferred there immediately. [12]

By use of the H.M.S. Dove survey chart and the topographical details shown in the Collingwood watercolour, it is possible to locate Swinhoe's house as having stood on the west side of Lane 19, Hai-an Road, Chihou [高雄市旗津區海岸路19巷].

McPhail Building
天利洋行的建築物

　　1864年11月〔清同治3年〕，天利洋行曾有一塊在旗後的地被永久出租，這份永久租賃權狀契約如圖1-4所示，之所以可以證明這塊地在旗後，證據在於契約上明白地寫著此地北方為潟湖。[13]

　　郇和在1865年8月30日寫給威妥瑪公使的信中如此描述這棟向天利洋行租的屋子：「由一個頗具規模的碼頭通往一個長長的庭園，從石階拾級而上，就能進入玄關大廳，左右兩翼有兩個長的大房間，形狀是66尺×20尺。右邊的大房間可當辦公室用，它的後面有兩個小房間可充當僕人的待命準備室。左邊的大房間及其後面的小隔間分別給巡補房、監獄及儲藏室。」[14]

　　郇和對這棟房子的描述，可以跟另一個人在後來對打狗領事館的描述做對照，這是在代理領事官雅妥瑪〔Thomas Adkins，又譯湯瑪斯·艾勒勤〕1867年11月28日寫的一封致其父親的家書中被發現。他是這麼寫的：

　　領事館是這裡最好的房子，但是您若是看到我使用的空間，一定會覺得莞爾。這房子的設計極為簡單，房子的低層原來計畫做為倉庫使用，有一條相當寬的走道在中間，兩側各有三個大房間。樓上的格局設計重覆樓下的。屋子前面有一座陽臺。地板鋪著瓷磚，窗戶很小，配上拙劣的石灰粉刷牆面。這裡的天氣尚未冷到必須生火取暖的程度，所以屋子內沒有設計壁爐，我猜想這房子在夏天應該會很涼快—畢竟這才是最重要的一點。我前面窗外的景色相當宜人，靠近我前庭園牆的就是港口—它的入口剛好在我視野的極左側，兩邊分別是柴山與薩拉森山頭〔Hill of Apes and Saracen's head，或稱薩拉森頭，即今之旗後山〕。[15]

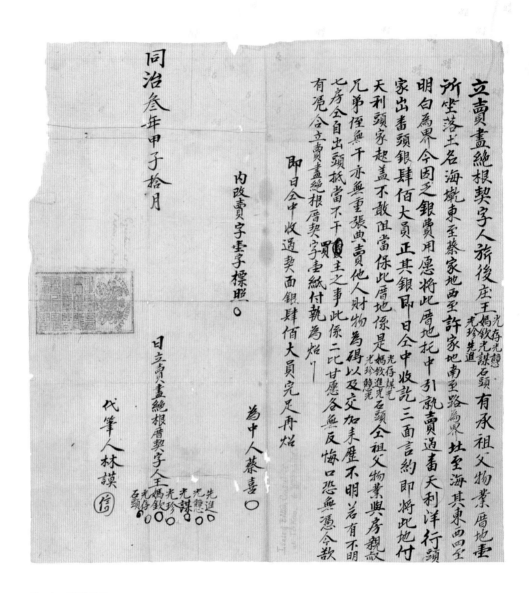

圖 1-4：天利洋行地契
天利洋行地契，其上標示"英國打狗領事館租約"。

Image 1-4 : McPhail Deed
Deed of Lease in Perpetuity granted in November 1864 to Messrs McPhail & Co, and marked 'Lease of British Consulate at Takao'.

很明顯地，雅妥瑪於1867年信中所描述的房子與郇和於1865年談的是同一棟建築。此外，雅妥瑪提到打狗港入口呈現在建築物最左邊，這點毋庸置疑地證明了此棟領事館建築是位於旗後。

根據郇和提到的1865年所測繪的海事圖（圖1-2），以及他與雅妥瑪對領事館建築的描述，我們可以精確地判斷天利洋行這棟洋樓的位置。在1865年海事圖上顯示的一座大建築物，位於第一個陸上領事館東南方（在地圖上，首處陸上領事館被標為英國領事館「Eng. Consulate」），也位於「市集」的右邊，可以推定它就是後來成為第二個旗後領事館的那棟天利洋行建築物。我們可以看到第二個旗後領事館正好在天后宮〔Tien-hou Temple〕的東邊，而在一張署名「打狗─德辛·韋伯」〔Ta-kau. – Dessin de Th. Weber〕的版畫中，我們可以看到這棟洋樓，如圖1-5所示。在此畫中，我們可以清楚地看到一棟長形的白色建築，它的二樓有五個窗戶一字排開，正好在版畫中心處的右邊，它就是第二個在陸上的旗後領事館。

我們可用一張1866年4月代理領事官倭妥瑪的手繪地圖：〔見圖1-6〕來更進一步地確認第二個旗後領事館的位置，這張圖的內容畫的是「臺灣府到打狗港的路徑」〔route from Taiwanfu to Takau-kon〕。此圖顯示了倭妥瑪往來臺灣府與打狗領事館時所行經的路線。圖中，我們很清楚地看到領事館是位在潟湖南方的旗後。此外，從倭妥瑪在1866年4月25日為這趟旅程寫下的註解中，我們得到以下這段清楚的解釋：

打狗被潟湖隔為兩個村落，北邊正是大家口中的打狗，南邊則是旗後或被當地人以閩南話稱「Kiao」。雖說（打狗）那邊的環境已開始改善，但居民仍然不多，旗後的聚落建於沙洲上，包括有領事館與主要外國人聚落，以及約上千個中國人居住……。我到臺灣府旅程的第一部份是走水路，因為我們必須從旗後越過潟湖……。[16]

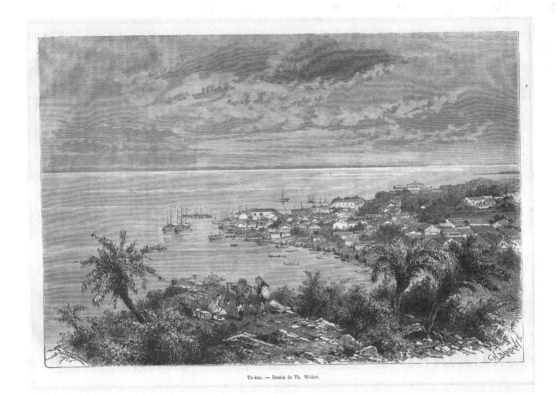

Ta-kao. — Dessin de Th. Weber.

圖 1-5：打狗—德辛・韋伯
湯瑪士・韋伯根據一張約翰湯森於1871年拍攝之旗後照片所雕製版畫，出現在法國插畫雜誌《天主教會》上。 這棟天利建築物，後來成為
英國領事館，被認為是長型建築， 有五個窗戶沿著二樓一字排開， 就在韋伯版畫正中央的右側。
（作者私人收藏，版權所有，翻印必究）

Image 1-5：Ta-kau. – Dessin de Th. Weber.
Engraving by Thomas Weber after an 1871 photograph of Chihou by John Thomson, which appeared in the French illustrated
magazine Les Mission Catholiques. The McPhail building, in 1871 being used as the British Consulate, is presumed to be the long
pale building, with five windows running along its second storey, just to the right of the centre of Weber's engraving.

倭妥瑪提到旗後位於一塊沙洲上的資料能讓我們瞭解更多領事館的歷史。另一個稍後到任，一樣代理老是缺席的郇和的代理領事官固威林〔William Marsh Cooper，又譯威廉‧馬許‧固威林〕曾在1869年9月對駐京公使阿禮國抱怨道：「住在一塊富鹽分的沙洲上，使我們無法像駐在其它港口一般，利用從家鄉帶來的種子種植蔬菜。」這個證據又一次顯示了在旗後的天利洋行建築至少在1869年仍然被用來當做英國領事館，而以前的歷史研究者卻認為這時領事館早已經在哨船頭〔Shao-chuan-tou〕山丘上了。[17]

郇和領事在1865年的信中更寫著，雖然天利洋行比較希望簽一個長的租約，「他們也同意用16000銀元或鷹洋〔Mexican Silver Dollar，譯注：當時的國際通貨—墨西哥銀元〕的價格把土地連同建築物的全部權利售出。」[18]

在倭妥瑪之後、雅妥瑪之前，同樣也到打狗代理郇和職務的代理領事官賈祿〔Charles Carroll，又譯查爾斯‧賈祿〕，在任內巧遇天利洋行戲劇性的破產事件（即使一再缺席，郇和仍然保有領事一職，直到1873年才卸任）。賈祿在1867年4月21日寫信催促拉塞福‧阿禮國爵士馬上把天利洋行這棟建築物買下，他提到英國政府以每年2400元的租金跟天利簽訂五年租約，並有權在任何時候以16000銀元把此棟建築買下，在信中也提到當時租約才過了一年。這意味著英國領事館是從1866年4月開始租用這棟建築。賈祿信中更進一步提到天利洋行的買辦盜取超過30000銀元的現金後逃走的事。他期待購買這棟建築的事能在阿禮國爵士與克里斯曼少校來訪前做出決定。[19]

1867年，英國政府曾派遣一位皇家工程師—克里斯曼少校—前往亞洲各地測量已經用的或尚在計畫中的領事館用地。在1867年7月，在視察完畢後克里斯曼所寫的報告中，忠實地留下這段紀錄：領事館是向一家「數週前破產，於是名下產業必須被出售的公司」，以「每年2400銀元承租五年的合約，並附帶隨時可用16000銀元買下之選擇權」的條件租來：「……　（雖然）這房子本身並非那麼適合當領事館，原因在於上層的房間只能用來做為居住空間。」發生在1867年5月、留下清楚紀錄的天利洋行破產事件，以及克里斯曼提及的購買金額，或更正確地說永久租賃天利這棟建築所須花費的數目正是郇和寫給威妥瑪大使信中所說的價格這兩件事，再一次證明這兩人所指的領事館乃是天利洋行的這棟位於旗後的建築。[20]

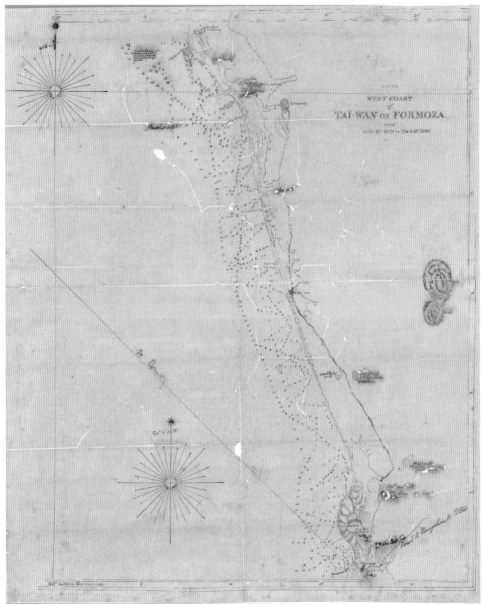

圖 1-6：瓦特斯（倭妥瑪）地圖：打狗到臺南
地圖，取自湯瑪士·瓦特斯於1866年4月25日之快信，顯示從臺南到位於旗後之打狗英國領事館的路徑。
（版權屬於英國政府，文件MPK 1/478，版權所有，翻印必究）

Image 1-6 : Watters' Map: Ta-kau-Kon to Taiwan-foo
Map, extracted from Thomas Watters' despatch of 25 April 1866, showing the route from Taiwan-foo to the British Consulate at 'Ta-Kau-Kon', which is located at Kî u (Chihou).

1868年8月，邊阿蘭〔Allan Weatherhead Bain，又譯艾倫‧威勒赫‧班〕受無償債能力的天利產業委託，把天利洋行這棟建築以一個未公開的價格賣給德記洋行〔Tait & Co〕，一般相信交易價格正好償還了天利對德記尚未清償的債務。有趣的是，英國外交部檔案附件裡的一份中文地契（圖1-4）上被做了註記：「天利洋行租打狗英國領事館這塊地的租約。」[21]

在天利洋行發生破產事件的期間，天利洋行事實上正負責運輸打狗領事館的公款資金，這是因為天利洋行有定期的商船往返打狗、香港以及廈門之間，也因為理應負責運送領事館官方信件與公款的英國皇家海軍砲艦只能不定期偶爾到訪。天利洋行攜款潛逃的買辦所帶走的三萬銀元中，包含了由香港帶過來、數目可觀的領事館公款。英國政府發現他們此時在事實上擁有天利的這棟建築，又同時被一個五年租約綁到1871年春天；眼下天利已經破產，而且又因為丟失公款而欠政府一筆款項，原本英國政府可以行使選擇權買下這棟建築，但他們斷然拒絕了，而是要求天利洋行用每年2400銀元的租金來抵償因丟失公款而欠英國政府的債務。雖然阿禮國記錄這筆債款僅有3000銀元，不過正確數目似乎更多，因為1868年整年租金仍可以使用欠債相抵，英國政府不用額外付錢。[22]

諷刺的是，盡心盡力促成這樁租賃案的郇和可能從未入住過旗後天利洋行建築。上頭派他去中國大陸主理廈門領事館，他於1866年3月1日離開，而反觀天利洋行這棟建築，很明顯地直到1866年5月1日才租出去，而真正有人進駐使用大約是5月中之後了[23]

這棟建築物本身，在1868年德記洋行〔Tait & Co〕買下之後，仍舊作為英國領事館使用。一直到1879年春天，領事館的租約才終於結束，此時哨船頭山丘上新建的領事館官邸也正式交給英國領事館使用。之後，天利洋行的這棟建築在1884年6月被賣給陳順和〔Chen Shun-ho〕。

§

McPhail & Co had permanently leased a plot of land in November 1864 (Ching Tung-chih

3rd year [同治 3 年]) at Chihou, as proven by the reference to the Lagoon being to the North given in the Deed of Lease in Perpetuity, shown as Image 1-4. [13]

In his 30 August 1865 despatch to Thomas Wade, Swinhoe described the building thus: "On entering the hall by stone steps from the long courtyard which is approached from the harbour by a substantial jetty, you find on the right and left two long boarded rooms 66 X 20 feet. The right of these would serve for the offices and the two small rooms beyond on the same side for the servants' waiting rooms. The large room on the left of the hall and the two small rooms in its rear would serve for the constable, the jail, and public storerooms". [14]

Swinhoe's description can be compared with a later description of the British Consulate at Takow found in a letter from Acting Consul Thomas Adkins [雅安瑪] to his father, dated 28 November 1867. Adkins wrote as follows:

The Consulate is the best house here. But you would smile could you see my quarters. The plan of the house is simple in the extreme. The lower storey was originally intended for a wharehouse [sic]. It consists of a broad passage flanked on either side by 3 large rooms. These rooms and passage are reproduced in the upper story. There is a Verandah in front. The floors are of tiles, the windows are small & the walls are very badly whitewashed. The weather is not cold enough for fires so that fireplaces are not required. I should think the house will be cool in the summer - that after all is the main point. The outlook from my front windows is rather nice. Close to the wall of my front Court is the harbor - its entrance just visible on the extreme left flanked by the Hill of Apes and Saracen's head. [15]

Clearly, the building that Adkins describes in 1867 is the same one that Swinhoe had described in 1865. Moreover, Adkins' description of the harbour entrance being to the extreme left of the building indisputably places the Consulate on Chihou.

From the 1865 Admiralty Chart (see Image 1-2) mentioned by Swinhoe and from the descriptions of the building by Swinhoe and Adkins, it is possible to fix the location of the McPhail building precisely. The large building shown on the 1865 Admiralty Chart to the south east of the first on-shore Consulate, which is marked on the chart as 'Eng. Consulate'), and to the right of the 'Market Place', can be presumed to be the McPhail building which became the second Chihou Consulate. The second Chihou Consulate appears to have been located just to the east of the T'ien-hou Temple [天后宮], and can be seen in the engraving entitled 'Ta-kau. – Dessin de Th. Weber', shown as Image 1-5. This second on-shore Consulate surely appears as the long pale building, with five windows running along its second storey, just to the right of the centre of the engraving.

Further confirmation of the location of the Consulate being at Chihou can be found on a sketch map (see Image 1-6) drawn in April 1866 by Acting Consul Thomas Watters showing the route from Taiwan-foo to 'Takau-kon [打狗港]'. This map shows the route taken by Watters when travelling between Taiwan-foo and the Consulate, which is clearly shown to be on the southern side of the Lagoon at Chihou. Moreover, Watters' accompanying description of this journey, dated 25 April 1866, contains the following clear explanation:

> *Takow is divided by the lagoon into two villages, the Northern being Takow proper and the Southern Chihou or as the natives name it Kiao. ... [The Takow] side, though at present beginning to improve is still very thinly peopled. Kiao, which is built on a sand-spit, contains the Consulate and the principal foreign hongs besides about one thousand Chinese. ...... The first part of the journey to Taiwanfoo is by water for we must cross the lagoon from Kiao ....*[16]

The reference Watters makes to a 'sand-spit' is instructive. A later Acting Consul, William Marsh Cooper [固威林], similarly substituting for the ever-absent Consul Robert Swinhoe, in September 1869 complained abour the cost of living to the British Minister, Sir Rutherford

Alcock, that: "Living on a spit of salt sand, we are unable to raise vegetables from home seed as at other ports." This again shows that the McPhail building on Chihou continued to be used as the British Consulate at least until 1869, and long past the time when previous researchers have claimed that the Consulate was located on the hill at Shao-chuan-tou. [17]

Consul Swinhoe, in his 1865 letter, had further written that, although McPhail & Co preferred a long lease, 'they have consented to sell all right and title to house and ground for the sum of Sixteen Thousand [Mexican Silver] Dollars [$16,000]'. [18]

Acting Consul Charles Carroll [賈祿], again standing in officiating for Swinhoe who however remained Consul until 1873, and who followed Thomas Watters and preceded Thomas Adkins, was in charge of the British Consulate at Takow at the time of McPhail & Co's spectacular bankruptcy in 1867. Charles Carroll urged upon Sir Rutherford Alcock the immediate purchase of the building in a letter dated 21 April 1867, describing the terms upon which the British Government held the house as a lease for five years at $2,400 a year with the option of purchase at any time for $16,000, and stated that only one year of the lease had expired. This implies that the building was originally leased in April 1866. Carroll further reported that McPhail's compradore had absconded with over $30,000 in cash. Acting Consul Carroll looked forward to a decision on this matter before the expected visit by Alcock and Major William Crossman. [19]

In 1867 the British government had sent Major William Crossman, a Royal Engineer, to survey the British Consular sites, either existing or proposed, across Asia. In Crossman's subsequent July 1867 report, it is duly recorded that the Consul had leased "premises at $2,400 per annum for five years certain, with the option of purchase at any time for the sum of $16,000" from a firm that "has become bankrupt within the last few weeks, and the property will have to be sold ⋯ [although] the house itself is not very suitable, as the upper rooms only can be made available for a dwelling house". The well-documented collapse of McPhail & Co's business in May 1867, and the fact that the purchase, or more correctly the permanent lease, option amount is precisely as proposed by Swinhoe in his letter to Wade, again lead to the conclusion that the building is the McPhail building at Chihou. [20]

The McPhail building was sold by Allan Weatherhead Bain [邊阿蘭], on behalf of the insolvent McPhail estate, to Tait & Co [德記洋行] in August 1868 for an undisclosed amount but believed to be as settlement of McPhail & Co's outstanding debt to Tait & Co. Interestingly, the Chinese land deed (see Image 1-4) attached to the British Foreign Office file has been annotated 'Lease of British Consulate at Takao (to?) McPhail & Co'. [21]

At the time of McPhail & Co's collapse, the company was in charge of the transport and supply of Consular Funds, due to the company's frequent voyages to Hongkong and Amoy and the very infrequent visits of the Royal Naval gunboats that were supposed to carry the official Consular mails and funds. The Consular Funds were required for the payment of Consular wages and sundry expenses. The absconding compradore of McPhail & Co had taken the sum of $30,000 in company funds, which included a considerable amount of the Consular Funds that they had been entrusted to carry across from Hongkong. Finding themselves in possession of the McPhail building and bound by a five year lease that was not scheduled to expire until Spring 1871, the British government, rejecting the option of purchasing the building outright, decided to settle with the estate by writing down their debt by $2,400 each year in lieu of rental. Although Alcock recorded this debt as being only $3,000, it appears to have been more as the entire year's rental for 1868 was still offset against the amount owing. [22]

Ironically, Swinhoe probably never lived in the McPhail building that he had so earnestly requested. He was ordered to the mainland to officiate at the Amoy Consulate and left on 1 March 1866, whereas the McPhail building was apparently not leased until 1 May 1866 and not occupied until well into May 1866.

As for the building itself, after passing into the hands of Tait & Co in 1868, the McPhail building continued to be used as the British Consulate until the end of April 1879, when the lease was finally terminated and the newly-built Consular Residence on the hill at Shao-chuan-tou was handed over to the British Consul. The building was subsequently sold to Chen Shun-ho [陳順和] in June 1884. [23]

Swinhoe's Departure
郇和的離去

　　如同上述記錄所示，郇和懷孕的妻子克莉絲汀娜，此外可能還有他們的兩個年輕小女兒，在1865年左右已來到打狗與他會合，就在位於打狗潟湖南岸的第一個英國領事館啓用之後。克莉絲汀娜·郇和當時是打狗唯一的一位外國女性，正在懷孕的她運氣相當不錯，因爲馬雅各醫師〔Dr James Laidlaw Maxwell：又譯詹姆斯·雷德勞·麥斯威爾醫師〕正好在1865年5月29日抵達打狗。郇和的第三個孩子在同年10月2日於打狗出生，取名爲羅伯·阿弗烈·郇和〔Robert Alfred Swinhoe〕，據說是從荷蘭統治時期以後，第一個在臺灣出生的西方嬰兒。在克莉絲汀娜產後休息完後，郇和在馬雅各醫師的建議下，陪伴他的妻子兒女一行於11月到廈門，克莉絲汀娜的父母施敦力夫婦〔Stronachs〕是廈門傳教士，他的姊妹卡洛琳·郇和嫁給柏威林〔William Henry Pedder：又譯威廉·亨利·佩德〕，他是廈門當地的領事。雖然郇和在12月時回到打狗，1866年2月底他又馬上被派回廈門，留下倭妥瑪由3月1日起開始管理臺灣領事館的業務。[24]

　　1866年4月4日，郇和被任命爲廈門的代理領事官，但同時仍保留英國駐福爾摩沙領事的職位。事實上，一直到1873年的9月爲止，郇和都仍然保有臺灣領事的職位，不過這中間他只回過福爾摩沙一次，而且還是很短暫地停留，時間是1869年初，爲的是要處理與樟腦貿易及傳教活動相關的事件，這些事件曾導致代理領事官約翰·吉必勳〔John Gibson〕在1868年11月時，戲劇性地採取未經上級授權的艦砲外交。[25]

§

　　As recorded above, Consul Robert Swinhoe had been joined at Takow by his pregnant wife Christina and, presumably, his two young daughters after the opening of the first British Consulate on the southern shore of the Takow Lagoon. Christina Swinhoe, as the only foreign woman, was fortunate that Dr James Laidlaw Maxwell [馬雅各] was to arrive on 29 May 1865 during her pregnancy. Swinhoe's third child, named Robert Alfred Swinhoe, was born on 2 October 1865 at Takow, reputedly the first Western birth on Taiwan since Dutch times. After Christina's confinement, Consul Swinhoe, upon the advice of Dr Maxwell, escorted his wife and children in November 1865 to Amoy, where her parents, the Stronachs, were missionaries and Robert Swinhoe's brother-in-law William Henry Pedder [柏威林], who had married his sister Caroline Swinhoe, was Consul. Although Swinhoe returned to Takow in December 1865, he was ordered back again to Amoy at the end of February 1866 leaving Watters in charge of the Taiwan Consulate from 1 March 1866. [24]

On 4 April 1866 Swinhoe was ordered to remain in Amoy as Acting Consul whilst retaining the position of British Consul to Formosa. In fact, Swinhoe was to remain the Consul for Taiwan until September 1873, though he was to return to Formosa only once, and then briefly, in early 1869 to handle problems related to the camphor trade and missionary activities, which had led to the dramatic and unauthorised use of gunboat diplomacy by Acting Consul John Gibson [吉必勳] in November 1868. [25]

Diplomatic Indifference
不變應萬變的外交態度

　　繼1868年底因艦砲外交而導致同年11月英國海軍陸戰隊奇襲並佔領安平的風暴後，英國政府決定對清廷採取懷柔態度以彌補破損的關係。發生在臺灣的暴動，包括對外國傳教士的人身攻擊、焚燬佈教所，以及圍繞著臺灣道臺梁元桂的樟腦獨賣權所發生的爭論，這一連串的紛爭與動盪讓英國人開始考慮要不要關閉臺灣領事館。1868年7月1日，代理領事官吉必勳剛剛接任代理領事官全美生〔George Jamieson〕的職位，就被梁道臺否定他的領事權力；隔天，德記洋行駐臺的經理人就被刺殺，吉必勳察覺到自己處境艱難，迫不得已使用了武力。但是，英國外交部隨即對動武這件事感到懊悔，因此下令在中國禁止使用如此挑釁的行動。考量當時的情況，英國擁有許多殖民地，為了管理不斷擴展壯大的大英帝國，已經挪不出更多資源且自顧不暇，所以沒有任何意願去醞釀與策劃滿清帝國的崩解。[26]

　　在上述的動盪之後，因為英國在中國的外交事務上打算扮演一種誠懇合作的角色，所以英政府表面上顯得很樂意來解決領事館人員對居住品質低劣的不滿，因此在臺灣府城（譯注：安平）租了一棟新房舍。1869年7月，代理領事官固威林〔Cooper〕接替了運氣不佳、任內碰上棘手問題的吉必勳，固威林也只在旗後這間「環境惡劣的領事館」待了七個月，之後就因為罹患熱病而離開臺灣。固威林試圖以回家渡假休息的名義返回英國，不過卻因為病況嚴重而在途經香港時被放下船，如此他至少可以在平靜中等待死亡來臨。事實上，固威林後來幸運地渡過難關活了下來，不過他極有可能是最後一位還試圖把領事館設在旗後的領事。實際上，之後上任的領事都是自己安住在臺灣府城，而派助理官駐守旗後。[27]

　　臺灣府城的新領事館，於1872年向許建勳租用，是棟位於府城知府衙門〔Prefect's yamen〕東牆的傳統中式建築，這個位置讓領事能與道臺有迅速即時的溝通。當1875年英國領事事務部門的阿赫伯〔Mr Herbert James Allen, 又譯赫伯特‧詹姆斯‧艾倫〕，前來府城拜訪時，在福爾摩沙南方的領事駐守處確實就在此棟中式建築裡，因為他曾描述自己當時在「環境舒適的英國領事衙門」享受過一段愉快的停留。[28]

　　1870年，英國政府考慮要關掉福爾摩沙的領事館，或者是將它降級成為隸屬於廈門領事館的副領事館。此時的外相克拉林登伯爵〔Earl of Clarendon〕想要採取駐京公使阿禮國的建議，裁撤或降級福爾摩沙領事館。然而外相卻在1870年6月27日過世，實際上就是死在他的辦公室內。同日繼任為外相者是習於緩事緩辦的格蘭維爾伯爵〔Earl of Granville〕。他馬上決定不須採取任何行動來改變現狀，不須關閉福爾摩沙領事館，也無須費事進行降級。他主導下的英國外交保持著以不變應萬變的原則，持續到1874年他的任期結束。[29]

　　這段時期所採取的互相配合、以不變應萬變的外交原則，反映在現實上就是在1871年至1875年間，幾乎沒有任何來自打狗或臺南的領事報告出現於紀錄上。[30]

　　然而，1874年後班傑明・狄士芮利〔Benjamin Disraeli〕回任首相後，英國在亞洲地區開始展現一種更為果決斷然的態度：積極確保據點來做為海軍船艦與商業汽船的加煤站：試圖阻止其他西方勢力如俄羅斯與法國、還有國力開始增強的日本，對羸弱中國的蠶食侵略。日本遠征軍在1874年為了報復原住民而登陸琅嶠灣〔Liangkiau Bay〕的事件，導致英國政府由1870年代中期之後重新燃起對福爾摩沙的興趣與重視，即便當時基隆煤礦的質與量都已經大幅降低，但還有其他重要的戰略與外交考量讓英國不能放棄臺灣。[31]

　　當時中國與大不列顛之間有好一些問題需要被釐清，其中一個就是英國臣民在中國內陸旅行與居住的權益。英國主張這是在1858年簽訂天津條約〔Treaty of Tientsin〕後英國人理當享有的權利，但卻遭中國官方強烈的質疑反對。經過一連串困難的協商，總算雙方達成協定，於是1876年9月在芝罘〔Chefoo〕簽署一個新的增定條款，是為芝罘協定〔Chefoo Convention〕。因為某些歷史上的混淆，我們事實上錯把芝罘稱為煙臺〔Yantai〕。[32]

　　駐京公使威妥瑪雖然從1876年11月到1879年6月曾離開北京回到英格蘭，但他在煙臺協定成功簽署後，得以把更多的心力轉移到行政事務上，例如福爾摩沙領事館的建造，以及選派一位自邱和1866年初離開以來，首位視事的福爾摩沙總領事。1877年11月，有雅芝

〔Archer Rotch Hewlett，又譯亞契‧羅區‧有雅芝〕被指派爲駐福爾摩沙總領事，一直以來他都在北京的英國公使館擔任威妥瑪公使的漢文副使，他很明顯地是繼12年多以前的郇和之後，第一個住在福爾摩沙的英國總領事。

從1870至1871年間，有雅芝已曾在打狗擔任約兩年之久的代理領事。1877年11月甫一抵達福爾摩沙，他很快地就著手處理這個島嶼在被忽略的這幾年中堆積如山尚未解決的問題。事實上，極有可能因爲有雅芝有著在1870年前後榮景可期的打狗擔任過代理領事官的經歷，所以才促成了1878年與1879年之間英國領事公館與領事辦公室在哨船頭興建一事。

§

Following the turmoil surrounding the use of gunboat diplomacy in late 1868 that had culminated in the storming and occupation of Anping by British marines in November, the British government decided to take a much more conciliatory attitude toward the Ching authorities. The disturbances in Taiwan, which had seen fatal attacks on foreign missionaries and the burning of foreign missions as well as disputes over the camphor monopoly rights of the Taiwan Tao-t'ai, Liang Yuan-kuei [梁元桂], the British began to consider the closure of the Taiwan Consulate. Acting Consul Gibson had taken over from Acting Consul George Jamieson on 1 July 1868 only to have his authority rejected by Tao-t'ai Liang: the following day Tait & Co's Agent on Taiwan was stabbed and Gibson found himself in an impossible position. The use of force was deplored by the British Foreign Office and led to the curbing of such provocative actions in China. The British already had their hands full and resources at full stretch in managing a sprawling empire and had no wish to precipitate the collapse of the Ching Dynasty. [26]

In their newly cooperative role in China, the British were seemingly content to meet their Consular staff's objections to sub-standard accommodation at Takow by renting a new premises in the capital of Taiwan-foo. Acting Consul Cooper, who relieved the hapless Gibson in July 1869 and who spent a mere seven months at the 'wretched consulate' before fever drove him off the island. Attempting to reach England on Home Leave, Cooper became so ill that he disembarked at Hongkong so that he might die on land in comfort. Cooper in fact survived but may well have been the last Consul to attempt to reside permanently at Chihou. Indeed, the practice soon became for the officiating Consul to reside at Taiwan-foo and his Assistant to reside at Chihou. [27]

The new British Consulate, located at Taiwan-foo, and leased in 1872 from Hsu Chien-hsun [許建勳], was a traditional Chinese building on the eastern wall of the Prefect's yamen, ensuring prompt communication with the Tao-t'ai. This was certainly the southern Consular seat in 1875 when Mr Herbert James Allen [阿赫伯] of the British Consular Service visited Taiwan-foo, as he describes his pleasant stay 'in the hospitable yamen of the British Consul'. [28]

In 1870 the British government considered either closing the Consulate on Formosa, or of making it a Vice-Consulate under the Amoy Consulate. The Foreign Minister of the time, the Earl of Clarendon, was inclined to follow the advice of Alcock, the British Minister at Peking. However, Clarendon was to die on 27 June 1870, literally in his office, and was succeeded as Foreign Minister by the dilatory Earl of Granville on the same day. Granville soon resolved that no further action should be taken on the closure or downgrading of the Formosa Consulate and remained largely indifferent to British foreign interests throughout his tenure which lasted until 1874. [29]

As a reflection of this cooperative period of indifference, virtually no Consular report emerged from either Takow or Tainan between 1871 and 1875. [30]

However, with the return of Benjamin Disraeli as Prime Minister in 1874, the British were to take a much more assertive role in Asia: securing the 'coaling stations' for the naval and mercantile steamers; and seeking to stop the encroachment of other Western powers, such as Russia and France, and of the newly powerful Japan upon a sickly China. The incursion of the Japanese punitive expeditionary force, which landed at Liangkiau Bay [琅嶠灣] in 1874, led to a reassertion of British interests in Formosa from the mid-1870s, despite the extent and quality of the Keelung coalfields having been largely discounted. [31]

Of the several questions that needed to be clarified between China and Great Britain were the rights of British subjects to travel and reside in the interior of China. This assertion of what the British considered to be a right under the 1858 Treaty of Tientsin [天津條約], was strongly disputed by the Chinese authorities. However the tenuous negotiations finally reached resolution and a new treaty revision was signed in September 1876 at the Treaty Port of Chefoo [煙臺], and known as the Chefoo Convention [煙臺協定]. Through some historical confusion Chefoo was actually named Yentai [煙臺]. [32]

Despite taking leave to England from November 1876 until June 1879, the British Minister at Peking, Sir Thomas Wade, was now able to turn his attention to more administrative matters, such as the construction of Consular buildings on Formosa and the stationing of the first Consul on the island since the departure of Swinhoe in early 1866. In November 1877, Archer Rotch Hewlett [有雅芝], who had been Wade's Assistant Chinese Secretary [漢文副使] at the British Legation [英國公使館] in Peking, was appointed Consul to Formosa and was seemingly the first British Consul to reside on the island since Swinhoe some dozen years earlier.

Hewlett had already spent nearly two years, from 1870 to 1871, at Takow as Acting Consul and, after his arrival on Formosa in November 1877, promptly set about resolving the outstanding issues on the island after the years of neglect. Indeed, it was perhaps the very fact that Hewlett had experienced Takow in its days of promise around 1870 that led to the construction of the British Consular Residence and Consular Offices at Shao-chuan-tou in 1878 and 1879.

Setting up of British Consulate at Takow and on Chihou

Notes to Chapter One
第一章註解

1. FO 228/313, Taiwan 1 & 4.

2. Coates, Patrick D., The China Consuls, Oxford University Press, 1988, pp. 319-321; Hall, Philip B., Robert Swinhoe (1836-1877) FRS, FZS, FRGS: A Victorian Naturalist in Treaty Port China, The Geographical Journal, Vol 153, No 1, March 1987, pp. 42-43; FO 228/330, Peking 87; FO 228/374, Tamsuy 11; and The Gentleman's Magazine, Vol. 217, p. 392.

3. Carrington, George W., Foreigners in Formosa, 1841-1874, Chinese Materials Center Inc., San Francisco, 1977, p. 179; and FO 228/374, Taiwan 25 & 32.

4. Lo Hui-min and Bryant H., British Diplomatic and Consular Establishments in China: 1793-1949, SMC Publishing Inc., Taipei, 1988, Vol. 2, p. 429; Mayers, William Frederick (with revisions by G. M. H. Playfair), The Chinese Government: A Manual of Chinese Titles, Categorically Arranged and Explained, with an Appendix, Kelly & Walsh, Shanghai, 1897, p. 146.

5. Coates, pp. 320 ff.

6. Permanent lease. The Ching government did not allow foreigners to purchase land outright. 'Permanent lease' or 'perpetual leases' could however be granted by the Chinese land-owner to the foreigner giving him 'the right to use' the land. Under Japanese rule, foreigners in Taiwan were able to convert such permanent leases into full ownership under (Taiwan) Ordinances Nos 3, 4 and 5 (1907). FO 678/3156; see Oakley, David C., The Foreign Cemetery at Kaohsiung, Taiwan Historica [臺灣文獻館], Vol. 56, Issue 3, 2005, pp. 265-295, p. 282.

7. FO 17/476, Legation 117, Alcock to Stanley, 20 July 1867; FO 228/505, Hewlett to Wade, Tainan 11, 16 May 1871, Enclosure 1, Carroll to Foreign Community, Consular Notification; British Parliamentary Papers [B.P.P.], Vol. 2, Consular Establishments, Irish University Press, 1971, p. 231; Oakley, David C., The Foreign Cemetery at Kaohsiung, Taiwan Historica [臺灣文獻館], Vol. 55, Issue 3, 2005, pp. 265-295, pp. 270-271.

8. B.P.P., Vol. 2, pp. 436-438, Cooper to Alcock, 26 September 1869; WORK 10/33/10, pp. 37-40, Wade to Granville, 14 July 1871, and O.W.L. to Treasury, 5 February 1881.

9. FO 678/3012; G.R.O. Death Certificate, Chelsea No. 410, Robert Swinhoe died 28 October 1877 at 33 Carlyle Square, aged 41.

10. 1871 England Census return for Chelsea, RG 10/80, Page 8, Swinhoe; FO 228/420, Swinhoe to Wade, 30 December 1865, Birth Entry for Robert Alfred Swinhoe born Takow on 2 October 1865; and FO 228/397, Takow 27, 30 August 1865.

11. FO 228/397, Takow 27.

12. Collingwood, Cuthbert, Rambles of a naturalist on the shores and waters of the China Sea, John Murray, London, 1868, pp. 38-46.

13. FO 678/3130.

14. FO 228/397, Takow 27.

15. Warwickshire County Record Office, Thomas Adkins, member of the Diplomatic Service in China: correspondence mainly addressed to his father at Milcote, 1855-79, (CR 3554). Letter from Takow, dated 28 November 1867.

16. MPK 1/478; FO 228/420, Takow 8, 1866.

17. B.P.P., Vol. 2, p. 436.

18. FO 228/397, Takow 27.

19. Pickering, William A., Pioneering in Formosa, Hurst and Blackett, London, 1898 (Reprinted by SMC Publishing, Taipei, 1993), pp. 170 ff.; WORK 10/435, Carroll to Alcock, 21 April 1867; and WORK 10/435, Carroll to Crossman, 24 April 1867.

20. B.P.P., Vol. 2, p. 231; Pickering, pp. 170 ff.

21. FO 678/3130.

22. B.P.P., Vol. 2, p. 436; FO 17/476, Legation 117.

23. WORK 10/33/10, O.W.S. to O.W.L., 4 August 1879; FO 678/3130.

24. Hall, p. 41; Lo & Bryant, p. 430.

25. Coates, p. 322; Coates, pp. 325 ff; Lo & Bryant, p. 430; Foreign Office List, Statement of Services, 1877.

26. Gordon, Leonard H. D., Taiwan and the Limits of British Power, 1868, Modern Asia Studies, 22, 2 (1988), (pp. 225-235), p. 234; FO 228/459, Gibson to Alcock, Taiwan, 4 July 1868; FO 228/459, Gibson to Alcock, Takow Office, 10 July 1868; FO 228/459, Gibson to H.M. Senior Naval Officer at Taiwan and Takow, Takow Office, 22 August 1868; FO 228/459, Gibson to Alcock, Takow Office, No. 35, 25 November 1868.

27. FO 678/3186; Coates, p. 328.

28. FO 678/3034; and Allen, Herbert J., Notes of a Journey through Formosa to Taiwanfu, Proceedings of Royal Geographical Society, Vol. 21 (1876-7), pp. 258-265.

29. Yen, Sophia Su-fei, Taiwan in China's foreign relations 1836-1874, Hamden, Conn., 1965; pp. 114-120; and WORK 10/99, Buckler to Treasury, 11 November 1874.

30. Coates, pp. 328ff; and FO 678/3034.

31. Bax, Bonham W., The Eastern Seas, London, John Murray, 1875, p. 90.

32. Pelcovits, Nathan A., Old China Hands and the Foreign Office, Octagon Books, New York, 1969, pp. 101-130.

英領館新的一頁：
英國領事館在打狗置產
以及租賃領事官邸土地

*Planning the new British Consular
properties at Takow, and Leasing
the Site for the Consular Residence*

TAKO

PLAN OF CONSULAR SITE

B.

GRAVE YARD

SHARP SLOPE

GRAVE

I, Lin Ta Sin, having on the 20th January 1877, by deed leased to H.M.'s Chief Commissioner of Wako & London in perpetuity, through Francis Julian Marshall, acting for and on his behalf, a piece of ground at Takar, I hereby declare that the ground so leased is represented on this plan as comprised within a blue line.

20   FEET = 1 INCH

Signed by the abovenamed
Lin Ta Sin in presence at
Takar the 15th day of June 1877.

Introduction
緒論

　　完成於打狗一地租賃土地事宜，使得領事館建築本體終能順利興建，這段期間關鍵的英國領事官員是有雅芝〔Archer Rotch Hewlett ，1838-1902，又譯亞契‧羅區‧修雷特〕，他是在1877年11月被指派爲領事官的。雖然名義上他是被派來福爾摩沙的第四任領事官，但實際上他是自郇和之後首位長期駐在島上的領事官。[1]

　　紀錄上顯示有雅芝是一位和藹可親且正直盡責之人，他是英格蘭米德塞克斯郡〔Middlesex〕一位富裕外科醫生的第三個兒子，在1858年以二十歲之齡，由倫敦大學國王學院的中國課程結業後，加入英國派駐中國的領事部門。他在1870年代中期擔任北京英國公使館〔the British Legation at Peking〕的助理中文秘書〔Assistant Chinese Secretary；或稱漢文副使〕一職，這不僅證明了他使用中文的能力，也使得他可以因職務之便接觸到一些重要人士，比方說駐京公使威妥瑪〔Thomas Francis Wade〕。[2]

　　有雅芝在1870年元月剛到福爾摩沙時，擔任的是代理領事官與翻譯官的工作，一直服務到1871年底，幾乎有兩年之久。正好就在他即將再次被派任到福爾摩沙之前，亦即1877年，翻譯官的職位被廢止。然而，在1840年代，英國派駐中國的領事外交工作開始時，許多領事官們缺乏執行外交事務所需的中文溝通能力，因此才徵召翻譯官來協助他們。雖然所有被徵召入選加入英國派駐中國領事部門的人士，皆能從擔任實習翻譯官〔Student Interpreter〕這個職位開始，他們之中大多數後來會成爲辦事員，或副翻譯官，但只有很少數脫穎而出成爲翻譯官。領事館人員的階級（以及1869年時的年薪概算），由高至低如下：領事官〔Consul〕800英鎊; 副領事官〔Vice-Consul〕600英鎊; 翻譯官〔Interpreter〕600英鎊; 副翻譯官〔Assistant〕400英鎊; 而實習翻譯官〔Student Interpreter〕是200英鎊。[3]

　　1870年代早期，有一個懸而未決的問題困擾著領事部門，那就是該不該繼續在福爾摩沙設英國領事館。固威林〔William Marsh Cooper〕，這位在1869年繼臉上無光而引退的約翰・吉必勳〔John Gibson〕之後，在島上僅待了六個月的代理領事官，他的意見是英國應該將領事館從福爾摩沙撤去。這樣的意見或態度是受到了1868年的教案與樟腦油專賣糾紛事件所影響而產生的，這些動盪最後導致了臺灣人激烈的排外風潮，進而激發英軍以狂風暴雨之勢佔領安平。迂衡形勢，1870年代早期，對於福爾摩沙南部的外貿發展而言，是特別關鍵的時期。

1870年，嘗試在衝突與混亂之中恢復福爾摩沙南部秩序的人，就是有雅芝。他的行動包括約束某些無法無天的外國商人之行徑，最著名的就是逮捕怡記洋行的必麒麟〔William Alexander Pickering，又譯威廉・亞歷山大・畢格林〕；再者，他保護政府與商賈的財產權，包含正式設立打狗外國人墓園〔Takow Foreign Cemetery〕。在他出任領事初期，他的副翻譯官是霍必瀾〔Pelham Laird Warren，又譯佩漢・萊爾德・華倫〕，此人後來成為在臺灣擔任領事時間最久，而且也可以說是所有臺灣領事中表現最傑出的一位，本書將於第五章對其職業生涯再作更深入探討。[4]

法蘭西斯・朱利安・馬歇爾（在中方文件中僅稱其為「馬委員」。譯注：馬歇爾於1876年之後擔任英國上海工部衙門的代理量地官，是規劃設計打狗英國領事館的要角）在後來曾提及代理領事官亞歷山大・費里德〔Alexander Frater〕於1877年5月時向上級請求把新領事館建在安平，因為那裡是大多數進出口貿易的集散地；然而，公使威妥瑪與有雅芝兩人均反對這個意見，所以這件事沒有進一步的發展。由於有雅芝曾經是駐北京公使威妥瑪的助理中文秘書，所以他與威妥瑪可以說是關係匪淺；我們可以推斷有雅芝提出的看法必定是建立於1870至1871年那段時間他待在打狗的經驗上。[5]

有雅芝於1877年重返福爾摩沙南部時，打狗已經變得跟他當年離開時不一樣了。大約從1872年起，也就是1871年他離開後不久，外國商賈開始把營運據點轉移到安平。根據與道臺定保〔Tao-t'ai Ting Pao〕簽訂的海埔海灘章程〔Sea Beach Regulations〕，清廷允許商賈們可以填海造地，只要他們繳交一份租金，作為維持安平的海軍兵工廠〔Naval Arsenal〕之經費。於是，商賈們開始在當年荷蘭人所建的熱蘭遮城〔the old Dutch Fort of Zelandia〕北邊那塊地方填海造地。[6]

有好幾個原因造成了商賈遷移到安平，但其中最主要的理由是打狗潟湖的持續淤積變淺。雖然清廷一再保證要疏濬打狗港，但不論是抽取港底淤沙，或是禁止鹽農與蚵農擴張到越來越淺的水域，當局都沒有拿出任何實際作爲。因此，在當時船體隨時代演進越來越大，吃水量也隨之增加，但是港口本身卻日漸變淺。更嚴重的是，在港口入口要進入潟湖處有一個隨著浪潮而移動的巨大淤積沙洲，在海象較差的日子裡特別危險，文獻記載顯示，當時發生的許多船難與溺水事件，起因就在於嘗試通過打狗港入口時遇上這塊淤積沙洲。[7]

即使有以上這些難題，有雅芝之所以繼續支持將領事館建在打狗而非安平，可能主要是基於對清廷裡改革派的丁日昌的信任。丁日昌是李鴻章提拔的門生，李鴻章則是滿清末年的重臣，丁在平定太平天國之亂時因表現傑出而嶄露頭角。1875年之時，丁日昌與英國公使館的中文秘書在北京相見，有雅芝是這個中文秘書的助理，而威妥瑪公使是其上司，據說丁日昌「以熱誠而親切的態度接待他，兩人無拘無束地交談」。丁日昌於1876年被派任爲福建撫臺，當時行政轄區包括臺灣。丁日昌是因爲他的傑出能力而出人頭地，不是經由古老過時的科舉制度受到拔擢，他很執著地相信中國必須要進行西化才能具備與世界諸國競爭的實力。他在1876與1877年間來到臺灣，在臺南府與打狗間架設了中國第一條電纜，也在基隆開採煤礦。他的計畫也包含了疏浚打狗港，讓汽船得以入港停靠；還有修築一條貫通福爾摩沙南北的鐵路。有雅芝本人針對1878年時丁撫臺可能是被迫退休一事，曾有過以下的描述：

　　……對福爾摩沙而言，最具政治影響力的事件，要算是〔1878年5月7日〕丁撫臺退休一事了。他那種開明進步的政策方針對福爾摩沙資源的開發貢獻良多，而……任何評論如果沒有指出他退出福建省（當時臺灣是其下一府）的當權行列是一件讓人扼腕的事，都不算完整交代實情。……在打狗，丁撫臺本來已經在盤算籌畫一些港口改善方案，要讓打狗港在任何季節都能安全地讓最大的輪船進出。如今〔這計畫〕已經被擱置下來，而我必須很遺憾地說，〔這計畫〕敗部復活的希望很渺小。[8]

即使打狗港的情況是這樣的嚴峻，到了1878年，建造領事館的計畫還是早就開始啓動。

雖然有雅芝領事官對於把領事館建在打狗而非某些人屬意的安平港這個決策，具有重要的影響力，但實際上，這決策的制定最早可以回溯到1867年。負責建造位在中國與日本境內的英國領事館建築的單位是設於上海的工部衙門〔the Office of Works at Shanghai〕，隸屬於英國財政部〔the British Treasury，又譯度支部〕。在接下來的兩段文章篇幅裡，我們將檢視上海工部衙門的建立、它的決策系統，以及那些與建造打狗領事官邸與辦公處息息相關的重要官員與人士。

§

The key British Consular officer during the period of finalizing the leasing of sites for the construction of the Consular buildings at Takow was Archer Rotch Hewlett [有雅芝] (1838-1902), who was appointed Consul in November 1877. Although nominally the fourth Consul to be appointed to Formosa, he was apparently the first since Consul Robert Swinhoe to reside on the island. [1]

Described as an amiable and conscientious man, Hewlett was the third son of a well-to-do Middlesex surgeon and had joined the China Consular Sevice in 1858 at the age of 20 from the China Class at King's College, London. During the mid-1870s Hewlett had served as an Assistant Chinese Secretary [漢文副使] to the British Legation at Peking [英國公使館], testifying not only to his skills in Chinese but also giving him access to men such as the British Minister to China, Thomas Francis Wade [威妥瑪]. [2]

Hewlett had first come to Formosa as Acting Consul and Interpreter [翻譯官] in January 1870 and had remained for almost two years until the end of 1871. The post of Interpreter was abolished in 1877, shortly before Hewlett was appointed again to Formosa. However, in the earliest days of the China Consular service in the 1840s, many of the Consuls lacked the necessary Chinese language skills and so interpreters were recruited to support them. Although all recruits to the China Consular service subsequently began as Student Interpreters [實習翻譯官], most would simply become clerks, or Assistants, and only the select few would become Interpreters. The rankings of seniority (and approximate salaries in 1869) were as follows: Consul [領事官] (£800); Vice-Consul [副領事官] (£600); Interpreter [翻譯官] (£600); Assistant [副翻譯官] (£400); and Student Interpreter [實習翻譯官] (£200). [3]

Overhanging this earlier period around 1870 was the uncertainty about whether the British Consulate should remain on Formosa at all. William Marsh Cooper [固威林], who spent a scant 6 months on the island as Acting Consul following the unceremonial removal of Acting Consul John Gibson [吉必勳] in 1869, was of the opinion that the British should withdraw. This followed on from the 1868 troubles over missionaries and the camphor trade, which had culminated in intense anti-foreign agitation and the British storming and occupation of Anping. Thus, the early 1870s were a particularly important period in the development of foreign trade in South Formosa.

It was Consul Hewlett who sought to bring order to South Formosa in 1870, both in terms of the freewheeling activities of the foreign traders, notably arresting William Alexander Pickering [必麒麟] of Elles & Co, and of the property rights of the government and merchants, including the formal establishment of the Takow Foreign Cemetery [打狗外國人墓園]. Throughout this early period his Assistant was Pelham Laird Warren [霍必瀾], who would later become the longest-serving and arguably the most illustrious Consul to have resided on the island and whose career is looked at in some detail in Chapter Five. [4]

Francis Julian Marshall (identified in Chinese documents only as 'officer Ma' [馬委員]) was later to relate how Acting Consul Alexander Frater [費里德] had, in May 1877, made a plea for the new Consulate to be built at Anping, where most of the foreign trade was then being transacted; however, Wade and Hewlett had both opposed the idea and nothing further was done. Having been an Assistant Chinese Secretary to Wade, the British Minister at Peking, Hewlett was on familiar terms with Wade and must have based his opinion on his experience of Takow as it was in 1870 and 1871. [5]

PLAN OF CONSULAR SITE

By the time that Hewlett returned again to South Formosa in 1877 Takow had changed considerably. Starting from around 1872, and thus soon after Hewlett's departure in 1871, the foreign merchants had begun to shift their bases of operations up to Anping. Under the Sea Beach Regulations [海埔海灘章程], confirmed by Tao-t'ai Ting Pao [定保], the merchants were able to reclaim land from the sea and pay a rental towards the upkeep of the Naval Arsenal at Anping. The merchants set about reclaiming the area of Anping that lay to the immediate north of the old Dutch Fort of Zelandia [熱蘭遮城]. [6]

There were many reasons for this move to Anping, but one major cause was the continued shoaling of the Takow Lagoon. Despite repeated promises, the Ching authorities had failed to take any action to either dredge the harbour bottom or to curtail the incursions of salt farmers and oyster cultivators into the increasingly shallow waters. Thus, at a time when ships were increasing in size, with correspondingly deeper draughts, the harbour was getting shallower. Moreover, a large and shifting sand bar just outside the harbour mouth made entry into the Takow Lagoon particularly treacherous during periods of rough sea, and numerous wrecks and accidental drownings are recorded as having taken place just outside the the harbour entrance due to the problems of crossing the bar. [7]

Hewlett's continued support for building the Consulate at Takow rather than at Anping probably had much to do with his faith in the progressive Ting Jih-chang [丁日昌]). Ting was a protégé of Li Hung-chang [李鴻章], the leading statesman of the late Ching dynasty, and had first risen to prominence during the Taiping rebellion [太平天國之亂]. In 1875 Ting had met the British Chinese Secretary, to whom Hewlett was an Assistant and Wade the Minister, in Peking, "received him with great cordiality ⋯ and spoke very freely." He was appointed Governor, or Fu-tai [撫臺], of Fuchien Province, which then included Taiwan as an administrative territory, in 1876. Ting had risen to prominence through ability, and not through the archaic examination system, and believed passionately that China needed to Westernize in order to compete in the world. He had come to Taiwan in 1876/77 and built the first telegraph line in China between Taiwan-foo and Takow, and developed the coal mines at Keelung [基隆]. His plans included dredging Takow Harbour so that steamships could enter the port and building a railway from the north to the south of Formosa. Hewlett himself described Governor Ting's probably forced retirement in 1878 in the following terms:

The event of the greatest political significance ... so far as Formosa is concerned, is the retirement of Ting Footai, which took place on [7 May 1878]. His enlightened policy has done much to develop the resources of Formosa, and ... any notice would be incomplete that did not deplore his withdrawal from the Executive of the Province of which this Island is a Department. ... At Takow, the Footai had in contemplation harbour improvements calculated to make this a port of refuge accessible at all seasons for even the largest class of vessels. [This work has] come to a standstill now, and there is, I regret to say, little to encourage a hope that [it] will be renewed. [8]

However, by 1878, the construction of the Consular buildings was already under way.

Although Consul Hewlett had had an influential voice in the decision to build at Takow rather than at the preferred port of Anping, the decision to build at Takow had effectively been taken as far back as 1867. Responsibility for the construction of Consular buildings in China and Japan rested with the British Office of Works [英國工部衙門] at Shanghai, which was an agency then overseen by the British Treasury [財政部]. The establishment of the Office of Works at Shanghai, its system of decision-making, and the key officers and staff connected with the construction of the Consular Residence and the Consular Offices at Takow is examined in the following two sections.

TAKOW

Planning the new British Consular properties at Takow,
and Leasing of the Site for the Consular Residence

PLAN OF CONSULAR SITE

The Office of Works at Shanghai
上海的工部衙門

　　本書的第一章曾提到皇家工程師克里斯曼少校〔見圖2-1〕與阿禮國爵士如何在1867年來到打狗勘察領事館預定地，以及評估是購買已租出的天利洋行建築，亦或是建造一棟新館舍的各種可能性。

　　這趟勘察之旅來自於英國財政部的要求，因為英國財政部認為如果在日本與中國的全部領事館建築都能因應使用的目的來設計建造，並且直接由財政部來管控，將能達到最佳的成本效益。然而，在此時工部衙門尚未於上海設立，而克里斯曼被要求僅就1867年各地之情況來評估實際的建館可能性與優缺點，而非全盤考量財政部的計畫。[9]

　　一份日期為1866年2月16日的英國財政部文件，記錄了以下的指示：

　　　行文給皇家工程師克里斯曼少校，告訴他女王陛下的政府已經決定要派一個皇家工程部門的官員，報告及安排英國駐中國與日本的領事暨法律機構之建造與維護。由陸軍大臣〔Secretary of State for War〕指派他執行此任務，並且也得到皇家陸軍元帥兼陸軍總司令的首肯。[10]

　　威廉・克里斯曼少校〔稍後成為爵士，1830-1901〕是一位皇家工程師，來自一個富有的英國地主家族。在肯特郡查塔姆的皇家軍事工程學院經過一段時間的訓練後，他於1848年得到軍團聘任，成為新成立的英國皇家陸軍工程部少尉。在查塔姆，他所上的課程很可能包括測量、估算及建築營造。1850至1860年代期間，克里斯曼為英國政府在澳洲、英國與加拿大，完成許多重要的測量與工程任務。在澳洲期間，克里斯曼曾負責西澳大利

圖 2-1：威廉‧克里斯曼
克里斯曼爵士，大約1860年任皇家工程部上校時所攝，他創設上海工部衙門。
（照片1348B/3，來自Battye圖書館憁誠授權，版權所有，翻印必究）

Image 2-1 : William Crossman, R.E.
Sir William Crossman, photographed as a Captain in the Royal Engineers around 1860, who established the Office of Works at
Shanghai in 1867.
(State Library of Western Australia 1348B/3. Courtesy Battye Library. All Rights Reserved)

亞當時唯一的深水港亞伯尼的工事，並且在1855年時娶了亞伯尼港主管的女兒為妻。當克里米亞戰爭在歐洲爆發時，他回到英國替戰事部門工作，在普里茅斯進行加強防禦工事之工程。1861年時，由於英國擔心美國內戰的動亂會向外擴張，他被派往加拿大各處旅行視察，並於稍後被任命為加拿大一地的皇家國防委員會的祕書長。到了1866年，他已經升為軍團長官，具備陸軍少校官階，非常得到當局的敬重。[11]

　　1866年3月克里斯曼遵照上述的任命，由英格蘭的南安普頓出發，赴香港與中國等地，去調查設於中日的領事館舍與地點，並作成報告。在1866年之前，設於中國的領事建築如果不是購自港埠地區的英商，就是由香港的量地官〔Surveyor-General〕部門所設計建造，這次的調查任務克里斯曼也曾向香港的量地官諮詢。完成在香港的工作後，他再繼續前往上海，於1866年5月24日抵達上海。[12]

　　決定要成立一個監督中國與日本兩地領事館舍興建的專責部門，這件事無疑是財政部與外交部共同策劃推動的。在一份1865年財政部的文件中，很詳細地列出了他們期待克里斯曼少校可以扮演的角色與功能。財政部的考量是雇用一位私人建築師來負責此事將極為昂貴，然而當時文官體系中又沒有任何建築專家能擔此任，所以他們決定由皇家工程師中找一位有經驗的官員來負責。這位官員必須能夠判斷領事建築需要滿足那些使用及居住功能，負責取得適合的土地，並且提出建造計畫與設計，取得工事所需建材，能監督工事之進行，並且支付款項給所有參與工程的人。[13]

　　前面已經說明過，1867年之前，領事館舍建造與維護任務都是由香港的量地官部門負責。然而，在1854年，英國政府將香港的治理由外交部轉交由新成立的殖民地辦公室管理，從此香港的治理與中國其他地方的外交事務分屬不同的政府部門管轄。當中國僅開放五個港口提供英國貿易與領事業務時，這種情況尚不會造成問題，但是到了1858年天津條約簽署之後，中國增加了十一個港口開放貿易，而且英國政府在北京開始設立公使館，行政系統必須改變的需求就變得一清二楚。外交部逐步地轉移出一些工作到其他部門，例如把訓練實習翻譯官的工作轉至北京公使館；伴隨著1869年殖民地辦公室自己即將設立會計支部的計畫，外交部發現他們迫切需要建立一個新的系統來與位高權重的財政部進行直接溝通折衝，克里斯曼少校即是肩負這項任務。[14]

PLAN OF CONSULAR SITE

　　回到領事館興建的正題，1867年，在南福爾摩沙建造領事館的計畫決定要暫緩實行，因爲郇和購置來建造領事館的打水灣土地被認爲不適合蓋領事館。此外，克里斯曼覺得英國政府有道義上的責任，必須繼續履行郇和已經開始跟人家洽談的天利洋行建物之租約，即使比較起來它相當昂貴。因此他建議英國政府繼續與當時已經破產的天利洋行的債務清算人維持租約，直到能找到更合適的領事館地點爲止

　　可是，在1867年這趟拜訪福爾摩沙港埠的旅途中，刻苦堅忍的淡水副領事官額勒格里〔William Gregory，又譯威廉‧格里哥利〕在北福爾摩沙的艱苦居住狀況讓克里斯曼少校與阿禮國爵士頗感驚訝。阿禮國向外交部報告說「他發現副領事官很可憐地寄居在偏僻道街中的一間小廟，四方皆被中式房舍與茅屋所夾繞」，而克里斯曼則在向財政部的報告中說領事館官員們「已經在一個我懷疑任何英國人能否住得了一個禮拜的房子裡，住了五年之久。」[15]

　　因爲淡水領事館的情形被認爲比其他地方更急需解決，於是英國財政部在1867年編列了預算來購買土地，以便興建領事公館與領事辦公處。同年11月，代理副領事官何爲霖〔Henry Frederic William Holt，又譯亨利‧斐德烈‧威廉‧赫特〕依據羅勃‧亨利‧伯斯〔Robert Henry Boyce〕的指令，取得一片廣大土地的永久租約，其中包括舊紅毛城〔the old Dutch Fort〕的土地。蓋館舍使用的建材用船運到淡水，土地則由伯斯下令整平，這一切都是爲了準備在舊紅毛城旁建造一棟領事官邸。但意外的是，1869年突然來了一道停止工事的命令，而且將建材運往廈門。[16]

　　從以上所描述發生在淡水的故事〔我們稍後將更仔細地探討〕，我們可以知道由伯斯擔任工部督導官的工部衙門在1867年已經在上海成立。當伯斯出任代理量地官的這段期間，克里斯曼正好留在中國擔任工部的量地官，直到1869年爲止，這期間克里斯曼的傳記裡有一段令人感到好奇的紀錄，披露出他在從事的其他活動。傳記中提到在1867年首次的福爾摩沙之行後，他又在1868年時伴隨著一隊水手與海軍陸戰隊，再次回到福爾摩沙。這讓我們不得不推測他們這隊人登陸的地方正是安平，不過有關這次行動的其他描述在傳記中付之闕如（譯注：本書作者的推測是這次行動就是1868年英國海軍陸戰隊強襲安平的事件，見第一章）。[17]

克里斯曼本來的背景是建築基地量地官與行政官，雖然他之前在澳大利亞的工程經驗也包括了非軍事性的公共工程，不過因爲他的年資較長，不能讓他持續地待在遠東地區。於是，英國財政部需要另覓一個能長期派駐在上海的量地官，讓他致力於設計與建造位在中國及日本境內的領事館舍。因爲如此，伯斯於1867年被英國財政部派來輔助克里斯曼。

另一位皇家工程師，羅勃‧亨利‧伯斯（1834-1909）生於愛爾蘭。1861年英國的戶口普查顯示，他與夫人露薏莎住在威爾斯的潘布魯克〔Pembroke, Wales〕，當時他是工部皇家工程部門的監工技師〔Clerk of Works〕。伯斯在1867年被財政部派到上海，出任第一位專業的公共工程師及建築師，然後在1872年的一封信中，透露出他成爲在上海的工部助理量地官。到了1874年，伯斯成爲量地官，而根據資料所示，當時負責中國與日本通商口岸方面業務的大英工部衙門地址位於上海的圓明園路〔Yuen-ming-yuen Road〕上，地點正好在上海英國領事館的範圍裡。[18]

1876年，就在成功爭取到購買打狗領事館舍土地的預算後，伯斯卻因身體健康持續地欠佳而返回英格蘭，顯然直到1899年，伯斯才回到上海復職。在他離開後，他的工作由法蘭西斯‧朱利安‧馬歇爾〔Francis Julian Marshall〕這位代理量地官取代。[19]

馬歇爾（1833-1914）是軍械部〔the Board of Ordnance〕一位士官之子，軍械部這個單位就是英國陸軍與皇家工程部中工程師部門的前身。他先在多佛當木匠的學徒，後來才加入英國陸軍的皇家工程部。整個1860年代期間，我們可以看到在資料上他名列爲皇家工程部的監工技師。大約在1875年左右，馬歇爾被指派爲首席量地官伯斯的助理，當1876年伯斯因身體健康欠佳離開中國後，馬歇爾成爲上海工部衙門的代理量地官。雖說馬歇爾在東方的同僚中很有人緣，但他也同時被人家稱爲冷硬派，之所以有這樣的評價，可能是反應了他所處的一個沒有人會羨慕的工作崗位，這項工作被夾在錙銖必較的大英工部與慣於奢華的領事部門之間。就是這樣的馬歇爾，不僅成功取得興建打狗英國領事館舍的用地，同時也負責設計與起造哨船頭的這處領事館舍。[20]

克里斯曼、伯斯與馬歇爾都是皇家工程師部門的一員。一直到1897年馬歇爾退休之後，上海工部衙門才雇請了一位經過英國皇家建築學會〔the Royal Institute of British

Architects〕認可的建築師來進行設計工作。因此，所有在1867至1897年間興建的領事公館與辦公處，包含位於福爾摩沙的那些，它們的設計與監造都是出自於皇家工程師部門所徵召和訓練的人員之手。[21]

§

In the first chapter it was related how Major William Crossman, R.E., (see Image 2-1) and Sir Rutherford Alcock had come to Takow in 1867 to inspect the Consular premises and to assess the possibility of either purchasing the rented McPhail building or of constructing a new building.

This tour had been undertaken at the behest of the British Treasury who considered that it would be more cost-effective to have all the Consular buildings in Japan and China purpose-built for their intended uses and under the Treasury's direct control. However, at this stage there was no Office of Works at Shanghai, and Crossman had been chosen only to assess the situation as it stood in 1867. [9]

A British Treasury Minute, dated 16 February 1866, gives the following instruction:

Write to Captain Crossman, R.E., that Her Majesty's Government having determined to send an officer of Royal Engineers to report upon and make general arrangements for the construction and maintenance of consular and judicial properties in China and Japan, the Secretary of State for War（陸軍大臣）*, with the concurrence of his Royal Highness the Field Marshal Commanding in Chief*（皇家陸軍元帥兼陸軍總司令）*, has nominated him for this service.* [10]

Major (later Sir) William Crossman (1830-1901) was a Royal Engineer, that elite corps of man who were trained not only for the battlefield but also for civil works during peacetime. A member of a wealthy land-owning English family, Crossman had received his regimental commission as 2nd Lieutenant with the newly-formed British Army's Royal Engineers in 1848, after a period of training at the Royal School of Military Engineering in Chatham, Kent. At Chatham his courses would have included Surveying, and Estimating & Building Construction. During the 1850s and 1860s, Crossman had carried out much important surveying and engineering work for the British government in Australia, Britain and Canada. In Australia, Crossman had been responsible for works in the district of Albany, then the only deepwater port in Western Australia, and had married the Albany Harbour Master's daughter in 1855. Returning to Britain as the Crimea War disrupted Europe, he worked on strengthening the fortifications at Plymouth for the War Office. In 1861, with a spillover from the American Civil War feared, Crossman travelled throughout Canada and was there appointed Secretary of the Royal Commission on the Defences of Canada. By 1866 he had been promoted to a regimental rank of Captain, with an Army rank of Major, and was clearly held in high esteem. [11]

In March 1866 Crossman accordingly set out from Southampton, England, to Hong Kong, China, to inspect and make a report on the Consular buildings and sites in China and Japan. Prior to 1866, the Consular buildings in China had either been leased from local British merchants at the ports or had been designed and built by the Department of the Surveyor-General [量地官] in Hongkong, with whom Crossman consulted. From Hong Kong, Crossman continued on to Shanghai, where he arrived on 24 May 1866. [12]

The decision to establish a new office to oversee Consular buildings in China and Japan was undoubtedly taken by the Treasury and Foreign Office acting together. An 1865 Treasury Minute details the expected function of Major Crossman. As the Treasury considered that it would be too expensive to hire a private architect and that no architect in the Civil Service was available, they had opted to send an experienced officer from the Royal Engineers. The officer should be able to judge what accommodation was required, be able to obtain the site and prepare the plans for construction upon it, to obtain the necessary materials, and to supervise and make payments to those involved in the construction work. [13]

PLAN OF *CONSULAR SITE*

As has been mentioned above, prior to 1867 the construction and upkeep of Consular buildings was the responsibility of the Surveyor-General's Department in Hongkong. Yet, in 1854 British government oversight of Hongkong had been transferred from the Foreign Office to the newly-established Colonial Office [藩政院], thereby breaking the governmental link with the rest of China. Whilst there were only five Treaty Ports open to British trade and Consular activity, this did not pose too much of a problem, but with the opening of eleven additional ports and the establishment of a British Legation at Peking following the 1858 Treaty of Tientsin [天津條約], the need for change became clear. The Foreign Office progressively transferred functions such as the training of Student Interpreters up to Peking, and, with the planned establishment of the Colonial Office's own Accounts Branch in 1869, the Foreign Office saw the urgent need to establish a new system whereby they could communicate directly with the all-powerful British Treasury. [14]

In the event, it was decided in 1867 to defer any decision on the construction of Consular buildings in South Formosa, as the Freshwater Creek site, obtained by Swinhoe for that purpose, was deemed unsuitable. Moreover, Major Crossman, feeling that the British government remained morally bound by the expensive arrangement that Swinhoe had entered into on the McPhail building, recommended that the British Government continue to honour its leasing agreement with the liquidators of the by now defunct McPhail & Co until a more suitable site could be found.

However, during their 1867 tour of Formosan ports, both Crossman and Alcock had been appalled by the housing conditions of William Gregory [威廉‧格里哥利], the stoic British Vice-Consul up at Tamsui [淡水] in north Formosa. Alcock reported to the Foreign Office that he 'found the Vice Consul wretchedly lodged in a little Temple in a back street, shut in on every side by Chinese houses and hovels'; and Crossman reported to the Treasury that the Consular officers had had to live for 'five years in a house I wonder any Englishman could have occupied for a week'. [15]

The situation being considered more urgent up at Tamsui, the British Treasury thereupon allocated the 1867 funds for the purchase of a site for the construction of a Consular residence and offices on Formosa to Tamsui in preference to Takow. In November 1867 the Acting Vice-Consul, Henry Frederic William Holt [何為霖], obtained the Permanent Lease on a large site which included the old Dutch Fort [紅毛城], under the directions of Robert Henry Boyce [伯斯], the Superintendent of Works at the newly-established office of works for China and Japan in Shanghai. Materials were shipped to Tamsui and the site was levelled by Boyce in readiness for the erection of a residence adjacent to the old fort, whereupon, in 1869, orders came to stop the work and the materials were shipped across to Amoy. [16]

The episode at Tamsui, which is examined in more detail later, shows that the Office of Works, with Boyce as Superintendent of Works, had already been established at Shanghai [上海] in 1867. While Major Crossman remained in China as the Surveyor at the Office of Works until 1869, when Boyce took over as Acting Surveyor, there is a curious mention of Crossman's other activities in his biography. In his biography it is recorded that, after his initial visit to Formosa in 1867, Crossman had returned to Formosa in the company of a force of sailors and marines in 1868. One can only assume that the place he landed was Anping, but no other mention has been found. [17]

Crossman was primarily a site surveyor and administrator, and although his prior engineering experience had included civil works in Australia, his seniority did not allow him to stay indefinitely in the Far East. Accordingly, in order to design and erect Consular buildings in China and Japan a more permanent surveyor was needed at Shanghai. Thus in 1867 Boyce had been sent out by the British Treasury to assist Crossman.

Robert Henry Boyce (1834-1909), who was born in Ireland, was another Royal Engineer. The 1861 British census shows Boyce living with his wife, Louisa, in Pembroke, Wales, where he was the Clerk of Works in the Royal Engineering Department. Boyce was sent out to Shanghai by the Treasury as the first specialist civil engineer and architect in 1867, and an 1872 letter shows him to be the Assistant Surveyor, Office of Works at Shanghai. By 1874, Boyce had become the Surveyor, and the address of HBM Office of Works for the Treaty Ports of China and Japan is given as Yuen-ming-yuen Road, Shanghai [圓明園路, 上海], where it stood within the grounds of the British Consulate. [18]

In 1876, having secured the budget for sites for the Consular buildings at Takow, Boyce returned to England due to continued ill-health, apparently not returning again until 1899, and Francis Julian Marshall took over as the Acting Surveyor. [19]

Francis Julian Marshall (1833-1914) was the son of a Sergeant in the Board of Ordnance [軍械部], the provenance of the Royal Engineering Department of the British Army and the Royal Engineers. He began his career as an apprentice carpenter in Dover, after which he joined the Royal Engineering Department of the British Army. Throughout the 1860s he is listed as a Clerk of Works in the Royal Engineering Department. Around 1875 Marshall was appointed to Shanghai as the Assistant to the First Class Surveyor, Boyce, and in 1876, following Boyce's departure from China, became Acting Surveyor at the Office of Works at Shanghai. Despite being well-liked by his contemporaries in the East, Marshall was also described as a 'pretty callous' man, though this might be more a reflection of his unenviable position of being caught between a niggardly British Board of Works [大英工部] and an ever-clamouring Consular Service. It was Marshall who would not only obtain the Consular sites at Takow, but who was also responsible for the design and erection of the Consular buildings at Shao-chuan-tou. [20]

Crossman, Boyce and Marshall were all Royal Engineers, and it was not until 1897, when Marshall retired, that the Office of Works at Shanghai was to employ an architect qualified by the Royal Institute of British Architects to carry out the design work. Thus all the British Consular Residences and Offices built between 1867 and 1897, including those on Formosa, were designed, and the erection supervised, by men recruited from, and trained by, the Royal Engineers. [21]

The Mechanics of Consular Construction in China

建造中國領事館建築物的機制

　　就在上海工部衙門於1867年成立後，英國財政部使用了一套作業機制，為的是確保能充分控制與監督位於日本與中國通商口岸的領事館舍之建造事宜。所謂的通商口岸，指的是中國或日本開放，可以進行外國貿易的港口或地方，通常都是屈服在所謂的不平等條約之下才開放的。剛開始時，駐中國的領事單位與上海的工部會共同合作，一起決定新的領事館舍應該興建的適當地點，然後，再決定那些舊有館舍需要修繕與重建。

　　駐中國的領事部門〔The China Consular Service〕由英國駐北京大臣〔公使〕所代表，他通常會依賴駐在通商口岸的領事官或代理領事官向他彙報的資料來做決策；與此相同的，上海的工部則需要量地官或代理量地官到目標地現場勘察。駐京大臣會把他的意見呈報給倫敦的外交部，而上海的量地官則向位於倫敦的工部進行報告。

　　依據各地彙整的報告，位於倫敦的工部將為下一個會計年度〔4月1日至次年3月31日〕擬定一份歲出預算書，然後再把此預算書呈報給財政委員會。然而，在1870年之後，倫敦的工部在皇家授權任命的一位工部與公共建築首席委員，以及工部委員會的監督之下，被賦予自行決定預算的權力。在委員會的運作機制中，如果要進行有關領事館舍的"正式表決"之前，會將英國外交部的意見再拿出來檢討考慮，比方說歲出預算有多少可以花費在館舍的計畫上。

　　當英國財政部還掌控著審查及授權在日本與中國建造領事官舍的預算時，採用了一套嚴格的標準規範，根據該處領事官員的官階與薪水，來決定要建造那一種形式的官邸，而且通常會盡量設計成官邸與辦公處合併在同一棟兩層樓的建築物中。透過這種有系統的規畫，財政部希望能配合領事官員的官位層級來提供不同大小與機能配置的官邸住所：也就是說，領事官、副領事官或翻譯官的官邸，在設計中將包含他們的家庭成員居住的空間及生活機能，然而，領事助理或實習翻譯官則只能得到單身宿舍。我們有理由相信這種標準

PLAN OF CONSULAR SITE

規範在工部委員會具有權力決定預算後仍被繼續採用。[22]

　　假如委員會審查後同意，或說是預算表決通過的話，那麼申請的款項將可以在下一個
會計年度動支使用，也就是從當年的4月1日至隔年的3月31日。如果未經委員會同意，不可
追加預算，也不能將未使用完的預算保留到下一個年度。

§

After the establishment of the Office of Works at Shanghai in 1867, a mechanism was put into place which was intended to ensure that the British Treasury had full control and oversight over all Consular construction at the Treaty Ports [通商口岸] in Japan and China. The Treaty Ports were those ports or places that were opened by China or Japan for foreign trade, typically by the so-called Unequal Treaties [不平等條約]. The China Consular Service and the Office of Works at Shanghai would initially cooperate together to decide where the Consulates should be built and, later, which ones needed repair or rebuilding.

The China Consular Service, represented by the British Minister at Peking [駐京大臣], would generally rely upon the despatches from the Consul or Acting Consul at the Treaty Port; whereas the Office of Works would require the Surveyor or Acting Surveyor to make an on-site inspection. While the British Minister at Peking would make his recommendations to the Foreign Office in London, the Surveyor at Shanghai would make his report to the Office of Works in London.

The Office of Works in London would then prepare an Estimate of expected expenditure for the forthcoming financial year (from April 1 to March 31), and submit this Estimate to the British Treasury Board. However, after 1870 the Office of Works was empowered to make its own decisions under a First Commissioner of Works and Public Buildings, who was appointed by royal warrant, and acted in consensus with the Board of Works. At the Board of works level, the views of the British Foreign Office would again be taken into consideration as would the British Treasury's view of the amount of money available for expenditure, prior to the 'Vote' which determined approval.

The British Treasury, in authorising the erection of Consular buildings in Japan and China, had used strict guidelines, based on the rank and salary of the Consular officer, to decide on the type of Consular Residence to be built and normally sought to combine the Residence and Consular Offices into a single, two-storey Consulate building. The Treasury wished to provide accommodation that befitted the rank of the Consular officer: thus, while a Consul, Vice-Consul or Interpreter would be entitled to accommodation for their whole family, an Assistant or Student Interpreter would only be allowed bachelor quarters. It is believed that these guidelines were continued by the Board of Works. [22]

If approval, or the Vote, was granted, the submitted amount would be available for the duration of the forthcoming financial year that ran from 1 April to 31 March. The figure grant-ed could not be exceeded nor could it be carried forward to the next financial year without the express approval of the Board.

Leasing of Sites for Consular Residence
and Consular Offices
尋覓領事官邸與辦公處的建地

　　馬歇爾在1876年面對的第一個挑戰是，找到並正式取得打狗領事官邸與辦公處的用地。一開始的計畫是把官邸與辦公處蓋在同一塊土地上，但是在最後，馬歇爾選擇租下在哨船頭潟湖的北岸兩塊分開的土地。到了1877年，在「拖了整整十二個月、歷經令人痛苦疲累的延遲與談判之後」，馬歇爾終於可以向倫敦方面報告，他已經成功地取得這兩塊土地。[23]

　　官邸這塊地的租賃跟租賃辦公處那塊地的複雜度相比，算是比較簡單的，後者的過程將在第三章再做探討。

§

　　The first task confronting Marshall in 1876 was to secure the sites for the Consular Residence and Consular Offices at Takow. The original plan had been to build the Offices and Residence on the same site, but in the event Marshall chose to lease two separate sites on the north shore of the Lagoon at Shao-chuan-tou. By 1877, Marshall was able to report to London that he had successfully obtained the two sites 'after vexatious delays and negotiations extending over a period of twelve months'. [23]

　　The leasing of the site for the Consular Residence proved simple in comparison to the complexities of leasing the site for the Consular Offices, which is examined in Chapter Three.

Leasing of Site
for Consular Residence
領事官邸的土地租賃

馬歇爾在1877年7月寫給倫敦方面的信中提到，他已經得到一塊可建造領事官邸的土地，他是如此描述這塊土地的：

官邸用地：〔這塊地〕位於打狗港入口的西北方，坐落在高於海平面約100呎的高地上。這是港口附近最好的一個位置，居高臨下眺望東方的打狗港與聚落，西方與南方的海，在北方則是高突的一片山巒。土地的表面是崎嶇不平的岩石平臺。這塊地的地形位置，讓我們無法把它拿來做為領事辦公處，這是因為它的海拔高度使其遠離清帝國海關與商人們的辦公室，如果考量到領事業務裡那些商業方面的事務的話，這個位置對商人而言並不順路。因此我們必須再買第二塊鄰近的土地，用來建辦公室、巡捕的房間與監獄。[24]

紀錄顯示，山丘上官邸用地的總價是430.60元，相當於81英鎊，81這個數目是馬歇爾自己在1877年信中所提及的，雖然當年81鎊的價值換算成今日的幣值只能大略猜測，不過據推估，以2013年的物價指數推算約為8000鎊，或者新臺幣36萬元左右。[25]

1870年代那一段時間，建造福爾摩沙領事館的計畫，因為英國政府不確定是否要全面退出福爾摩沙，而被擱置。然而，1872年6月時，英國外相格蘭維爾侯爵〔Earl Granville〕決定了新的外交方針，英國領事館退出福爾摩沙的風險不復存在。1872年末，駐北京大臣公使，威安瑪爵士，突然對代理領事官額勒格里下了指令，要他在打狗取得一塊地；但是，此時有關購地的款項尚未完成預算的編列與審議，於是助理量地官伯斯必須

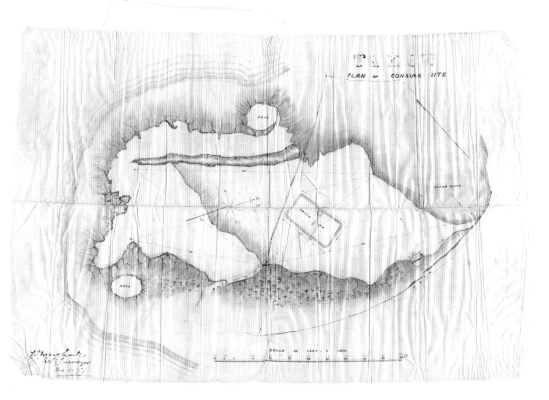

圖 2-2：1877年打狗領事館建地圖草稿
馬歇爾的1877年打狗領事館建地圖草稿，顯示哨船頭山丘上之空地與老墓園的位置。

Image 2-2 : Draft 1877 Plan of Consular Site at Takow
F. J. Marshall's 1877 draft Plan of the Consular Site at Takow, showing the vacant hill-top at Shao-chuan-tou and the position of
the old Grave Yard.

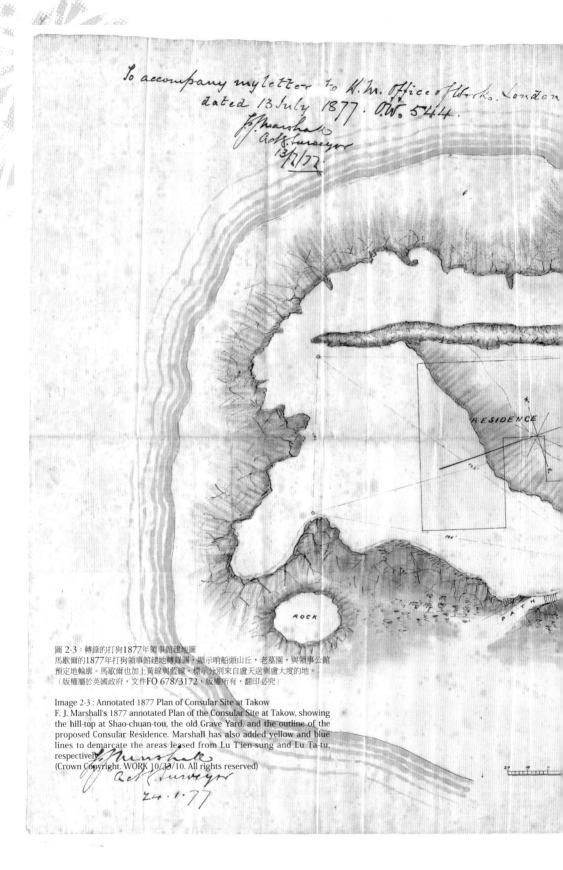

RESIDENCE

ROCK

PATH

圖 2-3：轉錄的打狗1877年領事館建地圖
馬歇爾的1877年打狗領事館建地轉錄圖，顯示哨船頭山丘，老墓園，與領事公館
預定地輪廓。馬歇爾也加上黃線與藍線，標示分別來自盧天送與盧大度的地。
（版權屬於英國政府，文件FO 678/3172，版權所有，翻印必究）

Image 2-3 : Annotated 1877 Plan of Consular Site at Takow
F. J. Marshall's 1877 annotated Plan of the Consular Site at Takow, showing
the hill-top at Shao-chuan-tou, the old Grave Yard, and the outline of the
proposed Consular Residence. Marshall has also added yellow and blue
lines to demarcate the areas leased from Lu T'ien-sung and Lu Ta-tu,
respectively.

F. Marshall
Act Surveyor
24.1.77

T A K O W
PLAN OF CONSULAR SITE

SHARP SLOPE

GRAVE YARD

GRAVE

PATH

E 20 FEET 1 INCH

I, Lu Ta Fu, having on the 20th January 1877 by deed leased to H. His First Commissioner of Works in London in perpetuity, through Francis Julian Marshall, acting for and on his behalf, a piece of ground at Takow, I hereby declare that the ground so leased is represented on this plan as comprised within a blue line.

Signed by the abovenamed Lu Ta Fu in my presence at Takow this 15th day of June 1877

W. Rath
Acting Consul

I, Lu Ta Fu, having on the 20th January 1877 by deed leased to H. His First Commissioner of Works in London, through Francis Julian Marshall, acting for and on his behalf, a piece of ground at Takow in perpetuity, I hereby declare that the ground so leased is represented on this plan as comprised within a yellow line. D

Signed by the abovenamed Lu Ta Fu in my presence at Takow this 15th day of June 1877.

W. Rath Acting Consul for Takow

在1873年10月向上級請求，取得自由裁量權，並在他預定的1874年打狗之行中就地談妥購地事宜，以便開始建造「上頭要求的領事館舍。」[26]

根據伯斯對興建領事館花費的估算，工部委員會在1875年時通過提撥212英鎊，用來購買建造打狗領事館舍的土地，計畫在1876至1877年間開始建造。然而，伯斯很快地就發現到他申請的經費總額將會不夠，於是，他在1875年9月要求重新投票表決，將預算提高到600英鎊，以用來取得一塊蓋領事館舍的建地。這個為數不少的預算增加，根據伯斯的說法，乃是歸因於打狗港的貿易景況蒸蒸日上。工部及時地在1876年1月6日撥下增加後的600鎊經費，這筆經費可以在1876/1877這個會計年度支用。於是，馬歇爾只花費600英鎊中的81英鎊就取得哨船頭山上的土地，而建造領事官邸的營建費用則另外再申請匡列。[27]

一開始的計畫本來是建造一棟既可以讓領事官員居住，又可以當作辦公處的建築，這是一種最常見的英國領事建築的配置方式。然而，到了1876年9月，當馬歇爾報告正在進行中的購地協商時，事情有所轉變，他在報告中提到目前的計畫是在山丘上建官邸，同時在山丘下另建一處建築當辦公處。這個決定與伯斯的想法剛好一致，似乎是基於同一個認知，認為不應該錯過在哨船頭山丘上蓋房子的好機會，但同時又覺得山丘上的建築物如果作為領事處的話，對於每天例行的商業活動實在太不方便，尤其是那些與船務及清帝國海關有關的業務。[28]

1877年1月，馬歇爾畫了一張用來建造打狗領事館的空地的配置草圖〔如圖2-2〕。這張配置圖中標示了一個"墓園"，早先的研究學者曾宣稱這張圖上的墓園就是最初的打狗外國人墓園。然而，馬歇爾在他1877年的信中對這個墓園的報告如下：

這是一個廢棄不用的墓園，其大小約58英呎長乘以31英呎寬見方，被一個低矮的泥牆圍起來，這個墓園佔去了一部份領事官邸建地。當然，在建造工事開始時，這墓園將會被移除；依照這個地方的習俗，移除前必須付一小筆的費用給逝去而埋骨於此之中國官紳的後代。[29]

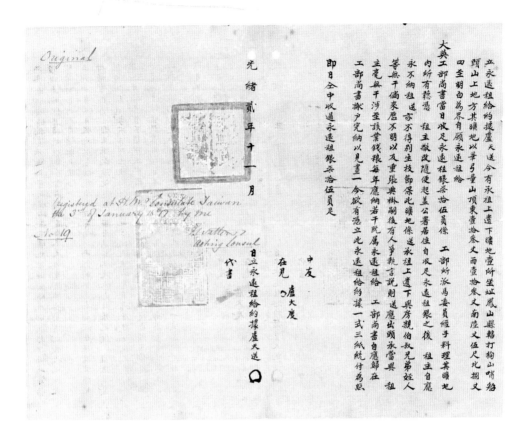

圖 2-4：領事館建地地契
盧天送於1877年2月2日釋出領事公館確切所在地之永久租賃權，給予馬歇爾的原始地契，馬歇爾代表女王陛下之工部。
（版權屬於英國政府，文件FO 678/3140，版權所有，翻印必究）

Image 2-4 : Deed of Perpetual Lease from Lu T'ien-sung for part of Consular Site
The original Deed of Perpetual Lease granted by Lu T'ien-sung to Marshall, acting on behalf of H.M. Board of Works, on 2
January 1877 for the actual site of the Consular Residence.

於是，馬歇爾很清楚地幫我們描述了這個墓地，陳述它的面積大小，也明白地指出這個被矮泥牆包圍的老墓園中埋葬的是一位中國官紳，或是清朝官員。他宣稱這墓園將會被移走，而且也會以金錢補償這位去世的官員的後人們。這個證據反駁了任何認為哨船頭山丘上緊鄰領事官邸的北邊，曾經有個外國人墓園的說法。[30]

在馬歇爾1877年7月的信中還附有兩張地契。這兩張地契是官邸土地的永久租約，由盧天送〔Lu Tien-sung〕與盧大度〔Lu Ta-tu〕兩位所簽署，官邸的土地是分兩次才轉讓給馬歇爾所代表的英方當局。因盧天送所簽的永久租約而轉讓給皇家工部委員會的土地，是領事官邸的確切所在地，於1877年1月2日〔光緒2年〕由馬歇爾代表簽約，並有代理領事官倭妥瑪〔Thomas Watters〕的連署，如圖2-3所示。此契約影本放在對頁。馬歇爾1877年7月信中所附的一張1877年領事館建地配置圖〔如圖2-4〕中，以黃線標示了從盧天送手中獲得的土地。第二張永久租約由盧大度在1877年1月20日簽署，由此而取得的土地是緊鄰預定建物北方的一塊地，在前述的圖中以藍線標界。以黃線標示的第一塊土地，其東、西、南向的邊界都在山丘頂部的邊緣，然而，以藍線標示第二塊土地，它的區域卻是延伸到山丘東西兩邊的山腳下。後來的歷史發展證明，這塊土地延伸至山丘腳下的界限引起了爭議。[31]

許妥瑪〔Thomas Francis Hughes，又譯湯瑪斯‧法蘭西斯‧休斯〕是當時駐打狗稅務司〔Commissioner for Customs〕，他曾在1877年3月寫信給馬歇爾抱怨邊界的事。清帝國海關〔The Imperial Maritime Customs〕早一年就在哨船頭山丘腳下買了一塊土地。在買地當時，海關以為他們的土地範圍自他們的後牆延伸出去，一直到達山丘頂端為止。許妥瑪矢言他們認定的地界是基於水陸洋行〔Brown & Co〕的地上物所有權，在海關取得之前是水陸洋行擁有此地的永久租賃權。如果真以海關所宣稱的以後牆為地界基準，馬歇爾的配置圖中的領事官邸地界確實侵佔到海關的土地。這個爭議最後以很紳士的方式解決。雖然馬歇爾的配置圖中的合法地界維持不變，英國政府同意不主張海關後牆內的土地所有權，而同樣地海關也同意不主張超過後牆界線的土地所有權。[32]

哨船頭南邊山腳下的土地具有複雜的歷史，但是深入瞭解後，它透露出很多早期打狗地區的風土人情。既然馬歇爾買來建領事館辦公處的土地正好位於哨船頭山腳下這塊地方，在下一章裡，我們就來細細檢視關於這塊土地令人好奇的故事。

§

In his July 1877 letter to London, Marshall announced that he had obtained a site for the Consular Residence. He described the site as follows:

Site for Residence. [This] is situated on the high land, about 100 feet above the level of the Sea on the North Western side of the entrance to the harbor of Takow. It is the finest site at the port, commanding a view of the harbor and settlement on the East, the Sea on the South and West, and a high range of mountains to the North. The surface of the ground is an uneven and rocky plateau. The situation of this land precludes it from being suitable as a site for Consular Offices from the fact that its elevation, and isolation from the Imperial Customs and the merchants' offices, rendering it rather an out of the way place for business purposes. It therefore became necessary to purchase a second and adjoining site upon which to erect offices, constable's quarters and gaol. [24]

The total cost of the land on top of the hill for the Residence is given as $430.60, equivalent to £81. The amount of £81 is that stated by Marshall in his 1877 letter; although the value of £81 today can really only be guessed at, it is calculated at around £8,000, or 360,000 New Taiwan Dollars, in 2013 money. [25]

Previous plans for the erection of Consular buildings on Formosa had been thwarted by the uncertainties around 1870 as to whether the British government would withdraw altogether from Formosa. However, in June 1872 the British Foreign Minister, Earl Granville, had removed any risk of the British Consulate being withdrawn from Formosa. In late 1872 the British Minister at Peking, Sir Thomas Wade, had promptly instructed Acting Consul William Gregory to secure a site at Takow; however, as no amount had yet been allocated for the purchase, Assistant Surveyor Boyce had to seek discretionary powers in October 1873 to purchase a site during his visit slated for 1874 in order to construct 'the Consular buildings required'. [26]

In 1875, the Board of Works had authorized the sum of £212, based on Boyce's estimate, for the purchase of a building site in order to erect a Consulate at Takow during 1876-77. However, Boyce quickly realized that the sum requested would prove inadequate, and therefore in September 1875 requested a new Vote to allocate £600 for the securing of a site. This need for such a sizeable increase in the amount required Boyce attributed to the more prosperous trading conditions at the port. The Board duly authorized the revised amount of £600 on 6 January 1876, to be expended during the financial year 1876/1877. Marshall had thus far spent only £81 of the allocated £600 in obtaining the land on the hill at Shao-chuan-tou, with the funds for the erection of the Residence being separately allocated. [27]

The original intention had been to build a single structure to house both the Consular officer and to serve as the Consular offices, being the most usual form of Consular building. However, by September 1876, when Marshall reported on the ongoing negotiations to purchase land for construction, he stated that the intention was now to build a Consular Residence on the upper site, with a separate building for the Consular Offices below. This decision, concurred with by Boyce, seems to have been taken on the grounds that, whereas the opportunity to build on such a fine site as that on the hill at Shao-chuan-tou should not be missed, any building up on the hill would be too inconvenient for the daily business that should be conducted at the Consular Offices, particularly with regard to shipping matters and the Imperial Maritime Customs. [28]

In January 1877 Marshall had drawn up a draft plan of the vacant Consular Site at Takow (see Image 2-2). On this plan is shown a 'Grave Yard', which has previously been claimed by researchers to have been the original Foreign Cemetery at Takow. However, Marshall reports on this grave yard in his 16 July 1877 letter as follows:

*A disused grave yard, that is, a space of 58 feet by 31 feet, enclosed by a low mud wall,
occupies a portion of it. This will of course be abolished upon commencing building
operations; to do which a small fee will, as is customary in this country, have to be paid to
the inheritors of the deceased mandarin whose bones now rest there.* [29]

Thus Marshall clearly identifies this graveyard, by giving the measurements, as the old
grave of a Chinese Mandarin or Ching Government Official, surrounded by a low mud wall.
He avers that the grave will be removed and compensation paid to the descendants of the
Mandarin. This refutes any suggestion that there was ever a graveyard for foreigners to the
immediate north of the Consular Residence on the hill at Shao-chuan-tou. [30]

Two Land Deeds were also enclosed in Marshall's July 1877 letter. These were the two
Perpetual Leases for the Residence site issued by Lu T'ien-sung [盧天送] and Lu Ta-tu [盧大度],
who had conveyed the property to Marshall in two separate transactions. The Perpetual Lease
granted by Lu T'ien-sung to Marshall, acting on behalf of H.M. Board of Works, on 2 January
1877 [光緒 年], and countersigned by Acting Consul Thomas Watters [倭妥瑪] is for the actual
site of the Consular Residence, and the Deed is shown as Image 2-3. The 1877 Plan of Consular
Site that was enclosed in Marshall's July 1877 letter (see Image 2-4) shows the land obtained
from Lu T'ien-sung outlined in yellow. The second Perpetual Lease, granted by Lu Ta-tu on
20 January 1877, is for the area immediately to the north of the proposed building, and is
outlined on the plan in blue. Whereas the first area, outlined in yellow, takes the crest of the
hill as its south, east and westerly limits, the second area, outlined in blue, extends down the
sides of the hill on its easterly and westerly boundaries. This extension of the boundary down
the hill was to prove contentious. [31]

Thomas Francis Hughes [許妥瑪], the then Commissioner for Customs [稅務司] at Takow,
wrote to Marshall in March 1877 to complain about the boundary. The Imperial Maritime
Customs [海關] had purchased the property at the base of the hill in the previous year. At that

time, the Imperial Maritime Customs had considered that their property extended beyond their rear wall and reached to the crest of the hill. This, Hughes affirmed, was based on squatter's rights that had accrued to Brown & Co [水陸洋行], the previous holders of the Perpetual Lease. The boundary shown on Marshall's plan encroached into the Imperial Maritime Customs property as defined by their rear compound wall. The matter was eventually resolved in a gentlemanly fashion. Although the legal boundary as marked on Marshall's map should remain unchanged, the British government agreed not to make any claim on the land within the Imperial Maritime Customs compound wall and the Imperial Maritime Customs agreed not to make any claims outside their compound wall. [32]

The history of the land at the southern foot of the hill at Shao-chuan-tou is extremely complex, but reveals much about the early days of Takow. As it was at the foot of the Shao-chuan-tou hill that Marshall was to lease the site for the Consular Offices, the intriguing story of the land there is examined in the following chapter.

TAKOW

PLAN OF CONSULAR SITE

Notes to Chapter Two
第二章註解

1. Lo & Bryant, Consular Establishments, Vol. 2, pp. 429-31; see FO 228, China: General Correspondence, Series I, 1861 to 1878.

2. Coates, p. 50 and p. 200. After 1854, many of the appointments to the China Consular Service were made at the recommendation of the China Class taught at King's College, London, then the only British institution teaching Chinese (see Coates, p. 75ff). See also Lo & Bryant, Consular Establishments, Vol. 2, p. 617.

   註：1854年後，許多到中國參加領事外交工作的職位是由倫敦國王學院提供的中文課程所推薦，當時那是唯一一教授中文的英國機構。

3. B.P.P., Vol. 2, p. 262, Alcock to Clarendon, 29 October 1869; and p. 479, Return of Student Interpreters in China, Japan, and Siam: 1847-72. Chinese Titles from W. F. Mayers' The Chinese Government.

4. Coates, p. 329; see also Pickering W. A. P., Pioneering in Formosa, London 1898, (Reprinted by SMC Publishing, Taipei, 1993) pp. 236-7; Oakley, David [李夢哲], The Foreign Cemetery at Kaohsiung [座落於高雄的外國墓園], Taiwan Historica, Vol. 56, Issue 3, Sept. 2005, pp. 265-295 [臺灣文獻 卷期56:3 民94.09頁265-295]. Lo & Bryant, Consular Establishments, Vol. 2, p. 430.

5. FO 228/1022, Marshall to O'Conor, 10 November 1885; FO 228/596, Frater to Fraser, 1 May 1877.

6. FO 262/958, Encl. Memo in Wileman to MacDonald, 2 May 1906.

7. see Davidson, p. 216 for following wrecks at Takow: Caroline Hutchings, 1874; Traviata, 1876; and Fyen, 1876. A notable, if slightly later, drowning was that of William Hopkins, an Irish seaman

from the barque 'West Glen', who drowned while crossing the sandbar at Takow on 20 July 1880, aged 24; Hopkins was buried at Takow Foreign Cemetery. For detailed information about William Hopkins, see the interesting research by Mai Han-ming [麥漢鳴] privately published as 魂歸原鄉 [A Soul Returning to the Hometown], January 2004.

8. Coates, p. 188-189; FO 228/616, Hewlett's Intelligence Report for May & June 1878.

9. B.P.P., Vol. 2, p. 210, Treasury Minute, dated 16 February 1866.

10. B.P.P., Vol. 2, p. 209, Treasury Minute, dated 16 February 1866.

11. Du Cane, Edmund F., The Late Major-General Sir William Crossman, Livesey & Co Ltd, Shrewsbury, 1902 (For Private Circulation), pp. 7-10; Fremantle Prison Research Files, Australia; Smithers, A. J., Honourable Conquests: An account of the enduring work of the Royal Engineers throughout the Empire, Leo Cooper, London, 1991, pp. 10-14, 28-29.

12. B.P.P., Vol. 2, p. 211, Treasury Minute, dated 16 February 1866; FO 17/1302, Crossman to Treasury, 30 May 1866.

13. B.P.P., Vol. 2, pp. 205-209, Treasury Minute, 22 December 1865.

14. The five Treaty Ports opened by the 1842 Treaty of Nanking [南京條約] were: Amoy [廈門], Canton [廣東], Foochow [福州], Ningpo [寧波], and Shanghai [上海]. The eleven additional ports were: Chefoo [芝罘 (煙臺)], Chinkiang [京江], Hankow [漢口], Kiukiang [九江], Kiungchow [瓊州], Nanking [南京], Newchwang [牛莊], Swatow [汕頭], Taiwan [臺灣], Tengchow [登州], Tientsin [天津]. British National Archives data.

15. FO 17/476, Alcock to Stanley, 20 July 1867;

PLAN OF CONSULAR SITE

Coates, p. 333; B.P.P., Vol. 2, pp. 224-234,
Crossman to Treasury, 18 July 1867.

16. WORK 10/435, Holt to Crossman, 18 February 1868.

17. Izumida, H., British Consular and Legation
Buildings in East Asia, Part I, Journal of the
Society of Architectural Historians of Japan, Vol.
15, pp. 93-104, 1990, p. 96; B.P.P., Vol. 2, p. 270,
Crossman to H.M. Consuls in China, 16 September
1869; Izumida, H., British Consular and Legation
Buildings in East Asia, Part II, Journal of the
Society of Architectural Historians of Japan,
Vol. 16, pp.78-91, 1991, p. 81; Du Cane, p.19.

18. MFQ 1/1017 reference to 31 August 1872 letter
from R. Boyce; The China Directory for 1874,
China Mail, Hongkong, 1874, Boyce's staff at
Shanghai are given as: Assistant – Assiter, Wm.,
Clerk – Donaldson, C. P. M., Clerks of Works –
Bennett, C. R., Hooper, John, and Power, W.

19. WORK 10/210, Marshall to Hughes, 24 March
1877; WORK 10/756; WORK 10/56/6; WORK
10/33/10, Marshall to O.W.L., 11 September 1876.

20. UK Census data; Titles taken from Post Office
Directory for London, 1882 et al.; Ruxton, Ian (Ed),
The Correspondence of Sir Ernest Satow, British
Minister in Japan, 1895-1900, Vol. 1, Lulu Press Inc,
2005, pp.250-3, Bonar to Satow, 8 October 1896.

21. Izumida, H., British Consular and Legation
Buildings in East Asia Part II, Journal of
the Society of Architectural Historians
of Japan, Vol. 16, 1991, p. 81.

22. B.P.P., Vol. 2, pp. 210 and 211, Treasury
Minute, dated 16 February 1866.

23. WORK 10/33/10, Marshall to O.W.L., 16 July 1877.

24. WORK 10/33/10, Marshall to O.W.L., 16 July 1877.

25. WORK 10/33/10, Marshall to O.W.L., 16 July
1877. Calculation based on UK Office of National
Statistics data. All amounts given in this section
are the actual values then stated. One British
pound in 1877 is calculated to be worth about
£100 in 2013. The dollar ($) amounts given
refer to Mexican silver dollars [墨西哥銀元],
commonly known as Foreign Eagles [鷹洋].

26. Granville Leveson-Gower, 2nd Earl Granville (11
May 1815–31 March 1891) was a member of
the Liberal Party and served as British Foreign
Secretary from July 1870 to February 1874 (Source:
Foreign & Commonwealth Office); WORK 10/99,
Buckler to Treasury, 11 November 1874; WORK
10/33/10, Boyce to O.W.L., 23 October 1873.

27. WORK 10/33/10, Boyce to O.W.L., 11 September
1875; Marshall to O.W.L., 11 September 1876;
and Marshall to O.W.L., 16 July 1877.

28. WORK 10/33/10, Marshall to
O.W.L., 11 September 1876.

29. WORK 10/33/10, Marshall to O.W.L., 16 July 1877.

30. WORK 10/33/10, Marshall to O.W.L., 16 July 1877.

31. FO 678/3140.

32. The Imperial Maritime Customs, despite being
almost exclusively staffed by foreigners, was a
Chinese government agency and thus able to
purchase property outright. WORK 10/210, Memo
signed by Marshall et al., dated 2 December 1878.

Chapter
Three

第3章

打狗英國領事辦公處
土地的租賃
Leasing of the Site
for the Consular Offices

Introduction
緒論

1876年，馬歇爾面對的第一個挑戰是，在打狗一地取得領事官邸與辦公處的建造用地。雖然原先的構想是把兩者蓋在同一個地方，然而伯斯與馬歇爾最後都決定在打狗港潟湖北邊的哨船頭，選擇租賃兩塊分開的土地分別興建。

在一年之內，馬歇爾已經成功地完成註冊登記，租下了哨船頭山丘上這塊地來作為領事官邸使用。然而位於官邸預定地山下的潟湖岸邊那塊領事辦公處建地的租賃過程，事後比較起來顯得複雜與冗長。

哨船頭南邊山丘腳下這塊地的土地所有權歷史相當複雜，但是卻透露出早期打狗的風土人情。既然這兩個領事館舍建築是在哨船頭同時起造，租賃領事辦公處建地的精彩故事，將在本章一一探討。

1877年7月16日，在馬歇爾寫給倫敦官方的一封關鍵信中，他提到自己已經取得一塊建造領事館辦公處的土地。他描述此塊土地如下：

辦公處用地：關於這塊辦公室與牢房的用地，是326英呎乘以100英呎見方的狹長土地，座落於前面最先提到那塊地（也就是領事官邸用地）的山丘下。這塊地是山丘下有一整塊填海造成、326呎乘以324呎見方大之土地的一部份。這塊地非常適合領事辦公處所需的各種機能，前方面對港口，方便商賈、船長艦長或其他種種人士來到領事館處理相關事宜。由此地往山丘方向將來須要開闢一條小徑，以作為與山上預定官邸間的通道。[1]

取得辦公處用地共花費2500銀元，大約相當於470英鎊，換算成2012年的幣值約等於47000英鎊。這樣看來，取得山下這塊地的經費佔工部委員會1876年1月爲購買領事館用地撥款600鎊的絕大部份，這筆600鎊的款項其中其實眞正支出的僅比550英鎊多一點而已。[2]

述說租賃與註冊登記哨船頭英國領事館辦公處土地所發生的故事，將把這個研究帶回到19世紀時，打狗與中國沿岸，外國商人前來貿易的最早時期。

哨船頭山丘下的土地原先爲寶順洋行〔Dent & Co〕所租下，但是爲何這塊土地後來成爲英國政府所有，當中的故事要從寶順洋行與其主要競爭對手怡和洋行〔Jardine Matheson & Co〕的種種恩怨開始說起。[3]

§

The first task confronting Marshall in 1876 had been to secure the sites for the Consular Residence [領事官邸] and Consular Offices [領事辦公處] at Takow. Although the original intention had been to build the Residence and Offices upon the same site, Boyce and Marshall chose to lease two separate sites on the north side of the Lagoon at Shao-chuan-tou.

Within a year, Marshall had successfully registered the site for the Consular Residence upon the hill at Shao-chuan-tou. Yet the leasing of the site for the Consular Offices, on the shore of the Lagoon below the Consular Residence site, proved to be a complex and lengthy affair.

The history of the land ownership at the southern foot of the hill at Shao-chuan-tou is complicated, but reveals much about the early days of Takow. Moreover, as these two Consular buildings were constructed simultaneously at Shao-chuan-tou, the intriguing story of the leasing of the site for the Consular Offices is examined in this chapter.

In his key 16 July 1877 letter to London, Marshall announced that he had obtained a site for the Consular Offices. He described the site as follows:

Site for Offices. With respect to the site for offices, gaol &c, this comprises a strip of land 326 feet by 100 feet, situated at the foot of the hill adjoining the first-named site [i.e. that of the Consular Residence]. It forms a portion of a large area of reclaimed ground measuring 326 feet by 324 feet. It is admirably adapted for the purposes required, having a frontage on the harbor, and within easy access of merchants, captains of vessels, or others having business to transact at the consulate. From this land a path will have to be formed on the hill side as a means of communication with the proposed residence above. [1]

The cost of the land for the Consular Offices is given as $2,500, then equivalent to approximately £470, and now equivalent to about £47,000 at 2012 prices. Thus this lower site accounted for by far the major part of the £600 authorised by the Board of Works in January 1876 for the acquisition of the Consular sites, of which just over £550 was actually spent. [2]

The tale of the leasing and registration of the site for the British Consular Offices [英國 領事處] at Shao-chuan-tou takes this study right back to the earliest days of foreign traders at Takow and on the China Coast during the 19th century.

The site at the foot of the hill at Shao-chuan-tou had originally been leased by Dent & Co [寶順洋行] but the story of how it came into the possession of the British government begins with Dent & Co's intrigues with their great rivals Jardine Matheson & Co [怡和洋行]. [3]

Leasing of the Site for the Consular Offices

W M Robinet & Co,
Jardine Matheson & Co, and Dent & Co
羅賓奈洋行、怡和洋行與寶順洋行

　　怡和洋行的起源可以追溯到1810年代晚期，不過直到1832年，它才開始用怡和這個名字。怡和洋行在1820年代在鴉片貿易中賺取到巨大的利潤，並且在1833年東印度公司〔East India Company〕的壟斷獨佔權結束後，怡和在1830年代也進入了茶葉貿易的市場。藉著它所擁有的快速帆船，怡和洋行不僅能躲避海盜，順利地在中國沿海運送鴉片，也能趕運當季最早收成的茶葉到達倫敦的市場，賺取高額的利潤。怡和洋行的成功吸引了其他英國貿易商的注意，當中最富競爭雄心的，莫過於早在18世紀晚期就有中國貿易經驗的寶順洋行了。寶順洋行特別想仿效怡和洋行在中國沿海的貿易成就，正因為這樣的競爭局勢，使得寶順洋行在1859年來到打狗，試圖大展身手。[4]

　　時間在1859年夏末，寶順洋行的奧利佛船長〔Captain Oliver〕率領著頂頂有名的寶順雙桅縱帆船伊蒙特〔the Eamont〕，裝載了巴特那〔Patna〕和貝拿勒斯〔Benares〕鴉片，抵達打狗港。奧利佛船長此趟由廈門至福爾摩沙的旅程，在1891年出版，林賽·安德森〔Lindsay Anderson〕所著的《一艘載運鴉片的快速帆船之巡航」〔A Cruise in an Opium Clipper〕一書中，記載得十分清楚。奧利佛船長僅被告知把鴉片運至打狗，以供應給一艘等待於潟湖中的收容船，而且也被告知說鴉片可以在此賣個非常好的價格。奧利佛船長發現在潟湖內，已經有一個馬修·魯尼船長〔Captain Matthew Rooney〕先在打狗港佔據了一個令人好生妒嫉的位置。[5]

　　魯尼船長，一個愛爾蘭裔美國冒險家，是第一個居住在打狗的外國貿易商。大約在1856年，美國公司羅賓奈洋行〔W. M. Robinet & Co〕已經在打狗設立了商貿據點。在1850年代末期，飄揚在打狗港的是美國國旗，以美國商人為主要勢力，而也許只是因為美國南北戰爭於1861年爆發，才使得美國沒能在中國地區的貿易中取得更大的佔有率及優勢。[6]

Leasing of the Site for the Consular Offices

CHINESE MANNERS AND CUSTOMS IN FORMOSA.

SUGAR GODOWN, OR WAREHOUSE.

圖 3-1：蔗糖棧房
版畫上的蔗糖棧房，或倉庫，出現在1859年11月5日的倫敦畫報。這被認爲是魯尼船長爲羅賓奈洋行在哨船頭建的棧房。
（作者私人收藏，版權所有，翻印必究）

Image 3-1 : Sugar Godown
Engraving of a Sugar Godown, or Warehouse, that appeared in the Illustrated London News of 5 November 1859. This is believed
to show the godown built at Shao-chuan-tou by Captain Rooney for Robinet & Co.
(Author's collection. All rights reserved)

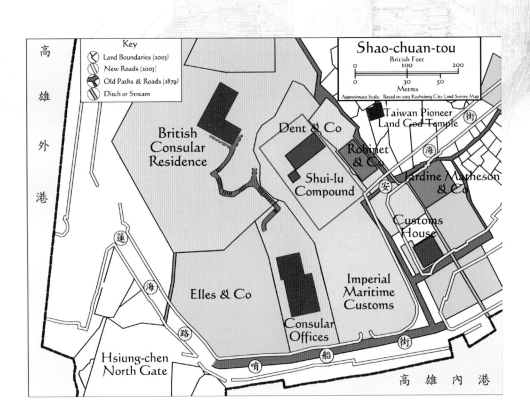

圖3-2：哨船頭地圖
哨船頭地圖，依比例繪圖，顯示出英國領事館建築，海關建築，以及羅賓奈洋行與怡和洋行的棧房。
（作者David Oakley私人收藏，版權所有，翻印必究）

Image 3-2 : Shao-chuan-tou Map
Map of Shao-chuan-tou, drawn to scale, showing the locations of the British Consular buildings, the Customs buildings, and the godowns of Robinet & Co and Jardine Matheson & Co.
(Copyright David Oakley. All rights reserved)

　　魯尼身為羅賓奈洋行的代理人，當時就在打狗潟湖的北岸，哨船頭山丘的東南方這個地方租了地，並利用堤防圈起了這塊地。當時，哨船頭大部份土地都屬於盧氏家族〔Lu family〕所有，魯尼就是向這個盧家租地。在那塊地上，他蓋了一個防波堤和一座貯糖倉庫〔如圖3-1〕。魯尼的倉庫，在1865年的海事圖上有被標示出來，是一棟長方型建築物，位於潟湖北岸一棟具有兩翼的長建築物之西北方〔參考第一章的圖1-2〕；而在一張哨船頭地圖上〔見圖3-2〕，它就是標示為羅賓奈洋行的那一棟建築物。

　　魯尼自己住在停靠在潟湖內的收容船上，他的鴉片與貴重物品也都存放在船上。當時，外國貿易商把船停泊在潟湖北岸，或是所謂的內港〔Inner Harbour〕，主要的考量是這樣比較安全，而當時打狗主要的聚落是位於潟湖南岸，用當地的方言稱Kîau的地方，也就是今天的旗後。

　　跟魯尼船長一樣，奧利佛船長也曾結識勇敢又有膽識的郭德剛神父，他是重建福爾摩沙多明尼克教會〔Dominican mission〕的人。郭德剛神父在1859年5月到達打狗，但在傳教過程中不幸地隨即遇上大災難，導致他被囚禁在鳳山〔Fengshan〕。他被魯尼船長救出後，繼續努力，創建了屏東縣萬金〔Wanchin〕聖母無原罪聖殿〔the Basilica of the Immaculate Conception，即俗稱的萬金聖母聖殿〕與高雄市的玫瑰聖母聖殿主教座堂〔the Holy Rosary Cathedral，俗稱玫瑰聖母堂〕。[7]

　　話說回來，寶順洋行不僅渴望在打狗建立自己的據點，也希望排除他們在貿易上最大的競爭對手，也就是供應鴉片給魯尼的怡和洋行。1859年12月，在被魯尼拒絕了數次之後，奧利佛船長終於成功買下魯尼在打狗的全部產業。魯尼的地產受到以十年為期的可更新租約所規範，而第一次簽租約是在1855年，從盧分來〔Lu Fen-lai〕與盧然老〔Lu Jan-lao〕手中租下。由魯尼手中轉移給奧利佛的區域包括從羅賓奈洋行倉庫後面到潟湖邊上的羅賓奈防波堤中間的全部土地〔這地區在前述的哨船頭地圖上是以橘色標示〕。奧利佛船長對擁有這個範圍內的土地產業仍覺得不夠滿意，於是他又在1859年12月〔咸豐9年12月〕簽了一個十年租約，把哨船頭南岸靠海的所有土地幾乎全都租下，由羅賓奈洋行倉庫往西邊延伸至井邊的大岩石〔見圖3-2〕，由他代表寶順洋行從盧天送手中租下。[8]

　　沙利文船長〔Captain Sullivan〕是怡和洋行在福爾摩沙的代理商，在這段期間他也正為了租用這一長塊連接海邊的土地在進行協商。在他眼中，寶順洋行上述的這筆土地交易唯一的目的就在於阻止怡和洋行在岸上建立據點。既然早先魯尼的鴉片貨源是由怡和洋行所提供的，寶順以為他們此舉不僅把這個顧客從怡和手中奪走，而且也阻擋了這家公司在打狗繼續貿易的任何機會。可是，就在一個月後的1860年2月，沙利文船長居然成功地在哨船頭取得另一塊土地，他似乎是以鴉片來直接支付土地費用，位置就在寶順洋行剛取得的土地東邊。在1865年海事圖上的長形、具有兩翼的建築物，以及在哨船頭地圖上以深綠色標示，時至今日還矗立在安海街的，就是沙利文船長在租來的土地上為怡和洋行所建造的倉庫。[9]

§

　　The origins of Jardine Matheson & Co go back to the late 1810s, although it did not gain its current name until 1832. Jardine Matheson profited immensely from the opium trade during the 1820s and also moved into the tea trade in the 1830s, after the monopoly of the East India Company [東印度公司] ended in 1833. With its speedy clippers Jardine Matheson was able not only to evade pirates to deliver opium along the China coast, but also to race the season's first teas to the markets in London where they commanded huge premiums. Such success attracted the attention of other British traders, with none being more aggressive than the prominent Dent & Co whose own China trade dated back to the late 18th century. Dent & Co was especially keen to emulate the success of Jardine Matheson in the China Coast trade, and it was this rivalry that first led Dent & Co to Takow in 1859. [4]

　　In the late summer of 1859 Captain Oliver of Dent & Co arrived at Takow carrying a cargo of Patna [巴特那] and Benares [貝拿勒斯] opium on board the famed Dent schooner, the Eamont. Captain Oliver's voyage from Amoy to Formosa is well documented in Lindsay Anderson's book entitled A Cruise in an Opium Clipper, published in 1891. Oliver had been told only that opium was being brought into Takow to supply a receiving ship and that the opium was fetching a very high price. Within the Lagoon Captain Oliver found that a Captain Matthew Rooney [魯尼] was already in jealous occupation of the northern shore of Takow harbour. [5]

Captain Rooney, an Irish-American adventurer, was the first known foreign trader to live at Takow. In about 1856 W. M. Robinet & Co [羅賓奈洋行], an American firm, had established themselves at Takow. In the late 1850s, it was the American flag that flew over the harbour at Takow and it was perhaps only due to the outbreak of the American Civil War in 1861 that the United States did not achieve greater dominance of the China coast. [6]

Rooney, W. M. Robinet & Co's agent, had leased and then embanked land on the northern shore of the Takow Lagoon to the south-east of the hill at Shao-chuan-tou. Most of the land at Shao-chuan-tou was owned by the Lu [盧] family from whom Rooney had obtained his lease. There he built a jetty and a warehouse for sugar (see Image 3-1). Rooney's warehouse is marked as the oblong building shown to the north-west of the long, two-armed building on the northern shore of the Lagoon upon the 1865 Admiralty map (see Image 1-2 in Chapter One), and as the Robinet & Co building on the Shao-chuan-tou map (see Image 3-2).

Rooney himself lived on the receiving ship, usually an old but spacious East Indiaman where he also stored his opium and treasure. At this time the foreign traders moored their ships on the north side of the Lagoon, or Inner Harbour [內港], principally for security as main village of Takow Harbour, called Kîau [旗後] in the native dialect, then lay on the south side of the Lagoon, at today's Chihou [旗後].

As well as Captain Rooney, Captain Oliver also met Father Fernando Sainz [郭德剛], the hardy priest who was reestablishing the Dominican mission in Formosa. After 200 years, Father Sainz had arrived at Takow in May 1859 but rapidly met with great adversities that saw him imprisoned at Fengshan [鳳山]. From there Sainz was rescued by Captain Rooney and intrepid father went on to found both the Basilica of the Immaculate Conception [聖母無原罪聖殿] at Wanchin [萬金] and the Holy Rosary Cathedral [玫瑰聖母聖殿主教座堂] in Kaohsiung [高雄市]. [7]

Dent & Co were keen not only to establish themselves at Takow but also to exclude their great rivals Jardine Matheson & Co who were supplying Rooney with his opium. In December

1859, after making several rejected offers to Rooney, Captain Oliver managed to buy out Rooney's business lock, stock and barrel. Rooney's property was held on a 10-year renewable lease, which had first been obtained in 1855, from Lu Fen-lai [盧分來] and Lu Jan-lao [盧然老]. The transferred site consisted of all the land from behind the Robinet & Co warehouse down to the Robinet jetty on the Lagoon (this area is coloured orange on the Shao-chuan-tou map). Not satisfied with only this holding, Captain Oliver then leased, again for 10 years, almost all the remaining foreshore of Shao-chuan-tou, extending westwards from the Robinet & Co warehouse to the large rock by the well (see Image 3-2), from Lu T'ien-sung [盧天送] also in December 1859 [咸豐 9 年12月] on behalf of Dent & Co. [8]

Captain Sullivan [沙利文], the Jardine Matheson agent for Formosa, who had also been negotiating for this stretch of foreshore, considered that this Dent transaction was solely to prevent Jardine Matheson from establishing themselves on shore. As Rooney had previously been buying his opium from Jardine Matheson & Co, Dent thought that they had not only wrested this customer from Jardine Matheson, but also had blocked any chance of the firm continuing to trade at Takow. Yet just one month later in February 1860, Captain Sullivan succeeded in obtaining another piece of land at Shao-chuan-tou, seemingly by paying in opium, immediately to the east of Dent's newly-acquired premises. The long, two-armed building shown on the 1865 Admiralty chart, and marked on the Shao-chuan-tou map in deep green, which still stands today in An-hai Street [安海街], shows the warehouse that Sullivan built on the site for Jardine Matheson & Co. [9]

The Shui-lu Compound
水陸大宅院

大約在1864年左右，水陸洋行〔Brown & Co〕接管了寶順洋行在廈門的部分業務，水陸這個名字是寶順洋行早先在廈門的前身公司。雖然廈門由水陸洋行接手，寶順仍持續在打狗的業務，在打狗他們的商務代理霍華船長〔Captain Howard〕，很顯然地在海岸邊蓋了一處住所。這個建築，後來被稱爲水陸大宅院〔Shui-lu compound〕，是在1865年之前所蓋的，因爲它出現在1865年英國海事圖上。我們知道寶順洋行在打狗也保有一艘收容船，三葉號〔the Ternate〕，就停在打狗港內用來存放鴉片與貴重物品。1864年11月7日，郇和最早在打狗設置的英國副領事館，就是在這艘寶順洋行的船上。[10]

1867年，發生了一場嚴重的商業蕭條，因而導致寶順洋行破產，一般都認爲這是因爲寶順與其競爭對手怡和洋行之間進行割喉戰的結果。因此在1867年早期，由於其財務問題，寶順洋行被迫從南福爾摩沙撤退。1867年，克里斯曼少校的打狗之行曾經視察過的就是寶順的產業。克里斯曼在報告中提到，這塊位於潟湖另一邊，與天利洋行建築遙遙相對的土地（譯注：即是位於打狗潟湖北邊的哨船頭上），地點更爲便利，而且有可能以比5000銀元多一些的價格就能買到。然而，他決定英國政府在道義上還是應該信守與天利洋行訂定的租約。於是乎，在哨船頭取得領事辦公處建地的機會一等就要等到另一個10年之後。[11]

1869年，寶順洋行破產後的兩年，水陸洋行正式接管寶順在打狗的資產，並開始以水陸洋行的名義在打狗經營生意。從此之後，水陸洋行接續著進行寶順洋行一直在做的築堤與海浦地填海造陸的作業。1870年，水陸洋行的代理商玻里多諾‧法蘭西斯科‧達錫華〔Polydoro Francisco da Silva〕根據海埔海灘章程，向英國代理領事，也就是前面提到過的有雅芝，申請一份證明，由中國官方保證水陸洋行進行填海造陸所取得的土地權益。租賃契約書正如水陸洋行期待的，由道臺黎兆棠〔Tao-t'ai Li Chao-tang〕於1870年9月[清同治9年9月]簽署。在1873年或該年前後，水陸洋行把它們的南部辦公室遷往安平，並把貿易活動的主要重心轉到北部的港口淡水；因此在打狗，它們只需要保留原先一小部份的土地。[12]

　　水陸洋行在打狗保留的土地是原先魯尼船長的物業，包括舊羅賓奈洋行倉庫。雖然這塊地是在1879年被正式轉移給水陸洋行的代理商朱利斯‧曼尼克〔Julius Mannich〕，稍後他以東興洋行〔Mannich & Co〕的名義進行貿易，但仔細查證後，這個物業轉移應該是在1873年所發生的。

　　當水陸洋行表示要釋出它們所擁有的舊羅賓奈倉庫以西的海岸地全部租賃權時，證據顯示是怡記洋行〔Elles & Co〕在打狗的代理商威廉‧亨利‧泰勒〔William Henry Taylor〕取得租賃權。這塊地包含原本由盧氏家族所出租的部份，加上利用防波堤由潟湖中逐漸填實造陸所形成的土地。

　　盧家租出的那部份土地後來被賣給清帝國海關〔Imperial Maritime Customs〕，在這筆交易中，海關因此取得水陸洋行的海岸舊居，也就是標示在哨船頭地圖的水陸大宅院。這棟宅院建築後來作為海關關長的官邸，一直到1891年關長把官邸遷往安平海邊為止。值得注意的是，哨船頭的海關房舍所在土地有一段時間都是由海關向泰勒承租，我們推測泰勒是當時持有租賃權的人。

§

Around 1864 Brown & Co [水陸洋行] had taken over part of Dent & Co's Amoy business, the name Shui-lu [水陸] being that of Dent's previous Amoy company. Dent continued on at Takow, where their agent, Captain Howard, apparently built a residence on shore. This building, known thereafter as the Shui-lu compound, was built prior to 1865 as it appears marked on the British Admiralty Chart of Takow of that year. Dent also maintained a receiving ship, the Ternate, within the Takow harbour to store opium and treasure. It was upon this Dent ship that Robert Swinhoe had first established the British Vice-Consulate at Takow on 7 November 1864. [10]

In 1867 there was a severe commercial depression and Dent & Co collapsed, this being often considered as a consequence of their cut-throat rivalry with Jardine Matheson. Thus in early 1867, Dent & Co was forced to withdraw from South Formosa due to their financial problems, and it was their property that Major Crossman had inspected during his visit in 1867. Crossman noted that this land, situated on the other side of the Lagoon from the McPhail building, was more conveniently situated and could have been obtained for little more than $5,000; however, he decided that the British government was bound by their rental agreement with McPhail. Thus the opportunity lapsed for another 10 years. [11]

A couple of years after Dent's failure, in 1869, Brown & Co [水陸洋行] formally took control of Dent's assets at Takow and opened their own business. Brown & Co thereupon continued Dent & Co's embanking and reclamation of the foreshore at Shao-chuan-tou. In 1870 the agent of Brown & Co, Polydoro Francisco da Silva [達錫華], applied to the British Acting Consul, who was none other than Hewlett, to request a Certificate for the reclaimed land from the Chinese authorities under the Sea Beach Regulations [海埔海灘章程]. The Deed of Lease was duly issued by Tao-t'ai Li Chao-tang [黎兆棠] in September 1870 [同治9年9月]. In or about 1873 Brown & Co removed their southern offices to Anping, and shifted the main focus of their trading activities up to the northern port of Tamsui [淡水]: they thus required to retain only a small portion of their land at Takow. [12]

The portion of land that Brown & Co retained at Takow was the original Rooney property and included the old Robinet & Co warehouse. Although this land was officially transferred to their agent Julius Mannich, later trading as Mannich & Co [東興洋行], in 1879, it would appear that the transfer actually took place in 1873.

When Brown & Co expressed their willingness to transfer all their leasing rights on the foreshore to the west of the old Robinet & Co warehouse, William Henry Taylor [泰勒], the Takow agent of Elles & Co [怡記洋行], apparently obtained the lease. The land consisted of the portion originally leased from the Lu family, plus the land that had been reclaimed from the Lagoon by embanking.

The portion originally leased from the Lu family was subsequently sold to the Imperial

Maritime Customs [海關], who thereby obtained the rights to Brown & Co's old onshore residence, marked as the Shui-lu compound on the Shao-chuan-tou Map. This building compound then served as the residence of the Commissioner of Customs until 1891, when the Commissioner transferred his place of residence up the coast to Anping. It is to be noted that the Custom House site at Shao-chuan-tou had been rented by the Imperial Maritime Customs from Taylor, who presumably held the lease.

Status of Reclaimed Land
填海造陸土地的歸屬情況

　　至於水陸洋行名下的那些填海造陸而來的土地，乃是由黎兆棠道臺在1870年簽發的文件所保證的。然而在1873年，夏獻綸道臺〔Tao-t'ai Hsia Hsien-lun〕簽發了另一份新的證明書，其中包含了自1870年以後再造陸形成的土地之權益，有效期限爲50年。由此可見，泰勒很可能也代表怡記洋行在1873年取得這片海埔地的權利，可是這個產權轉移卻從未向中國或英國官方註冊登記。[13]

　　大英工部在1876年就開始著手進行租賃領事辦公處土地的作業，在當時他們就在土地界線處放置了界碑〔如圖3-3〕。怡記洋行對工部表示願意切分這片堆填造成的岸邊土地的東邊部份，轉讓給他們作爲英國領事辦公處。然而，馬歇爾馬上很清楚地發覺到，問題不只是這塊填海造出的地持有人仍然是水陸洋行，而且這個證明書的有效期限僅有50年，而不是英國政府所需的永久租賃權。雪上加霜的是，這片海埔地與原來的哨船頭陸地從未被測量過，所以沒有人清楚正確的地界。

　　面對這樣的狀況，馬歇爾遂要求領事館取得一份新的永久租約，因而在1877年3月〔光緒3年2月〕代理領事官佩福來〔George Macdonald Home Playfair，又譯佩費爾〕要求道臺夏獻綸〔Tao-t'ai Hsia Hsien-lun〕讓英方將原來的證明書換爲永久租約。新契約是在1877年3月14日由夏道臺簽署，接下來水陸洋行在1877年6月28日把該處土地全數轉移給怡記洋行。而怡記洋行就在同一天，亦即6月28日，再把此片土地的一部份，轉讓給擔任英國工部首席委員代理人的馬歇爾。這兩個轉移案子居然發生在同一天，這件事清楚地顯示了英國工部針對存在於怡記與水陸洋行之間的土地轉讓已經預先做了安排規範，才能讓事情這麼有秩序地發展。[14]

　　有雅芝雖在1877年11月就被派爲領事官，但是直到1878年5月1日才到達打狗就任。有雅芝領事在到達後，即刻著手爲臨海土地與填海所造之地，以新的簽約人的名義，申請分割後的新的永久租約。這些重新分配水陸洋行土地的新持有者如下：怡記洋行持有最西邊

圖 3-3：1876 VR/IMC 界碑石
1876年馬歇爾豎立的地界碑石，以顯示海關和英國領事館辦公室園區土地之間的界線。
（作者私人收藏，版權所有，翻印必究）

Image 3-3：VR/IMC 1876 Boundary Stone
1876 Boundary Stone erected by Marshall to show boundary between Imperial Maritime Customs (IMC) and H. M. British Consular Office compounds; VR is Victoria Regina.
(Photograph by author. All rights reserved)

的部份；英國皇家工部持有中間部份；而清帝國海關則持有最東邊的部份。有雅芝是一個辦事周到而一絲不苟的人，他的首件工作指示就是要求必須進行新的土地測量。[15]

1879年8月3日〔光緒5年6月23日〕，就在所有的土地租約文件終於要就緒前，夏獻綸道臺溘然而逝。夏道臺也許比領事或工部都更清楚明瞭這塊物業的情況，因為他自1872年4月〔同治11年2月30日〕開始擔任道臺。新道臺張夢元在1879年9月〔光緒5年7月21日〕上任，必須接手處理這個已提出申請的契約簽署案。更糟的是，有雅芝在1879年10月20日把領事權交給助理領事官何藍田〔William Holland，又譯威廉・賀蘭〕，離開福爾摩沙。[16]

§

The reclaimed portion was held under the Certificate that had been granted to Brown & Co by Tao-t'ai Li Chao-tang in 1870. However, a new Certificate, that included land that had been reclaimed since 1870, was issued by Tao-tai Hsia Hsien-lun [夏獻綸] in June 1873 for a duration of 50 years. This suggests that William Henry Taylor, presumably acting for Elles & Co, had obtained the rights to this foreshore also in 1873 but that the transaction had never been registered either with the Chinese or British authorities. [13]

H.B.M. Office of Works had begun the process of leasing the Consular Office site in 1876, at which time they had placed boundary stones (see Image 3-3). Elles & Co then offered to divide off the easterly portion of the reclaimed foreshore for the site of the British Consular Office. However, it was immediately apparent to Marshall that not only did the rights to the reclaimed land still reside with Brown & Co but also that the Certificate was valid for 50 years only, and not in perpetuity as the British government required. To add to the difficulties the reclaimed area and original site had never been surveyed so that the precise boundaries remained unclear.

Accordingly, Marshall requested the Consulate to obtain a new lease in perpetuity, and in March 1877 [光緒3年2月] Acting Consul George Macdonald Home Playfair [佩福來] asked Tao-t'ai Hsia Hsien-lun [夏獻綸] for the Certificate to be exchanged for a Perpetual Lease [永租]. The new Deed was issued by Tao-t'ai Hsia on 14 March 1877, whereupon Brown & Co transferred the whole site to Elles & Co on 28 June 1877. Elles & Co then transferred a portion of this site to Marshall, acting as agent for H.B.M. First Commisioner of Works, on the same date, 28 June 1877. That these two transactions took place on the same day clearly suggests the regularisation of an already existing transaction between Elles & Co and Brown & Co. [14]

Archer Rotch Hewlett, though appointed Consul in November 1877, did not arrive at Takow until 1 May 1878. Upon his arrival Consul Hewlett applied for new separate Perpetual Leases for the foreshore and reclaimed land to be issued in the names of the new leaseholders. These new leaseholders for the now transferred Brown & Co property were: Elles & Co, who retained the westernmost portion; H.M. Office of Works, who now held the central portion; and the Imperial Maritime Customs, who held the easternmost portion. First, being a thorough man, Consul Hewlett requested that a new survey be made. [15]

On 3 August 1879 [光緒5年6月23日], before all the documentation had been finally completed, Tao-t'ai Hsia Hsien-lun died. Tao-t'ai Hsia probably knew more about this property than either the Consul or the Office of Works, as he had been Tao-t'ai since April 1872 [同治11年2月30日]. The new Tao-t'ai, Chang Meng-yuan [張夢元], took over in September 1879 [光緒5年7月21日], and was left to deal with the issuance of the requested Deed. Moreover, on 20 October 1879 Hewlett handed over charge of the Consulate to the Consular Assistant, William Holland [何藍田], and left Formosa. [16]

Registration of Perpetual Lease
永久租約的註冊登記

　　很顯然地，準備測量土地所需文件與簽發新租賃契約所遭遇的主要難題之一，是英國政府與海關兩造之間有關土地界線的衝突爭議。在他啓程離開打狗十天之前，有雅芝試著尋求解決地界問題的方法，而且起草了一份最終版的「有關1878年12月達成的共識之備忘錄」，這份共識是當年他自己與代理量地官馬歇爾及海關稅務司好博遜〔Hobson，又譯哈布森〕所溝通建立的。在這份備忘錄中，記錄著他曾與盧天送討論到地界，而盧天送現在聲稱他僅只把山丘上的土地讓與英國政府，而至於山丘旁的土地，則是他以12銀元與一紙契約轉讓給清帝國海關。可是，好博遜發現上述的契約內容中有文字表示「若海關與領事館有任何爭議，他們兩造應共同協商解決」這樣的意思，因為如此，這份契約對保障權益而言，沒有很大的價值。馬歇爾堅持英國政府持有海關圍牆之外所有土地的這項主張，此堵圍牆明顯地是水陸洋行在沒有合法權利的情形下蓋在山丘下的。因此之故，後來各方一致的結論是海關後牆外所有的土地為英國政府持有，英國政府也同意放棄主張海關牆內之土地所有權。[17]

　　現在就土地界線問題，英國政府與中國海關達成一致協議，中國官方終於可以在契約簽署之前，針對哨船頭海埔地進行測量。因此，代理領事何藍田會同鳳山縣饒縣令〔Fengshan Magistrate Shao〕和打狗貿易主管—旗後通商分局鄧委員〔the Takow Trade Commissioner Teng〕為此地作了詳盡的測量。[18]

　　新的代理領事官，霍必瀾〔Pelham Laird Warren，佩漢·萊爾德·華倫〕，於1880年1月1日到達打狗，由助理領事官何藍田手中接下領事業務。1880年的1月22日〔光緒5年12月11日〕，張孟元道臺簽署了這個土地契約，之後在1880年6月4日，這份土地契約文件由代理領事官霍必瀾在打狗正式登記生效〔見圖3-4〕。[19]

　　正當英國政府正式取得領事辦公處土地權利進入了冗長的過程時，構成領事館舍的兩棟主要建築，雖是延了又延，已然在同一時間於打狗開始興建。我們將在下一章，也就是

Chapter 3 打狗英國領事辦公處土地的租賃

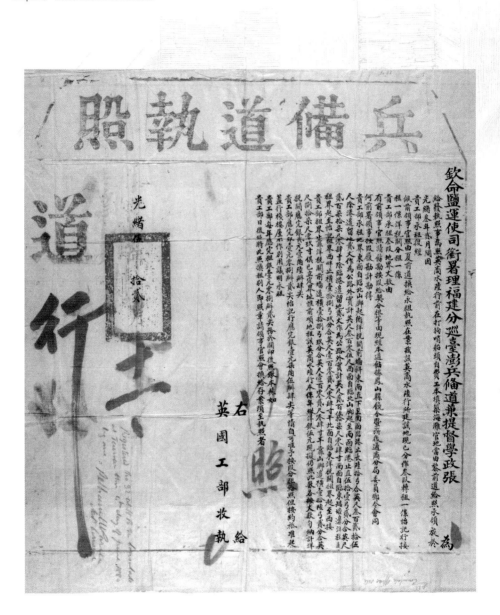

圖 3-4：領事館辦公室租賃地契
張道臺發出的英國領事館辦公室土地租賃地契，由代理領事霍必瀾在1880年6月4日於打狗註冊。
（版權屬於英國政府，文件 FO 678/3178，版權所有，翻印必究）

Image 3-4：Deed of Perpetual Lease for Consular Offices
Deed of Perpetual Lease granted to H.B.M.'s Office of Works for the site of the British Consular Offices issued by Tao-tai Chang and registered at Takow on 4 June 1880 by Acting Consul Warren.
(Crown Copyright. FO 678/3178. All rights reserved)

第四章，探討這兩棟矗立於打狗哨船頭的英國領事館建築物的設計與建造。

§

It appears that one of the major difficulties in preparing the documentation necessary for the survey of the site, and the issuance of a new Deed, was the contentious issue of the boundaries between British government land and that of the Imperial Maritime Customs. Ten days before his departure from Takow Consul Hewlett sought to resolve this issue of the boundaries and drew up a final 'Memorandum on the December 1878 Agreement' between himself, Acting Surveyor Marshall and Commissioner Herbert Edgar Hobson [好博遜]. In the memorandum Hewlett records that he had discussed the boundaries with Lu T'ien-sung who now claimed that he had only conveyed the land at the top of the hill to the British government and that he conveyed the hillside to the Imperial Maritime Customs for $12 with a Deed being drawn up. However, Hobson found that the Deed contained words to the effect that 'in event of any dispute the Customs & Consulate were to decide it together', so the value of this Deed was little. Marshall insisted upon the British government's claim to all the ground outside the Customs wall, which had been apparently built by Brown & Co upon the hillside without any legal right. Thus the consensus remained that all the ground outside the Customs back wall was held to be the property of the British government, and the British government agreed to abandon any claim to ground inside the Customs wall. [17]

Now that a consensus had been achieved between the British government and the Chinese Imperial Maritime Customs [海關], the foreshore at Shao-chuan-tou could at last be surveyed by the Chinese authorities prior to the issuance of the Deed. Accordingly, Acting Consul William Holland, together with Fengshan Magistrate Shao [鳳山縣饒縣令] and the Takow Trade Commissioner Teng [旗後通商分局鄧委員], made a detailed survey of the site. [18]

The new Acting Consul, Pelham Laird Warren [霍必瀾], arrived at Takow and took over from Holland on 1 January 1880. On 22 January 1880 [光緒 5 年12月11日] Tao-t'ai Chang Meng-yuan granted the Deed of Lease to H.B.M.'s Office of Works, and the Deed was then officially registered at Takow on 4 June 1880 by Acting Consul Warren (see Image 3-4). [19]

Whilst the long process of officially securing the rights of the British government to the site of the Consular Offices had been taking place, the two Consular buildings, though themselves delayed, had actually been erected at Takow. The next chapter, Chapter Four, looks at the design and construction of the two British Consular buildings at Shao-chuan-tou, Takow.

Leasing of the Site for the Consular Offices

Notes to Chapter Three
第三章註解

1. WORK 10/33/10, Marshall to O.W.L., 16 July 1877.

2. WORK 10/33/10, Marshall to O.W.L., 16 July 1877. Amounts are given in (\$) Mexican silver dollars and (£) 1877 British pounds.

3. Dent & Co operated under several names in China. Dent & Co used the name Pao-shun [寶順] in Foochow (see The China Directory of 1861) and also in Taiwan. The firm was known as Tien-ti [顛地] in Hong Kong (see The China Directory of 1861) and as Shui-lu [水陸] in Amoy until 1864, when they changed their name to Pao-shun and Brown & Co took over the name of Shui-lu (see China Directories for Amoy, 1861-63, 1864). Henry Donne Brown, the founder of Brown & Co, had been Dent's agent at Amoy. It is to be noted that, after the 1867 bankruptcy of Dent & Co, John Dodd continued to use the Dent company name [寶順] for his own company of Dodd & Co. For the sake of simplicity, I have consistently used the Pao-shun [寶順] name to refer to Dent & Co.

4. Bard, Solomon, Traders of Hong Kong: Some Foreign Merchant Houses, 1841-1899, Urban Council, Hong Kong, 1993, pp. 56-57, 65-68.

5. Both Patna [巴特那] and Benares [貝拿勒斯] opium came from the Bengal Presidency in the Northeast of India (while the Patna opium came in cakes packed into chests, the Benares opium, also in chests, came in rich round balls: the Benares product was greatly preferred in Formosa.); see, for example, p.86 from Lindsay Anderson's A Cruise in an Opium Clipper, Ibex, Melbourne, 1989 (This fascinating book was originally published in 1891 and describes the 1859 voyage of the Eamont to Takow under Captain Oliver.); A Receiving Ship was a heavily armed hulk, or decommissioned gunship, typically used to store the opium and the silver at a port.

6. Anderson, p. 197.

7. Fernandez, Fr. Pablo, One Hundred Years of Dominican Apostolate in Formosa 1859-1958, University of Santo Tomas, Manila, 1959 (Reprinted by SMC Publishing Inc., Taipei, 1994), pp. 41-51.

8. FO 678/3022; and FO 678/2999. See also Jardine Matheson (J.M.) Archives B8/6/5 and B8/6/9, reprinted in the Kaohsiung Historiographical Journal, Vol. 6, Issue 3 [高市文獻第6卷第3期], pp. 14-15.

9. J.M. Archives B8/6/9, B8/6/12 & B8/6/14. The plot measurements are precisely the same as those given in FO 678/3010.

10. see China Directories for 1862, 1863, and 1864.

11. Bard, pp. 56-57; B.P.P., Vol. 2, p. 231.

12. Davidson, pp. 176-177; Polydoro Francisco da Silva, a Portuguese citizen under British protection, was born in Macao (da Silva was one of two agents of Dent & Co in Amoy before becoming Dent's agent at Takow in about 1862, the other Dent agent at Amoy was Henry Donne Brown, who set up Brown & Co at Amoy, using Dent's Amoy trading name of Shui-lu [水陸].); FO 678/3177 (This Deed was translated by P. L. Warren, the Acting Interpreter at Takow in 1870.); FO 678/3022; and FO 678/3035.

13. FO 678/3178; WORK 10/33/10, Marshall to O.W.L., 16 July 1877.

14. FO 678/3178; and FO 678/3035.

15. FO 678/3178.

16. FO 228/661, p. 44; and FO 228/974, p. 106; see also 臺灣地理及歷史 卷九. 官職志 / 潘敬尉主編; 鄭喜夫纂輯, p. 24.

17. WORK 10/210. Memo by Hewlett on 1878
    Agreement between Hewlett, Marshall
    and Hobson, 10 October 1879.

18. FO 678/3178.

19. FO 228/974, Warren to Wade, 2 January 1880.

領事官邸與領事辦公處
之設計、材料與建造
Design, Materials and Construction
of the Consular Residence and
Consular Offices

SECTION 'B.B.'

EAST ELEVATION.

WEST ELEVATION.

PLAN
FOUNDATIONS ¹⁄A

[handwritten annotation at top: "to accompany my letter to H.M. office of Works. London. Dated 13 July 1877. O.W. 544. J. Marshall act[ing] Surveyor 13/7/77."]

Introduction
緒論

　　如同我們在第二章已經討論過的，在1867與1897年間，駐中國領事館舍的建造，是由英國陸軍皇家工程部裡徵召而來的人員所負責。皇家工程師對建築物的設計有相當老到的經驗，而且不僅僅侷限於防禦工事與監獄。倫敦最有名建築物中，有兩棟都是由皇家工程師所設計及建造的，它們是維多利亞與亞伯特博物館，以及皇家亞伯特廳，分別在1857年與1871年完成。

　　1877年2月，工部委員會總計核撥了1800英鎊給上海工部辦事處，做為在1877至1878年間在打狗建造一棟給助理領事官住宿的官邸。這樣的經費規模如何？為了做比較，我們應該還記得克里斯曼1867年的訪查打狗之行，理由之一是檢驗天利洋行的那棟建築以評估買下它的可行性。當時的估算曾記錄在英國國會的文件上，總值是3400英鎊，相當於16000元。這裡所謂的元，名義上是指香港元，但是香港的貨幣當時並沒有在商人之間取得足夠的信任，商人偏好使用西班牙或墨西哥銀元進行交易，這類銀元與香港銀元至少在名義上是可以等值換算的。1877年時，馬歇爾在報告上曾記述打狗領事官員當時是住在一棟租來的房屋中，而這當然就是我們前面提到的天利洋行那棟建築。[1]

　　等到1877年4月2日，馬歇爾一得到工部委員會的授權，他馬上就著手草擬建築工程計畫。同一時間，馬歇爾亦指示當時人在淡水監督該處官邸興建的上海工部辦事處監工技師〔Clerk of Works〕威廉・鮑爾〔William Power〕，即刻動身前來打狗監督新的建造工程。[2]

§

As has been discussed in Chapter Two, the Consular buildings erected in China between 1867 and 1897 were the responsibility of men recruited from the Royal Engineering Department of the British Army. The Royal Engineers had considerable experience in the design of buildings, and this was not merely limited to fortifications and gaols. Two of the most famous buildings in London, the Victoria and Albert Museum and the Royal Albert Hall, were designed and built by the Royal Engineers, with completions in 1857 and 1871 respectively.

In February 1877, the Board of Works allocated the sum of £1800 to the Office of Works at Shanghai for the construction of a Residence for a Consular Assistant at Takow during 1877-78. As a point of comparison it should be noted that one of the reasons for Crossman's 1867 visit to Takow had been to inspect the McPhail building with a view to purchasing it. The sum then stated in British Parliamentary papers was £3,400, equivalent to around $16,000. The dollars referred to were nominally Hongkong dollars, but these had failed to win acceptance amongst the traders, who preferred to use preferably the Spanish or otherwise the Mexican silver dollar which had virtual parity with the nominal Hongkong dollar. In 1877, Marshall noted that the Consular officer was currently living in a hired house, which was certainly the McPhail building. [1]

As soon as Marshall received authorisation from the Board of Works to build on 2 April 1877 he commenced to draw up plans for the building work. At the same time Marshall directed William Power, a Clerk of Works from the Shanghai Office of Works, then at Tamsui to oversee the construction of the Consular Residence there, to proceed to Takow to oversee the new construction work. [2]

To accompany my letter to H. M. Office
of Works. London. Lited 13 Juty 1877. O.W. 544.
J Marshale
act Surveyor
13/7/77.

Design of British Consular Residence
英國領事官邸的設計

　　如同第二章所言，原先的構想是在打狗建一棟包含官邸與辦公室的建築，供領事官員使用，這是英國領事館最常見的形式。可是，根據馬歇爾的報告，伯斯早在1875年3月就曾提出建議，最好在港口興建兩棟分開的建築做為領事館。1876年9月，馬歇爾報告中曾提到現在的構想是建一棟助理領事官等級所住的官邸建築，如果可能的話是規劃為單身者的宿舍，並兼具領事辦公室的機能；如此一來，另一棟分離的建築則充當巡捕的住所和牢房。他更進一步估算建助理領事官住所兼辦公室的費用是1800英鎊，而巡捕住所與牢房那棟的費用是1200英鎊。考量時間的限制，他提議將後者的工程暫時擱置，但他申請了用來蓋官邸的那1800英鎊。1877年2月，工部委員會如期地撥下總額1800英鎊的費用，作為在1877至78年間建造打狗助理領事官邸之費用。[3]

　　等到1877年4月馬歇爾著手草擬建築工程計畫之後不久，他就改變主意，覺得有必要把辦公室、巡捕住所與牢房一起建在山丘下的潟湖海埔地，而把官邸單獨留在哨船頭的山丘上，比較符合需求，於是他不得不在1877年7月再度修改這兩棟建築物的功能。如此一來，山上官邸將沒有辦公室的功能，空出來的閒置房間就被用來當臥室：就在這樣的情形下，這個官邸從助理領事官等級的單身宿舍升格為大小適合副領事官居住的公館。[4]

　　針對變更計畫，馬歇爾解釋道，因為官邸將建造在高於海平面100英尺的哨船頭山丘上，他想上到官邸的這段陡坡並不適合每日必須進行的治公事務。這些例行性業務牽涉到貿易，而這些商業相關業務不只是與船長的交易有關，也需要與清帝國海關密切合作，後者自1873年起，就已經在哨船頭山腳下建立起辦公據點。[5]

　　這些設計需要伯斯的建議，伯斯仍是負責中國及日本領事館舍的量地官，在領事館籌建的這段時間他正在英格蘭。儘管在1877年4月，馬歇爾已經命令他手下的監督技師威廉·鮑爾，經由廈門趕到打狗來參與領事館興建的工作，但是颱風季節的到來使鮑爾滯留在廈門，直到年底。這個建造時程上的延誤，讓伯斯能有更多的時間，針對哪種建築適合打狗

領事館，提供更多的建議，此時也正當他必須重新計算建築計畫的經費，以便納入由1878
年4月1日算起的下一個會計年度預算，以爭取工部委員會的許可。倫敦的工部辦公處根據
伯斯的建議，在1877年11月30日通知馬歇爾，依據新通過的預算，這棟建築必須規劃爲助
理領事官的官邸，它「應該樸實且牢固，而且由於打狗港白蟻肆虐，若非絕對需要，絕對
不准使用木料建材。」[6]

　　如同從馬歇爾爲打狗領事館官邸所繪的建築設計圖可以看到的〔圖4-1〕，這棟建築
物被設計爲一棟單層平房，具有木柱支撐的寬迴廊。這種平房設計是很典型的由印度起源
的皇家工程部作品。它那單層、輕巧的設計可能很像原先的淡水副領事官邸。在1867年
時，淡水領事官邸起先的設計是兩層樓的構造，然而在同年，北福爾摩沙發生大地震之
後，當時在淡水的代理領事官何爲霖〔Henry Frederic William Holt，又譯亨利・斐德
烈・威廉・赫特何爲霖〕說服了伯斯，輕巧的單層建築將會比較適合臺灣的情況。說起這
件事後來的發展，由於英國不確定是否繼續在福爾摩沙設立領事機構，淡水領事官邸直到
1876/1877年間才開始建造。[7]

　　雖然高於海平面，打狗領事官邸本身的水源供應來自建築北邊的一個天然泉源，這個
湧泉比迴廊地板高出64英呎。根據這些紀錄，泉源可能在領事官邸北邊約250公尺遠之處。
[8]

§

　　As stated in Chapter Two, the original intention had been to build a single structure at
Takow to serve as both a residence and offices for the Consular officer, this being the most
usual form of Consular building. However, according to Marshall, Boyce had recommended
as early as March 1875 that two separate buildings be erected at the port. In September 1876,
Marshall stated that the intention was to build one building to serve both as a Residence for
a Consular Assistant, which would have been bachelor quarters only, and as the Consular

TAK

CONSULAR

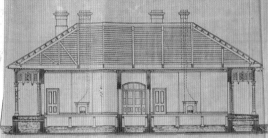

SECTION A.A.

FRONT ELEVATION

圖 4-1：1877年打狗領事館官邸建築設計圖
由代理量地官馬歇爾於1877年爲打狗領事館官邸建築設
計圖，此圖附在他於1877年7月13日的信中，一起寄到
倫敦工部辦公室。
（版權屬於英國政府，WORK 10/33/10，版權所有，
翻印必究）

Image 4-1 : 1877 Architectural drawings for Takow
Consular Residence
The Architectural drawings made by Acting
Surveyor Francis Julian Marshall for the Takow
Consular Residence in 1877, which were sent to H. M.
Office of Works, London, in his 13 July 1877 letter.
(Crown Copyright. WORK 10/33/10. All rights
reserved)

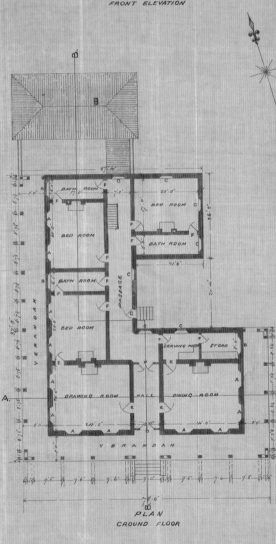

PLAN
GROUND FLOOR

SCALE 10

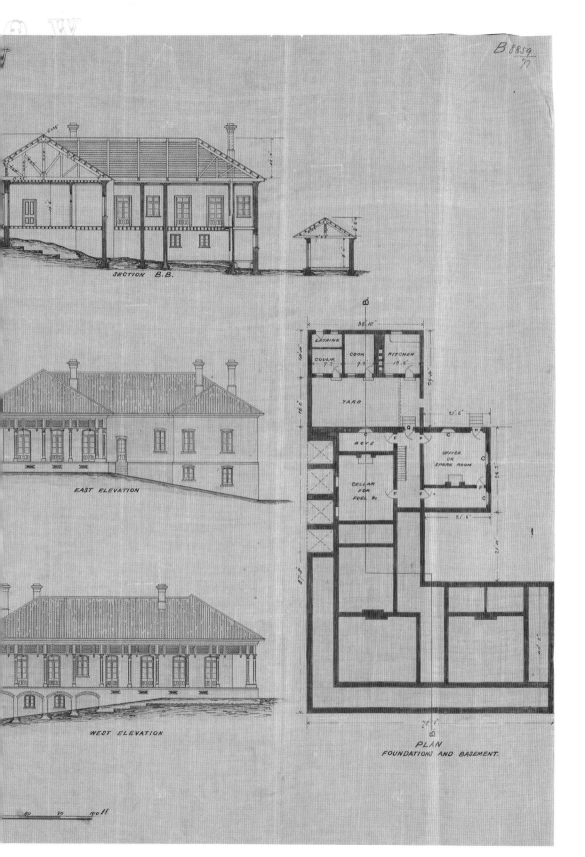

SECTION B.B.

EAST ELEVATION

WEST ELEVATION

B.

LATRINE
COOLIE 9.3
COOK 9.3
KITCHEN 13.6

YARD

BOYS

CELLAR FOR FUEL &c.

OFFICE OR SPARE ROOM

PLAN
FOUNDATIONS AND BASEMENT.

Offices; and that a separate building should therefore be erected for the Constable's Quarters and Gaol. He further estimated the costs of construction to be £1800 for the Residence for an Assistant with Consular Offices, and £1200 for the Constable's Quarters and Gaol. The latter building work he proposed be deferred due to time constraints, but requested the £1800 for the Residence. In February 1877, the Board duly allocated the sum of £1800 for the construction of a Residence for a Consular Assistant at Takow during 1877-78. [3]

Soon after Marshall commenced to draw up plans for the building work in April 1877, he determined that it would be necessary to build the Consular Offices together with the Constable's Quarters and Gaol down on the Lagoon foreshore, with the Consular Residence to stand by itself upon the hill at Shao-chuan-tou, and he was obliged to modify the separate functions of the two buildings again in July 1877. Thus the Consular Residence would have no Consular Office function, allowing the now redundant office rooms to be used as bedrooms: in this way the Residence changed from being a dwelling suitable for a bachelor, and became a Residence sufficiently large for a Vice-Consul. [4]

Marshall explained that, as the Consular Residence would be built 100 foot above sea level on top of the hill at Shao-chuan-tou, he reasoned that the steep climb up to the Consular Residence would make it unsuitable for day-to-day office matters. Such business affairs routinely involved trade matters, and not only meant transactions with ships' masters, but also required close cooperation with the Imperial Maritime Customs, who since 1873 had established themselves at the base of the hill at Shao-chuan-tou. [5]

The design needed the recommendation of Boyce, still the Surveyor for China and Japan, who was now living in England. Although Marshall had ordered his Clerk of Works, William Power, to proceed to Takow via Amoy in April 1877, the onset of the typhoon season left Power stranded at Amoy until the end of the year. This delay in the construction schedule allowed Boyce to offer further comments on the type of building that would be suitable at Takow, as he now needed to resubmit the construction of the building into the Estimate for the next financial year, beginning 1 April 1878, for approval by the Board of Works. On 30 November 1877, the Office of Works in London, acting on Boyce's recommendation, informed

Marshall that the building, with newly-approved budget, should be a Consular Assistant's Residence which "may be plain and substantial and that no timber may used except such as is absolutely necessary, owing to the prevalence of white ants at the Port." [6]

As can be seen from Marshall's architectural drawings for the Takow Consular Residence (Image 4-1), the building was designed as a single-storey Bungalow, with a wide Verandah supported by wooden pillars. The Bungalow design was typical of Royal Engineering Department work from India. The single-storey, lightweight design was probably very similar to that of the original Tamsui Vice-Consular Residence. The Tamsui building had initially been designed in 1867 as a two-storey structure, but after a massive earthquake in North Formosa in the same year the then Acting Vice-Consul at Tamsui, Henry Frederic William Holt [何爲霖], persuaded Boyce that a lightweight single-storey building would be preferable. In the event, due to uncertainties over the continued British Consular presence on Formosa, the Tamsui Residence was not built until 1876/1877. [7]

The Takow Consular Residence had its own water supply from a spring to the north of the building and some 64 feet above the level of the Verandah floor. This would place the spring about 250 metres to the north of the Consular Residence. [8]

Materials of Takow Consular Residence
打狗領事官邸的建材

　　關於木料建材的使用與白蟻帶來的侵害，馬歇爾沒有理會伯斯的建議與倫敦工部辦公處的禁止規定，在打狗領事官邸的設計上似乎用了相當多的木材。這可能是爲了讓大部份的結構先在中國大陸由熟練的木工造好，因爲當時的福爾摩沙缺少在地的熟練工匠，而且即使有也是距離遙遠聘雇不易，特別是福爾摩沙南部缺工更是嚴重。馬歇爾聲明這些建築將會是「福爾摩沙南部最早的一批異國建築物」，無視於郇和早在1865年就對天利洋行的建築做過類似的評斷。[9]

　　磚塊、花崗石、木造結構與其他材料，比方說鐵以及攪拌砂漿用的石灰，這些種種建材都是從中國大陸以船隻運來，在打狗港卸下，先擺放在港邊預定蓋領事辦公處的空地上。[10]

　　領事館舍使用的門窗、迴廊與屋頂都是在上海製造的。雖然1900年重新整修時所用的木材種類有被清楚地指定出來，但是我們卻沒發現任何文件提及1878/1879年建造時所用的木材種類。1900年重修時的合約有提到，屋頂木材支架使用了一種能抗白蟻的極堅硬之香坡疊木〔Yacal，譯注：產於菲律賓，密度高且重，龍腦香科喬木〕，屋頂鋪木與板條部份用的則是福州杉木〔Shamok，譯注：杉木，特色是輕巧耐用〕裁切。[11]

　　磚塊與屋頂用的瓦片全部都是在廈門燒製的。用來建造打狗領事館舍的進口磚瓦清楚地紀錄在由清帝國海關所製作的1878與1879年的打狗海關歷年貿易統計〔Takow Trade Returns〕，在這兩年都有剛好超過50萬片的磚瓦從廈門進口，這數目遠遠超過較早的任何年代，1875年除外。雖然目前山丘上的領事官邸構造，包括1900年重建的磚砌拱門迴廊，可能用了超過75萬片的磚瓦，但是原本的構造是以細的迴廊柱子來支撐木製屋頂，使用的磚塊必然少很多。1878/79年原始設計的磚塊與1900年的磚塊不同，它們的差異可以由大小看出：1878/79年較軟的磚塊很明顯地比1900年燒得很硬的磚塊來得大。[12]

威廉·鮑爾本來在1877年4月就被召集到打狗來監督當地領事官邸與辦公處的興建，不過卻因為沒辦法找到一艘汽船能從廈門載他到打狗而耽擱了行程。於是，在1877年5月1日，馬歇爾指示他留在廈門，安排磚塊、瓦片與花崗石裝船運送到打狗的事宜。可是，船班碰上6月開始的西南季風，這表示直到1877年11月前，將沒有任何東西可以被運過海峽。[13]

儘管後來這些材料及時地在1877/78年冬天運過海峽，真正的建築工事要到1878年春天後才開始進行。

§

Despite Boyce's comments and the strictures by the Office of Works in London about the use of wood and the predations of white ants or termites, Marshall seems to have used much timber in the design of the Takow Consular Residence. This may have been to enable much of the structure to be build on the Chinese mainland as local skilled workers were few and far between on Formosa at this time, and especially so in the south. Marshall claimed, despite Swinhoe's 1865 assertion to the same effect about the McPhail building, that these would be "the first foreign built buildings in the South of Formosa." [9]

The bricks, granite, woodwork and other materials, such as iron and the lime for mortar, for the construction of the buildings were shipped across from the Chinese mainland and unloaded at Takow, where they were initially stored on the vacant Consular Offices site. [10]

The doors, windows, verandahs and roofing were all made in Shanghai. Although the woods used in the 1900 renovation are clearly specified, no document has been found identifying the specific woods used in the 1878/79 construction. The contract for the 1900 renovation identifies the main roof timbers as being made from Yacal [香坡壘], an extremely hard wood that is termite-resistant, with the roof boarding and lath work being cut from Foochow Shamok [福州衫木] wood. [11]

The bricks and roofing tiles were all made in Amoy. The imports of the bricks for the Takow Consular buildings clearly show up in the 1878 and 1879 Takow Trade Returns prepared by the Imperial Maritime Customs, with the number of bricks and tiles imported from Amoy in both 1878 and 1879 being just over half a million units, which far exceeded all earlier years except 1875. Although the present structure on the hill, which includes the brickwork verandah arches from the 1900 reconstruction, may use over three-quarters of a million bricks, the original structure, with its slender verandah pillars supporting wooden slatting, would have used far fewer bricks. The original brickwork from 1878/79 can be distinguished from that of 1900 by the size of the bricks: the softer bricks from 1878/79 are noticeably larger than the hard-baked 1900 ones. [12]

William Power, who had been summoned in April 1877 to Takow to oversee the construction of the Consular Residence and Consular Offices, was unable to find a steamer to carry him from Amoy to Takow. On 1 May 1877 Marshall directed William Power to stay on at Amoy to arrange for the shipment of bricks, tiles and granite across to Takow. However, the onset of the southwest monsoon in June meant that nothing could be sent across until November 1877. [13]

Although the materials were duly taken over in the winter of 1877/78, the actual construction of the buildings did not begin until spring 1878.

Construction of Takow Consular Residence and Consular Offices
打狗領事官邸與領事處的建造

　　早在1877年7月時，馬歇爾發現他無法趕上工部委員會對打狗領事官邸建造工事所要求的期程進度。他的困難來自多種因素，但或許最主要的挑戰是來自於工部要求新的領事館工程要在會計年度內完成，會計年度是從4月1日起到下一年的3月底，可是福爾摩沙南部的建築工事卻會受到兩種盛行季風的控制影響。在南部這個地方，從5月到10月吹的是西南季風，經常導致陰雨連日，而且在7月後有颱風的機率會很高，這樣的氣候使得進入打狗港的過程充滿了危險；11月到次年4月吹的是東北季風，帶來晴朗天氣而且降雨機率很低。可見福爾摩沙南部適合建築工事進行的時段是11月到6月，這不僅當年如此，至今也仍然一樣，這樣的情況很清楚地與財政部會計年度（在3月底截止）內工事必須執行完畢的規定產生衝突。[14]

　　在幾乎沒有可能把建材運過瞬息萬變的臺灣海峽，也不可能在1877年底前展開任何建築工事的這種狀況下，馬歇爾預期領事館舍不可能會在會計年度結束的1878年3月31日前完工，於是他被迫要請求工部委員會在1878/79年度，再一次針對新編列的預算進行投票表決。[15]

　　這個新的預算表決，在1878/1879年度內提供了馬歇爾700英鎊的經費，但現在這筆錢已經不只是用於官邸的興建，同時也包含了領事辦公處的建造經費。然而到了1879年2月，馬歇爾明瞭他將會超支，於是他不得不要求在原來的700鎊之外，再多撥400英鎊，這次追加工部委員會同意了，但強烈地提醒馬歇爾，不得再增加任何預算。[16]

　　1878年初期，由於駐打狗的首席監工技師，人稱卡特曼先生〔Mr Cartman〕，很突然地在工程都尚未開始前辭職求去，馬歇爾不得不選擇一個臨時的監工技師，來監督打狗建築物的實際工程狀況。這個被選中的人是查爾斯‧梅維爾‧唐納森〔Charles Melville Donaldson〕。[17]

　　查爾斯・梅維爾・唐納森大約是在1823年生於蘇格蘭的格拉斯哥，原本是上海的船隻糧食供應商，經營聚盛洋行〔Donaldson & Co〕，其子為查爾斯・彼得・麥克阿瑟・唐納森〔Charles Peter McArthur Donaldson〕，1848年在中國出生，於1870年代早期就加入上海工部辦事處，一直擔任監工技師直到大約1890年。在1878年早期卡特曼無預警的離職之後，唐納森隨即被任命為工部駐打狗的總監督，他的任期由1878年3月25日開始，直到1879年6月30日領事館舍完工為止。有雅芝領事與馬歇爾兩人都極力稱讚唐納森在打狗盡心盡力毫不鬆懈的工作，並因此向倫敦方面建議，給他特別的獎賞報酬。但是倫敦官方因為擔心從此創下這種要求酬賞的先例，所以毫不遲疑地拒絕了。在打狗建築工事完成後，馬歇爾不再需要唐納森的服務，因此他在1879年7月22日返回他在上海廣東路1號的家；1891年4月2日，由神戶返回上海的途中，於海上去世。他的兒子唐納森繼續為工部辦事處服務，直到大約1890年才離職轉而為福利洋行〔Hall & Holtz〕工作，福利洋行是上海的第一家百貨公司。他死於1897年2月13日，被葬在上海的「新墓園」，就在他父親的墓旁。[18]

　　當建築工程開始後，堆放在山下空著的領事辦公處預定地的建材必須請當地工人，或所謂的「苦力」（coolies）背上山。為了這個目的，馬歇爾要求唐納森開闢一條到山丘上的新路徑，因為在這之前兩個領事館舍建地間並沒有路徑相連。

　　唐納森開闢的這條路是由山下領事辦公室後面繞上山丘，以對角線穿越的方式經過舊水陸洋行宅院後面的界牆（現在是清帝國海關的後牆），之後再連接另一條古老的登山小徑通往山頂官邸預定地的北邊（如圖4-3）。運到這裡後，建材才被安排、組合為實際建造時所需的形態。

　　從這條後來被稱為「唐納森的通道」〔Donaldson's Path〕的小路，可以眺望清帝國海關的官邸，這引起海關稅務司好博遜〔Herbert Edgar Hobson〕相當大的不悅。從稅務司好博遜與有雅芝領事之間有關小徑的通訊往返中，我們可以清楚地知道搬運建材上山的工作，在1879年5月時幾乎已經完成，可是這一條唐納森於1878年所建的通道，照理說應該是臨時性的，但搬運完成後卻仍舊開放著。有雅芝在離開打狗前不久曾寫道：

圖 4-2：1878年打狗領事官邸建造中的模樣（圖像解析度經過加強）。

Image 4-2 : 1878 View of the Consular Residence under Construction
Enhanced photograph of Shao-Chun-tou showing the Takow British Consular Residence under construction during 1878.
The building to the right of centre is the Shui-li Compound, used as the residence of the
Commissioner of the Imperial Maritime Customs; and further to the right can be seen the old Robinet & Co building.

圖 4-3：1904年時羅伯‧海斯汀的兒女們在領事石階（唐納森的通道）上。

Image 4-3：The Hastings children on the Consular steps c1904
Some of the children of Robert Hastings photographed on the Takow Consular steps just above the junction with Donaldson's Path, and just below the gate leading into the garden of the Consular Residence.

「談到通道本身與苦力使用這條通道的問題，對於海關官邸的住戶來說是令人厭惡的干擾，但在我看來則不過是「茶壺裡的風暴」。如果說真的有困擾，我們可以藉由提升圍牆的高度來解決，或者由海關方面來做，然後雙方再都各自種樹來將彼此區隔。現存的海關官邸可能再過幾年就會被拆除，而且我猜想沒有任何稅務司會想要再建一棟如同現在這棟一般，如此靠近山腳的新房子。」[19]

「唐納森的通道」在它通向山丘上領事官邸所在地剛開始的那一段非常的陡峭，接下來以對角線經過海關後牆的那一段則幾乎是平的。開始那一段非常陡峭的路段是用廈門所運來的花崗岩壓艙物打造石階，以及後來通道兩旁的石牆。在領事官邸的正門，或是面南的入口處，也用花崗岩打造了石階。

建造工程的主要承包商阿彭〔Apong，譯注：該人名可能是閩南語發音〕沒能履行合約，很明顯地他是在磚牆建好之後毀約，在1878年夏天時留下一棟完成一半的建物，如空殼般佇立在山丘上，如同圖4-2所示，該照片顯示山丘上只有空殼的領事官邸，亦可看到水陸洋行的宅院與羅賓奈洋行的舊建築。阿彭簽的契約規定，要在1878年6月30日前完成領事官邸的工程，然而根據馬歇爾的說法是他「工作的進度嚴重地落後以至於不能完成合約」。因為監工技師卡特曼先生無預警離職，馬歇爾被迫計畫在極短的時間內實際完成領事官邸的興建，從查爾斯‧梅維爾‧唐納森在3月25日到達後，直到1878年6月30日的合約終止日這段時間；然而，除此之外，我們找不到更多關於阿彭履約失敗的資訊。[20]

就在阿彭無法履約的事件發生後，馬歇爾馬上從上海送工匠渡海來打狗，用他們來監督及訓練打狗本地工人，因為「這幾棟建築是福爾摩沙南部首次出現的外國人蓋的建築物，於是很自然地，打狗當地人需要有人來教導如何去完成這樣的建築工事。」[21]

因為福爾摩沙南部有颱風來襲的風險，所以主要的建築工事只能在11月到次年6月這段時間進行，而且考慮到官邸的位置就在毫無遮蔽的哨船頭山崖上，因而官邸的工程要到1878年底才能安全地重新展開。然而證據顯示，在這幾個夏季月份，山下領事辦公處的準備工程有可能持續地在進行，包括建造地基和一道包圍館舍的圍牆。領事辦公處的預定地是一片開闊的海灘地，主要的地質是黑的海砂、淤泥，以及小塊的珊瑚石灰岩。為了讓這塊地基上面能蓋起量體沈重的領事辦公處，首先必須得改造地質，讓它成為穩固的地基。這就得利用從廈門開來的船隻艙底的壓艙物，這些船因為從廈門運來的都是一些輕便的貨物，如鴉片，所以來程時需要壓艙物，而回中國時則載滿了打狗港的糖。廈門船的壓艙物是由當地的粗砂、礫石以及花崗岩塊所組成；這些壓艙物被用來整平土地與填實地基，塊狀花崗岩則是被用在砌成圍牆的基座部分。[22]

背負著要趕在1879年的颱風季節來臨前，同時完成兩棟建築物的壓力，唐納森可以說是不眠不休地工作。有雅芝領事描述唐納森每天的工作是「從日出到日落，不僅平日工作，而且周日與假日也照常工作，在此種氣候下，這樣的辛勞對他的身體健康是極大的威脅。」唐納森自己曾談到他每天工作10個小時，在監督大部分是以日計薪的短期雇工，沒有任何當地通譯或助手的幫忙；更辛苦的是，因為人力不足，他自己一個人不得不工作到深夜，整理每天的帳目，計算並支付工人的薪水，也要持續保持官方的書信報告。[23]

領事官邸一如預定的期限，在1879年4月落成，而領事辦公處則於同年6月完工。換言之，這兩棟建築物都順利地在1879年颱風季節來臨前完成，可是唐納森不只沒有得到倫敦官方的金錢獎賞，甚至連書面嘉獎褒揚也沒有。[24]

§

As far back as July 1877 Marshall was having problems on meeting the Board of Work's requirements on the schedule for the construction of the Takow Consular Residence. There were many causes of his difficulties, but perhaps a crucial one was that, whereas the Board of Works demanded that new works be completed within the financial year that ran from 1 April to 31 March the following year, construction work in the south of Formosa was dictated by the onsets of the two prevailing monsoons. From May until October the southwest monsoon blows persistently in the south, bringing often rainy days together with the strong possibility of typhoons after July, and rendering the entrance to Takow harbour fraught with peril;from November until April the northeast monsoon blows, bringing fine weather with little possibility of rain. The period for construction in south Formosa was, and is today, from November to June, which clearly conflicted with the Treasury's financial year that ended in March. [14]

Faced with almost no possibility of getting the materials shipped across the treacherous Taiwan Strait nor of starting any construction work until the end of 1877, Marshall saw it would be impossible to complete the work before the end of the financial year on 31 March 1878, and was thus obliged to request a new Vote for 1878/79. [15]

The new Vote granted Marshall for 1878/79 was for £700, but now included the construction not only of the Consular Residence but also of the Consular Offices. Yet by February 1879 it was clear that he would overrun this budget and Marshall was forced to ask for an Excess of £400 on the £700, this the Board of Works agreed to but strongly cautioned Marshall against exceeding this amount. [16]

Due to the abrupt resignation in early 1878 of the first Clerk of Works stationed at Takow, named Mr Cartman, before the construction had even begun, Marshall was obliged to choose a new temporary Clerk of Works to supervise the actual construction of the buildings at Takow. The man chosen was Charles Melville Donaldson [查爾斯·梅維爾·唐納森]. [17]

Charles M. Donaldson, who was born about 1823 at Glasgow in Scotland, was a Ship Provisioner in Shanghai, trading as Donaldson & Co [聚盛]. His son, Charles Peter McArthur Donaldson, who was born in 1848 in China, had joined the Office of Works at Shanghai in the early 1870s and remained there as a Clerk until about 1890. Following the unexpected departure of Cartman in early 1878, C. M. Donaldson was appointed Superintendent of Works at Takow from 25 March 1878 until the work was finished on 30 June 1879. Both Consul Hewlett and Marshall were to highly praise Donaldson's unflagging work at Takow, recommending him to London for a special bonus. This request for remuneration was promptly rejected by London for fear of setting a precedent. Marshall no longer needed C.

M. Donaldson's services after the completion of the Takow buildings and he returned to his home at 1 Canton Road, Shanghai, on 22 July 1879; he died on 2 April 1892 at sea, returning from Kobe to Shanghai. His son, C. P. M. Donaldson, continued to work for the Office of Works until about 1890 when he went to work for Hall & Holtz [福利洋行], the first department store in Shanghai. He died on 13 February 1897 and was buried next to his father at the 'New Cemetery' in Shanghai. [18]

The materials that had been stockpiled on the vacant Consular Offices site now needed to be carried up the hill by local workers, or 'coolies'. For this purpose Donaldson was required by Marshall to cut a new pathway up the hill, as no roadway joined the two Consular sites.

The path that Donaldson made ran up the hill behind the Consular Office site and then was driven diagonally across beside the boundary wall behind the old Shui-lu compound, now occupied by the Imperial Maritime Customs, before joining another old track which took it up to the crest of the hill to the north of the proposed site of the Consular Residence (see Image 4-3). Here the materials were assembled for the actual construction work.

This pathway, known as Donaldson's Path, overlooked the Imperial Maritime Customs residence, causing considerable annoyance to the Commissioner of Customs, Herbert Edgar Hobson [好博遜]. From the correspondence that ensued between Commissioner Hobson and Consul Hewlett about the path, one can learn that the transfer of materials up the hill had been almost completed by May 1879, yet although the path was supposedly built by Donaldson in 1878 as a temporary one, it remained open. Consul Hewlett wrote shortly before leaving:

> As to the question of the path & its use by coolies being a nuisance to occupants of Customs residence I look upon it as more or less 'a storm in a teacup'. We can abate the nuisance if there is one, by raising the height of the wall, or the Customs can do this & each party can plant the other out. The present Customs residence will probably be taken down in a few years & I imagine no [Commissioner] will think of building a new house so near the foot

of the hill as at present. [19]

Donaldson's Path as it first climbed up the hill towards the site of the Consular Residence was very steep, whereas the diagonal part beside the Customs wall was almost flat. This steep first section made use of the granite stones in the Amoy ballasts to form steps and later a wall. Steps were also made to enter the Consular Residence compound from the front or southerly end (see Images 4-3 and 4-4)

The main contractor Apong defaulted, apparently after the brick walls had been built, leaving the half-finished building as a shell upon the hill during the summer of 1878, as can be seen in Image 4-2, which shows the Consular Residence as a shell upon hill, the Shui-lu Residence, and the old Robinet & Co building. Apong had contracted to complete the the Consular Residence before 30 June 1878, but, according to Marshall, "utterly failed to carry out his contract." Due to the sudden departure of Mr Cartman, Marshall had been forced to plan the actual erection of the Consular Residence in an extremely short period, running from the arrival of Charles Melville Donaldson on 25 March until the contracted date of 30 June 1878; however, no further information regarding Apong's default was found. [20]

Following Apong's default, Marshall resorted to sending workmen over from Shanghai to oversee and train the local workmen, as "these are the first foreign built buildings in the South of Formosa, and consequently, the natives had to be taught their work." [21]

As major building works could only be carried out from November to June, owing to the risk of typhoons in south Formosa, it was not until the end of 1878 that work could safely be resumed on the Consular Residence owing to its very exposed situation on the bluff at Shao-chuan-tou. However, it appears that, during these summer months, work on preparing the site for the Consular Offices, including building the foundations and a compound wall, could proceed. The site for the Consular Offices was open beachland mainly consisting of black sand, silt and small coral limestone rocks. To make the site suitable for the erection of the heavy Consular Offices, it was necessary to first provide a stable base. This was done by using the ballast from ships arriving from Amoy which were carrying only light cargo, such as opium, but would return to China laden with Takow sugar. This ballast consisted of coarse Amoy sand and gravel and lumps of granite; this was used to level the site and prepare the foundations, the lumps of granite were used to build the lower parts of the compound wall. [22]

Under the pressure of completing both the buildings before the onset of the 1879 typhoon season, Donaldson worked tirelessly. Consul Hewlett recounts how Donaldson worked every day "from sunrise until sunset, not only on weekdays, but on Sundays and holidays, and that at very great risk, in this climate, to his own health." Donaldson himself relates that he was working ten hours each day on supervising the workmen, who were mostly hired on a daily basis, without the aid of any local interpreter or assistant; moreover, he was obliged to work late into the night in compiling the daily accounts, in calculating and paying the workmen's wages, and in keeping up with the official correspondence. [23]

The Consular Residence was duly completed in April 1879 and the Consular Offices in June 1879. Thus both buildings were safely completed before the onset of the 1879 typhoon season, yet Donaldson received neither commendation nor monetary reward from London. [24]

The Finished
Consular Buildings at Takow
打狗領事館舍完工

馬歇爾在1879年8月寫了一封信給倫敦當局，其中夾附了一張剛剛完成的打狗領事館舍圖〔見圖4-4〕，他在信中報告說領事官邸於1979年4月26日啓用入住，而辦公處則是在6月份開始啓用。他也報告說那棟租來的旗後領事館舍，也就是大家所知道的原天利洋行建築，在4月底時被終止租約了。[25]

然而，在這兩個領事館舍基地仍有好幾項工作尚待完成。因爲在打狗當地找不到想要使用的那些材料，所以領事官邸的圍牆尚未建好。於是，在等待足夠的材料被當成壓艙物運來打狗港之前，馬歇爾只好先造了一道6呎高的竹籬笆來當暫時圍牆，因爲貨運費用太高，所以無法不用壓艙物來建造永久性的圍牆。我們可以據此推測，圍牆計畫用花崗岩塊來建造。此外，領事辦公處院子的地面填高工事尚未完成，但是他提到，物料（主要是廈門壓艙物）若是可以成功購得，填高工程便會繼續進行。[26]

§

In an August 1879 letter to London, in which he enclosed a plan of the newly-completed Consular establishment at Takow (see Image 4-4), Marshall reported that the Consul's Residence was occupied on 26 April 1879 and the Offices during June. He also reports that the hired Consular premises at Chihou, known as the old McPhail building, were relinquished at the end of April. [25]

Several items of work still remained to be carried out, however, at the two new sites. The enclosure wall of the Consular Residence had not yet been built as the desired materials

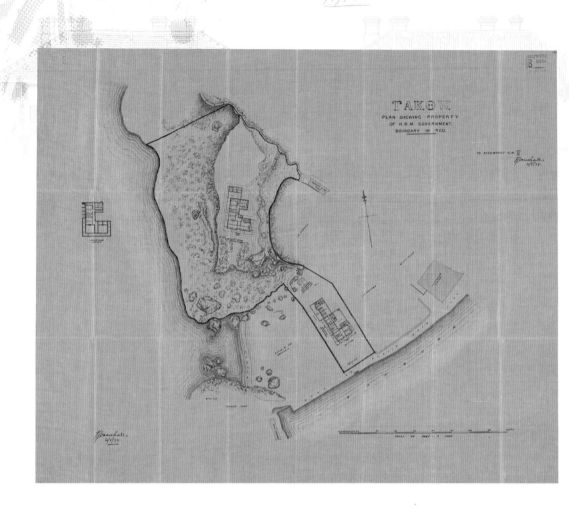

圖 4-4：1879年的圖，描繪了英國女王陛下擁有的打狗領事館物業。

Image 4-4 :　1879 Plan showing H. B. M. Consular property at Takow
Marshall's 1879 plan showing all the boundaries of the British Consular buildings at Takow.
This plan, which accompanied Marshall's August 1879 letter to H. M. Office of Works in London,
also includes the ground floor plan of the
Consular Offices and a modified plan for the basement of the Consular Residence.
(Crown Copyright. WORK 10/33/10. All rights reserved)

could not be found locally. Marshall had therefore erected a temporary 6-foot bamboo fence while he awaited sufficient material to arrive as ballast, the cost of freight being too high, to build the permanent enclosure wall. This suggests that a wall built from granite was intended. In addition, the raising of the ground level of the Consular Offices compound had yet to be completed, but he states that this would proceed as the materials, principally Amoy ballast, could be acquired. [26]

Consular Residence
領事官邸

有雅芝是第一個進駐使用新官邸的領事，針對這棟建築，他提供了以下描述：

「這個官邸居高臨下，眺望海和看向內陸的村落都是一覽無際，空間大小足以提供一位已婚或兩位未婚的官員居住。官邸內包括了一個客廳，一間餐廳與三間臥室，並配有一間書房、廚房與僕役房間」。[27]

對有雅芝而言，官邸的僕役房間成為他頭痛的難題。原先，設計了四個房間給官邸的僕役使用：其中兩個房間在官邸內部，另外兩房則在建築物後方的獨立小屋內。然而，後知後覺的馬歇爾似乎突然發現打狗當地的白蟻可能對建築造成極大的危害，其實伯斯在事先就曾警告過他白蟻的問題。因此馬歇爾下令把所有官邸前方〔朝南〕地窖房間裡所存放的箱子都清出來，移到其中一個僕役房，以免白蟻孳生，而這個僕役房可能就是送到倫敦的設計圖中〔如圖4-5〕標示著「男孩」的那個房間。在實際入住後，他更進一步發覺需要一個儲存柴火的房間，因此又更動了第二間僕役房作為此用途：這房間在設計圖中很真實地被標示為「燃料地窖」〔Cellar for Fuel &c〕。因此計畫中要給僕役使用的四個房間，到最後只有兩個維持原本計畫的用途。[28]

§

Hewlett, the first Consul to occupy the new Residence, offers the following description:

"The Residence, from which there is a commanding view of the sea and of the country inland, is sufficiently large for the accommodation of one married, or of two unmarried

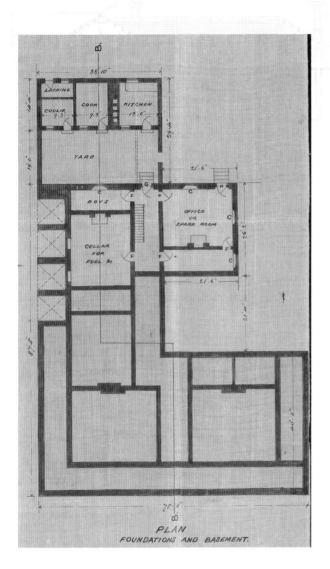

PLAN
FOUNDATIONS AND BASEMENT.

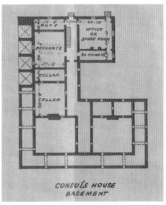

CONSULS HOUSE
BASEMENT

圖 4-5：1877年官邸地下室原始設計圖以及修訂過的1879年打狗領事官邸地下室設計圖。
〔兩張圖版權均屬於英國政府，WORK 10/33/10，版權所有，翻印必究〕

Image 4-5：Original 1877 Plan of Residence Basement & Modified 1879 Plan of Takow Residence Basement
Detail from Marshall's original 1877 plans for the Basement of the Takow Consular Residence (on right);
and 1879 modified version of the Basement plan (below left) from Marshall's
1879 Plan showing H. M. Consular property at Takow.
(Both images are Crown Copyright. WORK 10/33/10. All rights reserved)

officers. It contains a drawing-room, dining-room, and three bed-rooms, with a study, kitchen, and servants' apartments." [27]

The servants' quarters at the Consular Residence were a cause of concern for Consul Hewlett. Originally, four rooms had been planned for the household servants: two rooms under the house proper, and two rooms in the outhouse at the rear of the building. However, it seems that belatedly Marshall became aware of the great danger posed by white ants at Takow, about which he had been forewarned by Boyce. He therefore ordered that all the rooms in the front (south end) cellars to be cleared of the packing cases that were being stored there, and that they be moved into one of the servants' rooms, presumably that marked 'Boys' on the plans sent to London (see Image 4-5). He further discovered that a store-room for firewood was required, and therefore relinquished a second servants' room for this purpose: this is actually marked 'Cellar for Fuel &c' on the illustrated plan. Thus out of four rooms planned for servants, only two could finally be used as such. [28]

Consular Offices
領事館辦公處

　　在1879年8月的通信紀錄中，有雅芝也描述了新完工的領事館辦公處，他提到「堤岸碼頭區的辦公處包含了一間領事辦公室和一間綜合辦公室，綜合辦公室後面還設了官方抄寫員〔Writer，又譯書辦〕的住所」。[29]

　　領事辦公室的設計圖〔見圖4-6〕繪於1879年8月，詳細地顯示出房屋的分配位置。圖中可看出巡捕被安置在相當寬大的起居空間裡，有兩個臥室與一個起居室。在此圖中也顯示出牢房內設有三個拘留室。

　　然而，跟官邸的狀況一樣，有雅芝對於辦公處內缺乏領事館僕役的住處一事感到憂心。他寫道：「此處缺乏適當的居住空間給領事館的僕役，他們包含了四名船員〔他們的職責也包括擔任傳訊員〕，而且當我在此地時，僕役還包含了一名聽差〔Tingchai〕…馬歇爾…拒絕…安排更多的僕役起居空間，所持的理由是官方僕役不需要、也不應當住在領事館建築物內。針對這樣的意見，我所提出來的回應是，就我所知，領事館內的僕役對預防火警與竊盜事件是絕對必要的，只有在他們能住在領事館內，才能在任何的緊急狀況發生時提供他們的服務。」有雅芝也非常切中要害的指出，若是不在領事館內安排他們的住處，僕役們將會住在當時打狗的主要城鎮旗後，亦即港口的另一邊。[30]

　　為了平息這項異議，不過也謹記著自己有預算上的限制，馬歇爾取得倫敦方面的同意後，使用竹子、木板條與灰泥為材料，建造了領事館僕役的住處，並將支出控制在30英鎊以內。[31]

　　一位後來的領事，施本施〔William Donald Spence，又譯威廉・唐納德・史賓賽〕，曾提供更多有關這棟建築在1885年時被使用的詳細狀況〔見圖5-6〕。綜合辦公室在1885年當時被稱為船務辦公室〔Shipping Office〕，因為它主要的功能是辦理船舶到達以及離開打狗港時之登記報備。根據1864年稅務司威廉・麥斯威爾所頒布的打狗港海關章程以及領

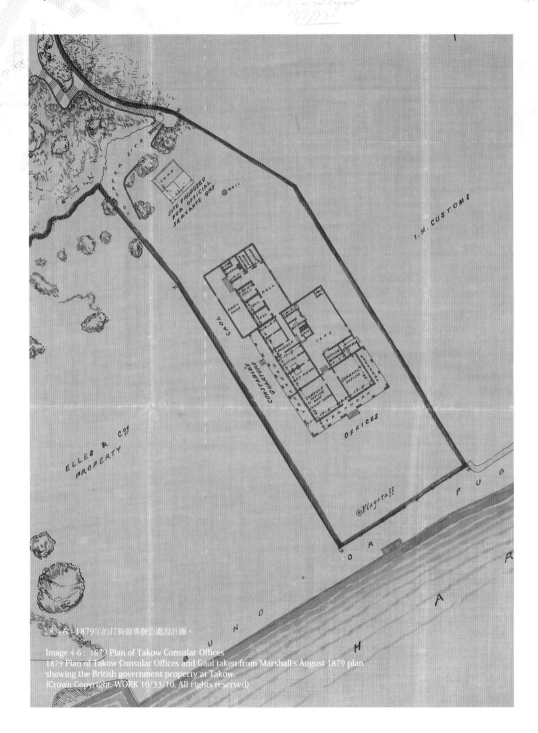

事邱和頒布的打狗港口章程，所有船長必須在到達港口的48小時內，把船隻文件與進口載貨單呈報給他們的領事；既然自從開港貿易的時期以來，英國領事也代理了丹麥、德國、法國與奧匈帝國的領事業務，這意味著幾乎所有到達打狗的船隻，都必須到這個領事船務辦公室登記報備。[32]

領事施本施1885年對此棟建築所作的描述中，在領事辦公室後方的兩個房間被標示為巡捕所使用的空間，巡捕睡在最靠近領事辦公室的房間。抄寫員顯然是住在綜合或是船務辦公室之後方，一間被標示為「辦公室僕役員」的小房間。辦公室傳訊員、船夫頭與守夜更夫則是全部睡在「一間獨立小屋」。船夫頭（head Gigman）是船員的領頭，負責管理繫在水岸階梯旁的領事坐船，從水邊的階梯上來可以進入領事辦公處；領事坐船是領事用於搭乘外出，稍候被移往安平。[33]

這裡的「獨立小屋」看起來很像是有雅芝曾經堅持要求，使用竹子、木板條與灰泥來為辦公室僕役蓋的住處，它不僅依照要求被建好了，而且也被妥善的使用。

§

In August 1879, Consul Hewlett also gives a description of the newly-completed Consular Offices, relating how the "Offices on the Bund lot include a Consul's Office and a General Office, in the latter of which accommodation is found for the [Chinese] Writer [官方抄寫員]." [29]

The plan of the Consular Offices (see Image 4-6), made in August 1879, shows the layout of the rooms in detail. The plan shows that the Constable had been allocated spacious quarters, with two bedrooms and a sitting room. The Gaol is also shown with three cells.

However, once again, Hewlett is alarmed at the lack of accommodation for the Consular servants. He writes that: "Very inadequate quarters have been provided for the Consular servants, who consist of four boatmen (who act also as Messengers), and, when I am here, of a Tingchai [聽差] as well. ··· Marshall ··· has declined ··· to furnish additional quarters on the ground that it is both unnecessary and undesirable that the official servants should reside within the Consular building. In answer to this, I have represented that, in my opinion, it is absolutely essential as a safeguard against fire and thieves, [and so that] their services [be] available for any emergency that might arise." Hewlett also makes the very valid point that servants would otherwise be living on the other side of harbour at Chihou, the main village. [30]

To meet this objection, yet clearly mindful of his budget constraints, Marshall obtained approval from London for the erection of quarters for the Consular servants, to be built of bamboo, lath and plaster, at a cost not exceeding £30. [31]

A later Consul, William Donald Spence [施本施], gives further details of the building as it was used in 1885 [see Image 5-6]. The General Office was by then described as the Shipping Office as its major function would have been the registration of ships arriving at and departing from Takow. According to the Takow Harbour Customs Regulations issued by Commissioner William Maxwell and the Consular Regulations issued by Swinhoe in 1864, all ship's masters were required to deposit their Ship's Papers and Import Manifest with their Consul within 48 hours of arrival at the port; since, throughout this period, the British Consul also represented Danish, German, French and Austro-Hungarian interests, this meant that almost every ship arriving at Takow had to register with the Consular Shipping Office [領事船務辦公室]. [32]

In Consul Spence's 1885 description of the building, the two rooms behind the Consul's Office were shown to be for the Constable, who slept in the room nearest to the Consul's Office. The Writer was apparently accommodated in the small room behind the General or Shipping Office that is marked "Office Servants". The Office Messenger, the head Gigman, and the Watchman all slept in "an Outhouse". The head Gigman was the head boatman, in charge of the Consular Gig that was moored beside the steps at the water's edge leading up to the Consular Offices; the Consular Gig was used to convey the Consul and was later moved up to Anping. [33]

It would seem that the 'Outhouse' was the bamboo, lath and plaster quarters for office servants, so strongly requested by Hewlett, and that these quarters were not only built but also put to good use.

Hewlett's Departure
有雅芝的離去

前面已經提過，有雅芝在1879年10月離開打狗。他被轉派到廣東〔Canton〕擔任領事，任期由1879年11月到1885年7月。然而，他在1883年7月時，明顯地受到精神崩潰的打擊，雖然他在1885年6月又回到領事的職位上，但兩個禮拜後，因為他仍然一直處在相當糟糕的狀態中，以致於廣東的醫官再度送他回家休息。他後來似乎恢復的情況良好，因為在回到英格蘭之後，他與年邁的母親同住到1890年代初期，然後於1894年至1898年間，出任英國駐瑞士日內瓦的領事。在1900年時，記錄上顯示他是住在法國東部離日內瓦不遠的一個小城，叫Bellegarde-sur-Valserine，在那兒他似乎與一名法國女士與她的兩個年輕女兒過從甚密，因為他在遺囑上把這幾位女士列為繼承人。在回到他姊妹位在英格蘭柏克夏的家中後，他就在1902年2月9日過世了。[34]

有雅芝離開打狗後，一開始由何藍田擔任代理領事官，但曾在1870及1871年擔任過有雅芝助理領事官的霍必瀾〔Pelham Laird Warren〕，後來回到打狗接替代理領事官的位置，並入住了打狗領事官邸。霍必瀾在福爾摩沙南部的故事將在第五章進行探討。

§

As previously stated, Consul Hewlett departed Takow in October 1879. He was transferred to Canton [廣東], where he served as Consul from November 1879 until July 1885. However, in July 1883 he apparently suffered a nervous breakdown and though he returned to his post again in June 1885, within two weeks he was still in such a poor way that the medical officer at Canton sent him home again. He appears to have recovered well, for, after returning to England and living with his aged mother until the early 1890s, he later acted as the British Consul at Geneva from 1894 to 1898. By 1900 he was recorded as living at Bellegarde-sur-Valserine in France, a short distance away from Geneva, where it appears he had a close association with a Frenchwoman and her two young daughters, as they are beneficiaries of his Will. Hewlett died on 9 February 1902, after returning to his sister's home in Berkshire, England. [34]

Initially William Holland stood in as Acting Consul, but Pelham Laird Warren, who had been Hewlett's Assistant in 1870 and 1871, returned to Takow as Acting Consul and took up occupancy of the Takow Residence. The story of Warren in South Formosa is looked at in Chapter Five.

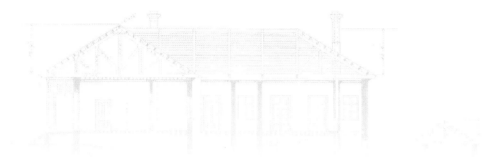

Notes to Chapter Four
第四章註解

1. WORK 10/33/10, Marshall to O.W.L., 11 September 1876 (This letter also relates that the 'consular officer at the port at present lives in a hired house'.); and B.P.P., Vol. 2, p. 210, Treasury Minute, 16 February 1866.

2. WORK 10/33/10, Marshall to O.W.L., 16 July 1877.

3. WORK 10/33/10, Boyce to O.W.L., 11 September 1875; WORK 10/33/10, Marshall to O.W.L., 16 July 1877; B.P.P., Vol. 2, p. 210, Treasury Minute, dated 16 February 1866, stipulates that Assistants were only entitled to bachelor quarters and not family residences, which were for Consuls, Vice-Consuls and Interpreters; WORK 10/33/10, Marshall to O.W.L., 11 September 1876 (This letter also relates that the 'consular officer at the port at present lives in a hired house'.)

4. WORK 10/33/10, Marshall to O.W.L., 16 July 1877; B.P.P., Vol. 2, p. 210, Treasury Minute, dated 16 February 1866.

5. WORK 10/33/10, Marshall to O.W.L., 16 July 1877.

6. WORK 10/33/10, Marshall to O.W.L., 16 July 1877; O.W.L. to Marshall, 30 November 1877; and Boyce Memo, 27 November 1877.

7. WORK 10/33/10, Plan B8859/77, 13 July 1877; King, Anthony D., The Bungalow: The Production of a Global Culture, Routledge & Kegan Paul, London, 1984, pp. 30-38; Davidson, p. 187; WORK 10/435, Holt to Crossman, 5 June 1868; and WORK 10/99, Marshall to O.W.L., 21 May 1877.

8. FO 678/3110.

9. WORK 10/33/10, Marshall to O.W.L., 19 February 1879.

10. WORK 10/33/10. Marshall to O.W.L., 16 July 1877; Marshall to O.W.L., 19 February 1879.

11. Yacal, Yakal or Yacul, [菲律賓] is a termite-resistant wood from South East Asia, Shorea obtusa, a member of the Dipterocarpaceae family and sold commercially as Taengwood 'Balau' [南洋欅木], 'Balau' is its name in Malaysia and Indonesia; FO 678/3158.

12. see Maritime Customs Annual Returns and Reports of Taiwan, 1867 – 1895, [清末臺灣 海關歷年資料] Institute of Taiwan History Preparatory Office, Academia Sinica, Taipei, 1997, Vol. 1, p. 384 and p. 437.

13. WORK 10/33/10, Marshall to O.W.L., 16 July 1877.

14. WORK 10/33/10, Marshall to O.W.L., 16 July 1877.

15. WORK 10/33/10, Marshall to O.W.L., 16 July 1877.

16. WORK 10/33/10, Marshall to O.W.L., 19 February 1879; O.W.L. to Marshall, 15 April 1879.

17. WORK 10/33/10, Marshall to O.W.L., 16 July 1877.

18. 1861 Scottish Census return for Barony, Glasgow, Page 17, Donaldson; Izumida, Part 2, p. 81; 1874 China Directory, Shanghai; Post Office Directory, London, 1882; WORK 10/33/10, Hewlett to Marshall, 12 June 1879; Marshall to O.W.L., 4 August 1879; Marshall to O.W.L., 22 August 1879; Donaldson to Marshall, 20 August 1879; O.W.L. to Marshall, 28 November 1879; FO 917/567, Will & Probate of Charles Melville Donaldson; see also Gratton, F. M., Freeemasonry in Shanghai and Northern China, Shanghai, 1900 (Reprinted by Ch'eng Wen Publishing Co, Taipei, 1971), p. 45; The New Cemetery is presumably the Pahsienjao Cemetery [八仙橋公墓], which opened in 1869; FO 917/763, Will & Probate of Charles Peter McArthur Donaldson.

19. FO 678/3036; and WORK 10/210, Memo by
    Hewlett on 1878 Agreement between Hewlett,
    Marshall and Hobson, 10 October 1879.

20. WORK 10/33/10, Marshall to
    O.W.L., 19 February 1879.

21. WORK 10/33/10, Marshall to
    O.W.L., 19 February 1879.

22. Findings of the architect Lin Shih-chao [林
    世超] during the 2012-13 excavation and
    restoration of the Takow Consular Offices.

23. WORK 10/33/10,Hewlett to Marshall, 12 June
    1879; Donaldson to Marshall, 20 August 1879.

24. WORK 10/33/10, Marshall to O.W.L., 4 August 1879.

25. WORK 10/33/10, Marshall to O.W.L., 4 August 1879.

26. WORK 10/33/10, Marshall to O.W.L., 4 August
    1879; Findings of the architect Lin Shih-chao
    [林世超] during the 2012-13 excavation and
    restoration of the Takow Consular Offices.

27. FO 228/974, Hewlett to Wade, 9 August 1879.

28. An earlier plan of the Takow Residence, contained
    in FO 678/3110, shows this 'Cellar for Fuel &c'
    room to be marked as being for 'Servants'; WORK
    10/33/10, Hewlett to Marshall, 5 June 1879.

29. FO 228/974, Hewlett to Wade, 9 August 1879.

30. FO 228/974, Hewlett to Wade, 9 August 1879;
    WORK 10/33/10, Hewlett to Marshall, 5 June 1879.

31. WORK 10/33/10, Marshall to O.W.L., 4 August
    1879; O.W.L. to Marshall, 28 November 1879.

32. FO 228/1020, Spence to O'Conor, 22 September

1885, Enclosure dated 8 September 1885; China
Directories for 1874 to 1884; FO 228/374, Swinhoe
to Wade, 21 November 1864, Enclosure 4.

33. FO 228/1020, Spence to O'Conor, 22 September
    1885, Enclosure dated 8 September 1885.

34. Coates, p. 200; Lo & Bryant, p. 617; 1891 England
    Census returns for Harrow, RG 12/1039, Folio 40,
    Page 19, Hewlett; Foreign Office records; 1902
    National Probate Calendar, p. 135, Hewlett, Archer
    Rotch; and Hewlett's Will, dated 20 February 1900.

清朝統治下的打狗領事館舍
The Takow Consular Buildings under Ching Rule

Introduction
緒論

　　打狗領事館官邸於1879年建好後，一直到清朝結束統治臺灣這一段時間，故事大多與領事霍必瀾〔Pelham Laird Warren，又譯佩翰·萊爾德·華倫〕有關。在1879年10月領事有雅芝離開後，首先由三等助理領事官何藍田〔William Holland〕接管領事業務，一直等到霍必瀾，當時的官位是一等助理領事官，在1880年1月1日接手後，代理領事官職位才換人。由於不久後即將到任的新領事官費笠士〔George Phillips，又譯喬治·菲力浦〕將駐蹕於臺灣府，於是，從1880年到1893年的大部份時間裡，霍必瀾就住在打狗的英國領事官邸。正因為霍必瀾停駐在福爾摩沙南部，透過他的報告，我們才得擁有日本統治臺灣前有關打狗與南福爾摩沙狀況之具有可信度的權威資料。

　　在霍必瀾於1893年離開福爾摩沙之後，胡力檣〔Richard Willett Hurst，又譯理察·威勒特·赫斯特〕接任領事，在其任內見證了整個島成為日本明治天皇〔Japanese Meiji Emperor〕轄下的領地。接下來的幾年，雖然新的日本統治政權進行了許多大幅改善打狗港狀況的措施，可是打狗英國領事館舍卻淪落到頹圮失修，最後在1925年被賣給日本官方當局。

§

　　The story of the Takow Consular Residence after its construction in 1879 until the end of Ching rule over Taiwan is largely the story of Consul Pelham Laird Warren[霍必瀾]. Following the departure of Consul Hewlett in October 1879, Third Assistant William Holland [何藍田], was left in charge until Warren, then a First Assistant, took over as Acting Consul on 1 January 1880. With the new Consul, George Phillips, expected shortly at Taiwan-foo, Warren took up residence at Takow. Warren was to be stationed in South Formosa for much of the period from 1880 through to 1893, and it is through his reports that an authoritative assessment of the situation at Takow and South Formosa prior to Japanese rule can be found.

After Warren's final departure from Formosa in 1893, Consul Richard Willett Hurst [胡力檣] took over and saw the island become a possession of the Japanese Meiji Emperor [明治天皇]. In subsequent years, despite the huge improvements the new Japanese rulers carried out at the port, the Takow Consular buildings fell into disrepair, and were eventually sold to the Japanese authorities in 1925.

Consul Pelham Laird Warren
領事霍必瀾

　　霍必瀾來自一個顯要的英國家族：他的曾祖父，理察・霍必瀾，曾是英王喬治三世的御醫；他的父親，理察・萊爾德・霍必瀾〔Richard Laird Warren〕，曾官拜英國皇家海軍上將。霍必瀾在1845年8月22日出生於德本郡〔Devon〕的Stoke Damerel，長大後進入澤西島上的維多利亞學院就讀，那是靠近法國北部外海的英倫海峽群島中的一個島。[1]

　　一般認爲霍必瀾曾受到英國外相的推薦，而進入英國在中國地區的領事服務行列，他是在1867年1月參加了由文官委員親自主持、競爭激烈的甄試。在1867年2月2日，他被指定爲實習翻譯官，之後他就啓程前往北京，在當時英國駐中國公使威妥瑪的指導下進行爲期兩年的語文訓練。他到達中國的時間點，正是中國剛剛要從1864年結束的太平天國之亂〔Taiping Rebellion〕的蹂躪中，逐漸恢復生氣的時候。[2]

　　當霍必瀾投身於中國領事服務行列時，其招募人員的方式正在發生改變。在1860年之前，領事人員的任命唯一的方式是恩賞推薦，並不需要任何的考試。但是從1861年起，有意申請加入者必須參加文官委員所主持的考試。早期，從1861年至1871年間，有資格參加這個考試的人選被限制在幾個經過篩選的愛爾蘭、蘇格蘭與英格蘭的大學或研究機構推薦的人，此外還有那些英國外相所推薦的人選。在1871年之後，整整有33年的時光，這個考試改爲對全部的大衆開放。考試通過的人馬上獲頒實習翻譯官的職位，並領有一份，在霍必瀾的時代，每年200英鎊的薪水。然後這些實習翻譯官被派遣到中國去，通常在那裡他們會花兩年的時間學習清帝國宮廷中使用的中國語文〔Mandarin，譯注：中國官方語言〕的說與寫。其中一小部份實習翻譯官能持續下去而升格成爲翻譯官；一些比較不幸的就無法再有陞遷的機會；然而，大多數的人接著都有機會被陞任爲三等助理領事官，這個職別在實質上只是辦公員，每年領300英鎊的薪資。[3]

　　霍必瀾在1869年11月18日被升爲三等助理領事官，並受命到打狗任職，在代理領事官有雅芝手下工作。有雅芝在1871年末離開福爾摩沙，當時霍必瀾雖只是一個小小的三等助理領事官，卻被留下來打理打狗和臺灣府（今臺南）的領事事務，一直等到副領事官額勒格〔William Gregory〕於1872年3月上任為止。[4]

霍必瀾在1871年參與了兩個意外事件的處理，這兩起事件的處理正好發生在英國外交部正在考慮是否撤除臺灣的領事館時，可以做為英國領事館在南福爾摩沙扮演的主要功能最好的示範。第一起事件發生在1871年7月，英國船隻Loudoun Castle號在福爾摩沙島南端外海發生海難；第二起事件發生在1871年12月，英國皇家海軍砲艦H.M.S. Dwarf號某些船員犯下無法無天之劣行。領事館有責任為商賈與水手提供協助，也必須調查所有發生在福爾摩沙近海外國船舶的海難與意外災害，如果領事館被裁撤，無法想見這些功能將如何能被執行。領事館第二個主要的功能是，調解中國人對在福爾摩沙的外國人經常發生之出軌行為的申訴並管控這些違紀洋人：H.M.S. Dwarf號砲艦的案例很顯然地也就是第二項領事功能的最佳範例。一群砲艦上的添煤水手越過旗後的潟湖來到苓仔寮〔Ling-a-liao〕這個地方，他們進入當地的媽祖廟偷走媽祖〔Goddess Matsu〕神像。事發之後，由於村民追得很緊，他們接著偷了一隻竹筏仔〔catamaran，閩南語Tek-pai〕，嘗試著橫渡潟湖逃回旗後，然而其中一人卻不幸落水溺死，他的名字是查爾斯・紐曼〔Charles Newman〕。這件事後續由霍必瀾與有雅芝出面與憤怒的村民斡旋，並且針對溺水而死的添煤水手寫了檔案報告。[5]

霍必瀾留在福爾摩沙南部一直到1873年6月，在那之後他被轉派到福州，到服務年資很深的領事官星察理〔Charles Anthony Sinclair，又譯查爾斯・安東尼・辛克萊〕手下擔任二等助理領事官，此人名聲極端不佳，因為他不僅對屬下，而且幾乎是對所有其他人態度惡劣所致。[6]

1874年，霍必瀾因其父親病重而回到英國。幸運地，在1874年之前，他已經完成5年的公職服務，所以根據英國財政部與外交部的規則辦法，他有資格要求財政部補助他回國所需旅費的半數。 他的父親，理察・萊爾德・霍必瀾上將於1875年7月29日逝世，死時有霍必瀾陪侍在側。處理好他父親身後諸事物後，霍必瀾隨即與遠房表妹，瑪麗・唐娜桑・漢培基〔Mary Donnithorne Humpage〕於1875年9月9日在倫敦的聖馬里波恩〔St Marylebone〕結婚〔見圖 5-1〕。[7]

次年（譯注：1876年）2月，霍必瀾已陞任一等助理領事官，帶著他的新娘瑪麗・唐娜桑・霍必瀾回到中國，在寧波〔Ningpo〕擔任代理領事官，他們的第一個孩子瑪麗・艾琳娜・霍必瀾〔Mary Eleanor Warren〕就在那兒出生。[8]

霍必瀾留在寧波，直到1877年中期，當領事固威林〔William Marsh Cooper〕終於接任爲止。在此之後，他受命在溫州一地成立新的領事館，這是在1876年煙臺條約簽訂後，新開放給外國人的通商口岸。在此地，他輪流擔任代理領事官與一等助理領事官，直到1879年，當他再度被派到福爾摩沙爲止。[9]

待在溫州的時候，他唯一的兒子，理察・萊爾德・霍必瀾〔Richard Laird Warren，又譯霍李家〕，於1878年8月9日出生，無疑地買威令〔Dr William Wykeham Myers，又譯威廉・韋克翰・梅爾〕這位有名的醫生必定曾參與他的接生，這位醫生是溫州唯一的開業醫師。1878年當時的溫州外國社群包含買醫師和他的家庭，霍必瀾和他的夫人瑪麗・唐娜桑・霍必瀾，一位領事館巡捕，加上一個傳教士，兩個商人，三個領航員與八個清帝國海關雇員。事實上，買醫生最年幼的女兒，夏洛特・康妮翰・史考特・梅爾〔Charlotte Cuningham Scott Myers〕在理察・萊爾德・霍必瀾出生後2個月也生於溫州，她的出生證明是由霍必瀾以當地代理領事的身分所註冊登記的。買醫師這幾位備受讚賞又多才多藝的女兒們，在中國的通商口岸間被譽爲“優雅三女神”〔Three Graces，譯注：源自希臘神話〕。[10]

買醫生家庭在1879年8月舉家遷往福爾摩沙，定居在打狗，就在港灣入口的南邊，一待就超過20年。他後來除了成爲打狗一地的社區醫師外，也被指定爲在旗後新建成的萬大衛紀念醫院〔David Manson Memorial Hospital〕的外科主任，這個醫院是在萬大衛醫師〔Dr. David Manson〕1878年突然過世之後，由旗後的大眾捐款所建，萬大衛醫師是萬巴德醫師〔Dr. Patrick Manson〕的弟弟。萬大衛醫師在1871年到1873年間是打狗的社區醫師，他也曾經在廈門和福州行醫。正因爲他在這三個港埠享有名聲，所以從外國居民那裡湧入的捐款相當充足，而且特別的是，也有來自福爾摩沙當地的中國要人慷慨解囊，於是外觀雄偉的萬大衛紀念醫院得以順利建成〔如圖5-2〕。[11]

圖 5-1：霍必瀾與瑪麗‧唐娜桑‧霍必瀾
佩翰‧萊爾德與瑪麗‧唐納桑‧霍必瀾的沙龍照，咸信是在1875年9月9日在倫敦的婚禮後不久所拍攝。
〔來自霍必瀾家族慷慨的授權許可，版權所有，翻印必究〕

Image 5-1 : Pelham Laird and Mary Donnithorne Warren
Studio photograph of Pelham Laird and Mary Donnithorne Warren,
believed to be taken shortly after their wedding in London on 9 September 1875.
(By kind permission of the Warren family. All rights reserved)

圖 5-2：萬大衛紀念醫院
這家紀念醫院於於1879年被建在旗後潟湖入口南面，爲了紀念萬大衛，他是萬巴德爵士的弟弟。
〔版權屬於Edinger收藏，版權所有，翻印必究〕

Image 5-2 : David Manson Memorial Hospital
The Manson Memorial Hospital was built on the south side of the Lagoon entrance at Chihou in memory of David Manson, the younger brother of Sir Patrick Manson, in 1879.
(Courtesy the Edinger Collection. All rights reserved)

　　1879年12月，霍必瀾加入早一步抵達打狗的買醫師，在1880年1月日來到打狗從何藍田手中接下領事的職務。那時，瑪麗沒有一起伴隨她的丈夫前來打狗，她陪伴著孩子留在寧波，並於1880年3月18日時，在那兒生下他們的第三個孩子，依瑟‧梅麗安‧霍必瀾〔Ethel Marion Warren〕。產下嬰兒後一個月，瑪麗、兩個較大的孩子與襁褓中的嬰兒，啟程到廈門，霍必瀾則由打狗渡海到那裡與她們會合，再一起回到打狗，並由他自己在打狗為依瑟的出生證明註冊登記。[12]

　　他在1880年1月1日由何藍田手中接管了福爾摩沙南部的領事館業務，之後他首先啟動的任務就是在1月底時召開一個有關在安平興建外灘的討論會議，這個政策象徵了打狗的重要性正在逐步下降。這個外灘〔Bund〕，或是稱為堤岸碼頭，其建造所需費用幾乎完全將由福爾摩沙南部的主要外商買單，由此可見安平自1870年以來的發展與進步。[13]

　　霍必瀾在1890年代的報告紀錄中曾提到1860年代的安平情況，它的範圍包括一個小漁村以及熱蘭遮城以北的一片廣袤的泥沙地區域，這片區域在潮水最高時會完全浸泡在水中。他還提到自1870年起，清朝政府允許外商從它那裡租用這些熱蘭遮城以北的泥沙平地，於是外商在這裡開始不斷填土築堤，因而在安平創造了一個外國人居住社區。1881年的7月，800呎長的外灘堤防，以及疏濬過的小港灣，終於在安平完工。這個工事的完成意味著貨運駁船現在可以直接到達小港灣岸邊的倉庫棧房。[14]

　　現在態勢很明朗了，至少在外商的眼中，安平從1870年起不僅變成他們在福爾摩沙南部比較中意的港口，而且其可以整年無休運作的貿易設施也漸漸變得比打狗優越。打狗港的問題一直都是潟湖不斷地淤淺與港灣入口處的沙洲障礙物。這個打狗沙洲障礙物半淹於水中，而且還會在打狗港入口外漂移。因為它的位置時常改變，所以海圖便失去指引的作用，為了安全入港船長真正需要的是一個平靜的海面，以及一位在地的領航員，使他們可以避開這個沙洲航行。這個問題最簡單的解決方式是使用挖泥船疏濬，以確保船隻行經港灣入口與內港下錨處的安全。有雅芝曾以為，提倡改革的福建巡撫丁日昌會信守他的承諾，疏濬打狗港，但是由於丁日昌在1878年5月突然被撤職，這個打狗港疏濬計畫看來前景渺茫。由於夏獻綸道臺於1879年8月去世，這讓霍必瀾認為疏濬橫亙打狗港口的沙洲這件事將遙遙無期。〔見圖5-3〕。[15]

　　1880年11月，皮耶‧腓特烈‧郝思義〔Pierre Frederick Hausser〕加入霍必瀾，成為福爾摩沙南部領事官僚的一員，而在緊接的12月，何藍田離開打狗前往倫敦。有關郝思義的種種，如他父親是倫敦的音樂教授等，下面將會有更多的介紹。[16]

　　隨著新領事喬治‧費笠士〔George Phillips〕在1881年2月13日到任，霍必瀾與他的家人被安排定居在打狗；當時在習慣上，領事官應該會駐守臺灣府，而助理領事官則在打狗。臺灣府（臺南）的領事館位於一棟雖然廣大但是搖搖欲墜的衙門裡，位置就在舊城池的中心地帶。因為霍必瀾駐守在打狗，打狗領事官邸首次被一整個家庭當做居所。在這之前曾使用過的兩位居住者，有雅芝是鰥夫，而何藍田則為單身漢。這次因為一個家庭進住而帶來的整套的家務運作，卻使得官邸一個始料未及卻相當關鍵的設計問題暴露出來。[17]

　　然而，就在1881年費笠士到任後的兩個月，霍必瀾和他的家人請假離開打狗，到廈門和歐洲旅行。很顯然地，以霍必瀾的官位及薪資而言，帶著太太與三個幼兒旅行並非易事，而且所費不貲。不過，現在霍必瀾又在中國的領事工作崗位上服務了另一個五年，如同上一次，英國財政部再一次支付了部份的費用：財政部補助官員一半的旅費，而對家屬的旅行補助則為三分之一。[18]

　　他的夫人瑪麗於1882年4月30日，在英國生下他們的第四個孩子，桃樂西‧霍必瀾〔Dorothy Warren〕。不過，他是在幾乎一年之後，於1883年3月31日回到打狗。那時，他只有在夫人，瑪麗，與新生嬰兒桃樂西的陪伴下回到打狗，其他的孩子則被留給霍必瀾那位寡居的祖母照顧，以便於他們能接受英國的教育。[19]

　　在這同時，費笠士已在1882年7月離開福爾摩沙，在交接空擋的短暫時間裡，把管理南福爾摩沙領事館的責任交給赫思義，直到副領事官湯瑪斯‧倭妥瑪〔Thomas Watters〕於7月底由淡水過來擔任正式領事官為止。就在1883年倭妥瑪重新把領事職權交回給霍必瀾時，他寫了一封信給北京的英國大臣公使讚許赫思義的真誠態度與能力。但赫思義是在1878年成為實習翻譯官，所以必須等到1886年才有首次升等的機會。[20]

　　在霍必瀾不在福爾摩沙的這段期間，關於改善臺灣府地區交通連絡或打狗港疏濬的事務絲毫不見進展。1883年時，買醫師的汽艇Scalpel號已經在安平與打狗間往返行駛，因為當時沒有固定的商船航班會來到打狗港。打狗港唯一還在進行的商業活動是在每年產糖季節時，約有５０艘運糖船會入港裝載糖，時間由４月到６月。雖然打狗港淤積情況惡化，但船隻還是來此裝載糖而不在安平，唯一的原因就是最佳的產糖區，現在的屏東縣到安平港間的道路狀況相當地差。除此之外，領事費笠士也觀察到，現在每家公司都在安平設了居所或倉庫，安平無可避免地會成為福爾摩沙南部的商業中心，除非打狗港入口的沙洲被移除，港灣疏濬，而且在打狗與臺灣府之間建造一條運河或道路，否則打狗注定沒落。[21]

霍必瀾當時雖是代理領事官，但他選擇住在打狗的新領事官邸，所以他的代理助理官赫思義就被派駐在臺灣府那個逐漸破敗中的衙門。與臺灣府城的老舊官邸相比，打狗的新領事官邸被買醫師描述為「坐落的地點優美，以及用講究且科學的方式來建造」在山丘平頂上。買醫師更進一步記錄下官邸的種種，廚房與其他獨立辦公室一起形成四方形庭院的北邊，庭院有高牆圍繞，南邊為領事官邸：由庭院可經由一扇門通往領事官邸的房子，房子上層就是主臥室〔見圖5-4〕。[22]

與此同時，安平因為大多數的外國商貿現在都在此進行，所以它跟臺灣府城做為主要領事業務據點所產生的機關分布配置，其中存在的缺點變得越來越明顯。根據海關章程〔Customs Regulations〕，到達的外國商船必須檢具船隻的註冊資料與載貨單等文件呈報領事館。然而，由臺灣府城內的領事館到安平港的旅程又長又不方便。因此，需要雇用一位臨時的船務辦事員駐守安平。由於這樣的安排很容易就會產生船長與貿易商雇傭的辦事員鑽漏洞的機會，霍必瀾認為這樣的安排無法令人滿意，故而要求在安平港正式建立一個船務辦公室。[23]

事實也顯示，居住在臺灣府裡那棟租來的領事官邸是有害健康的，特別是在雨季。1883年7月時，代理領事官霍必瀾考量赫思義日漸變差的健康狀況，不得不讓赫思義撤離臺灣府領事館，雖然事實上他從4月起才住在那兒，時間並不長。買醫師建議讓赫思義撤到打狗領事官邸居住，然而霍必瀾於此時發現，領事官邸的五個房間中，因為屋頂漏水的問題，在雨季時期只剩下三間的狀況適合人居住。由於他的夫人瑪麗與女兒桃樂西也住在官邸，無法提供空間給赫思義，不得已只好租用怡記洋行〔Bain & Co〕在打狗的房舍的半邊，給生病的赫思義休養居住。[24]

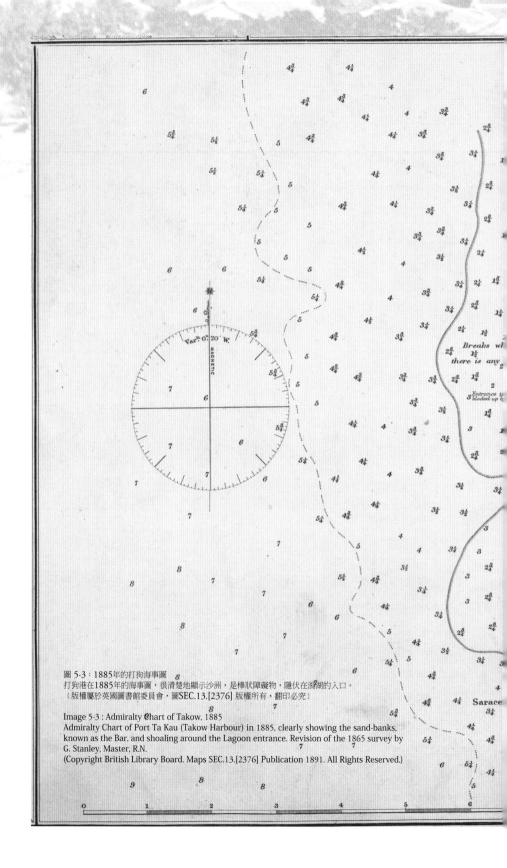

圖 5-3：1885年的打狗海事圖
打狗港在1885年的海事圖，很清楚地顯示沙洲，是棒狀障礙物，隱伏在潟湖的入口。
〔版權屬於英國圖書館委員會，圖SEC.13.[2376] 版權所有，翻印必究〕

Image 5-3 : Admiralty Chart of Takow, 1885
Admiralty Chart of Port Ta Kau (Takow Harbour) in 1885, clearly showing the sand-banks, known as the Bar, and shoaling around the Lagoon entrance. Revision of the 1865 survey by G. Stanley, Master, R.N.
(Copyright British Library Board. Maps SEC.13.[2376] Publication 1891. All Rights Reserved.)

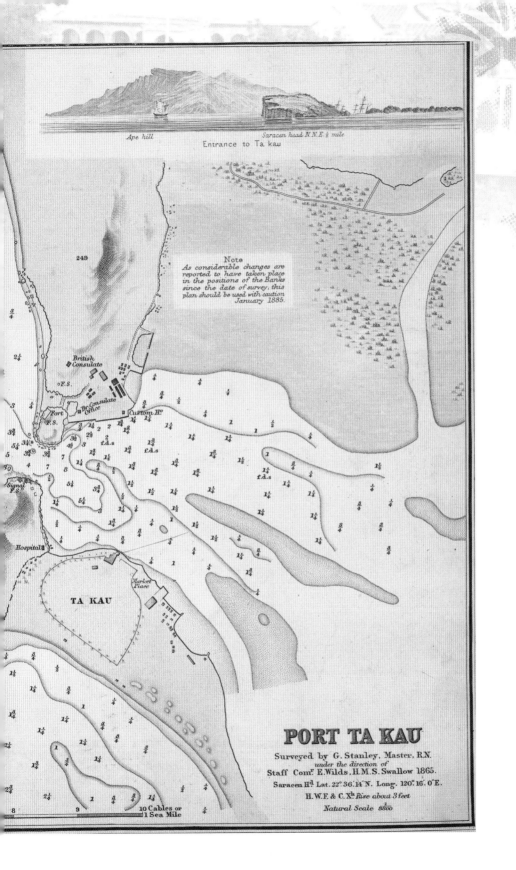

Ape hill   Saracen head N.N.E. ½ mile

Entrance to Ta kau

Note
As considerable changes are
reported to have taken place
in the positions of the Banks
since the date of survey, this
plan should be used with caution
January 1885.

British
Consulate

o F.S.

Port
F.S.

Br Consulate
Office

Custom H⁰

f.d.s

f.d.s

f.d.s

Signal
F.S.

Hospital

Market
Place

TA KAU

PORT TA KAU

Surveyed by G. Stanley, Master, R.N.
under the direction of
Staff Com⁻ E. Wilds, H.M.S. Swallow 1865.
Saracen H⁻ Lat. 22° 36′ 14″ N. Long. 120° 16′ 0″ E.

H.W.F. & C. X⁻ Rise about 3 feet

Natural Scale 8800

10 Cables or
1 Sea Mile

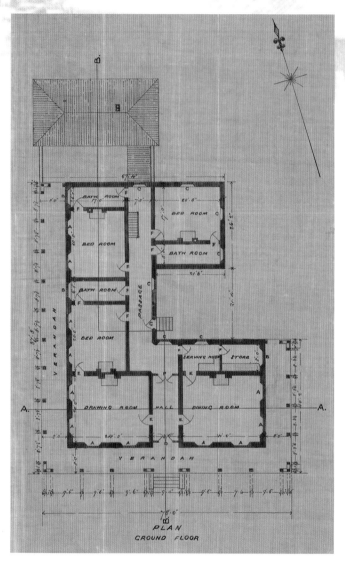

圖 5-4：打狗領事官邸的地面樓層設計圖
來自馬歇爾的1877年為打狗領事公館所繪建築設計稿細部，顯示梅爾醫師描述過的房間。
〔版權屬於英國政府，WORK 10/33/10，版權所有，翻印必究〕

Image 5-4 : Ground Floor Plan of Takow Consular Residence
Detail from Marshall's 1877 architectural drawings for the Takow Consular Residence, showing the rooms described by Dr Myers.

§

Pelham Laird Warren [霍必瀾] came from a distinguished British family: his great-grandfather, Richard Warren, had been a Physician to King George III; and his father, Richard Laird Warren, was an Admiral in the British Royal Navy. Pelham Warren was born on 22 August 1845 at Stoke Damerel in Devon, and educated at Victoria College on Jersey, one of the British Channel Islands that lie just off the coast of northern France. [1]

Warren is believed to have been recommended by the British Foreign Secretary for the China Consular Service, and took the competitive Examination before the Civil Service Commissioners in January 1867. He was appointed a Student Interpreter on 2 February 1867, whereupon he travelled out to Peking for two years' language training under the direction of Thomas Francis Wade [威妥瑪], then the Chinese Secretary at the British Legation. Warren thus arrived in a China still recovering from the ravages of the Taiping Rebellion [太平天國之亂] which had ended in 1864. [2]

The method of recruiting officers for the China Consular Service was changing at the time Warren entered the service. Until 1860 appointments were made solely by patronage and there was no examination required. From 1861, applicants were required to take an examination set by the Civil Service Commissioners. In the early years, from 1861 to 1871, this examination was restricted to nominations made by selected Irish, Scottish and English academic institutions, and also to nominations made by the British Foreign Secretary. After 1871, the examinations became open to all for the next 33 years. Successful applicants were given an immediate appointment as a Student Interpreter and a salary, in Warren's day, of £200 per annum. The Student Interpreters were then shipped out to China, where they usually spent 2 years studying written and spoken Mandarin, the language of the Chinese imperial court. A select few would continue on as Interpreters; an unfortunate few would not progress any further; yet most would subsequently be promoted to Third Class Assistants, in essence mere office clerks, drawing salaries of £300. [3]

Warren was promoted to Third Class Assistant on 18 November 1869 and ordered to Takow to serve under Acting Consul Hewlett. Hewlett departed from Formosa at the end of 1871 and Warren, though only a Third Assistant, was left in charge at Takow and Taiwan-foo until the arrival in March 1872 of Vice-Consul William Gregory [額勒格里]. [4]

In 1871, Warren was involved in two incidents which exemplify the main functions performed by the British Consulate in South Formosa at the time that the Foreign Office was considering its removal. The first, in July 1871, involved the wreck of a British ship, the Loudoun Castle, off the southern cape of Formosa; the second, in December 1871, concerned the lawless behaviour of some of the crew of a British naval gunship, the H.M.S. Dwarf. The Consulate was responsible to provide assistance to merchants and mariners, and to investigate all foreign maritime wrecks and disasters that occurred off the coasts of Formosa, and, if the Consulate were removed, it is hard to see how this function could have been performed. The second major function of the Consulate was dealing with Chinese complaints against, and the often errant behaviour of, foreigners in Formosa; and the H.M.S. Dwarf case certainly met these criteria. A group of stokers from the gunship had crossed the Lagoon from Chihou to Ling-a-liao [苓仔寮], where they had entered a temple and stolen an image of the Goddess Matsu [媽祖]. With the villagers in hot pursuit, the stokers had next seized a catamaran [Tek-pai, 竹筏仔] and attempted to flee back across the Lagoon, but one man, named Charles Newman, had fallen in the water and drowned. Warren and Hewlett were left to deal with the outraged villagers and to file a report on the drowned stoker. [5]

Warren remained in South Formosa until June 1873, when he was transferred to Foochow [福州] as Second Assistant under the long-serving Consul, Charles Anthony Sinclair [星察理], a man with the foulest of reputations for his dealings with subordinates and just about anybody else. [6]

In 1874 Warren returned to the United Kingdom where his father was gravely ill. Fortunately, by 1874 Warren had completed his first five years in the Service, and so, according to British Treasury and Foreign Office regulations, was entitled to take Home Leave with the Treasury paying half of his travel expenses. His father, Admiral Richard Laird Warren, died 29 July 1875, with Pelham Warren present at the death. Having sorted out his father's affairs, Warren promptly married his second cousin, Mary Donnithorne Humpage[瑪麗 · 唐納桑 · 漢培基], on 9 September 1875 at St Marylebone in London (see Image 5-1). [7]

In February the following year, Pelham Warren, now a First Assistant, returned to China with his bride Mary Donnithorne Warren, to take up the post of Acting Consul at Ningpo [寧波], where their first child Mary Eleanor Warren was born. [8]

Warren stayed at Ningpo until the middle of 1877, when the appointed Consul, William Marsh Cooper [固威林], finally took charge. Warren was then ordered to set up a new Consulate at Wenchow [溫州], which had been newly opened to foreigners under the 1876 Chefoo Convention [煙臺條約], and where he served intermittently as Acting Consul and First Assistant until 1879 when he was sent once more to Formosa. [9]

Whilst at Wenchow, the Warren's only son, Richard Laird Warren [霍李家], was born on 9 August 1878, and the birth was doubtless attended by Dr William Wykeham Myers [買威令], the sole medical practitioner at Wenchow. The foreign community at Wenchow in 1878 consisted of Dr Myers and his family, Warren and his wife Mary Donnithorne Warren, a Consular constable, plus one missionary, 2 merchants, 3 pilots and 8 Imperial Maritime Customs employees. Indeed, Myers' youngest daughter, Charlotte Cuningham Scott Myers[夏洛特 · 康妮翰 · 史考特 · 梅爾], was born at Wenchow two months after Richard Laird Warren and her birth was registered there by Warren as the Acting Consul. The much-admired and accomplished daughters of Dr Myers were to become known in the Treaty Ports of China as the Three Graces. [10]

he Myers family moved to Formosa in August 1879 and lived at Takow, on the southern side of the harbour entrance, for over 20 years. Dr Myers, in addition to becoming the Community Physician at Takow, Medical Offices for the Imperial Maritime Customs and for the British Consulate, was appointed the Surgeon-in-charge of the newly-established

David Manson Memorial Hospital [萬大衛紀念醫院] that had been erected at Chihou by public subscription following the sudden death in 1878 of Dr. David Manson [萬大衛], the younger brother of Dr. Patrick Manson [萬巴德]. David Manson had been the Community Physician at Takow from 1871 to 1873, and had also served at Amoy and Foochow. Such was his repute in these three ports that sufficient contributions were forthcoming from the foreign residents, and particularly from the local Chinese authorities in Formosa, to enable the magnificent David Manson Memorial Hospital to be erected (see Image 5-2). [11]

On 29 December 1879 Warren joined Dr. Myers at Takow and took over the Consulate from William Holland on 1 January 1880. Mary Warren did not immediately accompany her husband, as she stayed behind with the children back at Ningpo, where she gave birth to their third child, Ethel Marion Warren, on 18 March 1880. After one month, Mary Warren,, the two elder children and her baby proceeded down to Amoy, where Pelham Warren travelled across to meet them, arriving back at Takow where he registered Ethel's birth on 12 May 1880. [12]

Warren took over charge of the South Formosa Consulate from William Holland on 1 January 1880, and, indicative of the declining importance of Takow, one of his first tasks was to chair a meeting for the construction of a Bund [外灘] at Anping at the end of January. This Bund, or embanked quay, was to be paid for by nearly all the principal foreign merchants in South Formosa, and shows how far the development of Anping had advanced since 1870. [13]

Writing in September 1890s, to the British Minister Sir John Walsham Warren [華爾身] related that in the 1860s Anping had consisted of a small fishing village with the area to the north of Fort Zelandia [熱蘭遮城] being an open expanse of mud that was completely submerged at high tide. He added that, starting from 1870, foreign merchants had been allowed to obtain leases from the Chinese Government for these mudflats to the north of Fort Zelandia [熱蘭遮城], which they proceed to fill in and embank, thus creating the foreign settlement at Anping. The 800-foot long Bund, and the deepening of the creek, at Anping was completed in July 1881. The completion of this work meant that cargo lighters could now directly access the godowns situated along the creek. [14]

It is clear that, at least in the eyes of the foreign merchants, from 1870 Anping became not only the preferred port of South Formosa, but also that the facilities for year-round trade were becoming superior to those at Takow. The problems at Takow had always been the shoaling of the Lagoon and the Takow Bar. The Takow Bar was a submerged sandbank that shifted about just outside the harbour entrance. As its position constantly changed, charts were of little use but rather the ship's master needed a calm sea and a local pilot to be able to navigate over the bar. The simple solution would have been to use a dredger to keep both the harbour mouth and the inner anchorage safe for ships. Consul Hewlett had trusted that the progressive Fuchien Governor [福建巡撫] Ting Jih-chang [丁日昌] would carry through on promises to dredge Takow harbour, but with Governor Ting's sudden withdrawal from office in May 1878 the prospects looked slim. And with the death of Tao-t'ai Hsia Hsien-lun [夏獻綸] in August 1879, Warren considered that there was no longer any chance of the bar at Takow being dredged (see Image 5-3). [15]

In November of 1880, Warren was joined in South Formosa by Pierre Frederick Hausser [皮耶 · 腓特烈 · 郝思義], and the following month Holland departed for London. Of Hausser, whose father was a Professor of Music in London, more is written below. [16]

Following the arrival on 13 February 1881 of the new Consul, George Phillips, Warren and his family were accommodated at Takow; the practice then being that the Consul should be stationed at Taiwan-foo, and the Assistant at Takow. The consulate at Taiwan-foo was housed in a large, but decaying, yamen, located in the heart of the old walled city, which belonged to Hsu Chien-hsun, whose father was reputed to be one of the richest men in Formosa and to have been Captain Rooney's valued customer with Warren stationed at Takow, the Consular Residence was being used as a family dwelling for the first time. Regarding the only two previous occupants: Hewlett was a widower; and Holland was a bachelor. This full operation as a family household was later to expose an unintended but fatal design problem. [17]

However, exactly two months after Phillips' arrival in 1881, Warren and his family departed from Takow for Amoy and Europe on leave. Clearly, for an officer such as Warren, with a wife and three young children, this would have been no small undertaking and expense.

However, as Warren had by now completed a further 5 years' Consular service in China, the British Treasury again defrayed part of the expense: the Treasury paying half the officer's travel expenses and one third of his family's expenses. [18]

His wife, Mary, gave birth to their fourth child, Dorothy Warren, in England on 30 April 1882. However, it was not until almost a year later, on 31 March 1883, that Warren returned to Takow. He was accompanied only by his wife, Mary, and the new baby, Dorothy, as the other children had been left in the care of Warren's widowed mother, so that they could obtain a British education. [19]

Meanwhile, Phillips had left Formosa in July 1882, briefly handing over charge of the South Formosa Consulate to Hausser prior to the arrival from Tamsui [淡水] of Vice-Consul Thomas Watters [倭妥瑪] as officiating Consul at the end of the month. Upon restoring charge of the Consulate to Warren in 1883, Watters wrote to the British Minister at Peking praising Hausser's cordial manner and ability. Yet Hausser, who had become a Student Interpreter in 1878 on a meagre annual salary of £200, would have to wait until 1886 for his first promotion and a more fitting income. [20]

During Warren's absence nothing had happened either to improve the communications with Taiwan-foo or to improve the harbour at Takow. By 1883, Dr Myers' steam launch Scalpel was running between Anping and Takow, as there were now no regular trading steamers visiting Takow. The only business still being done at Takow was the loading of about fifty ships yearly with sugar during the sugar trading season, which ran from April to June. The sugar loading continued at Takow, despite the worsening harbour, due solely to the roads between the premier sugar districts in what is now Pingtung County [屏東縣] and the port of Anping being so bad. Moreover, Consul Phillips observed that Anping, where every firm now had either its residence or warehouse, would inevitably become the centre of the South Formosa business unless the Takow bar was dredged, the harbour deepened, and a canal or road constructed between Takow and Taiwan-foo. [21]

Warren, although now the Acting Consul, preferred to live at the new residence at Takow, so that Hausser, his Acting Assistant, was stationed in the decaying yamen up at Taiwan-foo. In contrast to the residence within Taiwan-foo city, the new Consular Residence at Takow was described by Dr. W Wykeham Myers as being "beautifully situated, [and] carefully and scientifically built" on the summit of a hill. Myers goes on to record that the kitchen and other out-offices formed the northern side of a quadrangular courtyard which was surrounded by high walls, with the southern side being formed by the Consular Residence: that side of the house could be accessed from the courtyard by a door, above which were the main bedrooms (see Image 5-4). [22]

Meanwhile, the shortcomings of the existing Consular arrangements up at Anping, where most of the foreign trade was now being transacted, and at Taiwan-foo were becoming very apparent. According to the Customs Regulations, incoming foreign ships were required to deposit their Ship's Papers and Import Manifests with the Consulate. However, the journey from the Consulate in Taiwan-foo out to the port at Anping was both inconvenient and lengthy. It was therefore necessary to employ a temporary Shipping Clerk at Anping. As this arrangement was prone to abuse by sea captains and the hired mercantile clerks, Warren deemed it unsatisfactory and urged that a Shipping Office be established at Anping. [23]

The rented Consular building at Taiwan-foo was also proving unhealthy, especially during the rainy season. In July 1883, Acting Consul Warren was obliged to withdraw Hausser from Taiwan-foo Consulate on account of Hausser's declining health, despite the fact that he had only been there since April. Dr. Myers advised that Hausser be withdrawn to Takow, yet Warren found that, out of the five rooms at the Takow Consular Residence, only three were habitable during the rains due to problems with the roof. With his wife Mary and daughter Dorothy at the Consular Residence, Warren was unable to provide space for Hausser, and was obliged to rent half of the house of Bain & Co [怡記洋行] at Takow as accommodation for the ailing Hausser to recuperate. [24]

Death of Mary Donnithorne Warren
瑪麗・唐娜桑・霍必瀾之死

1883年9月，才由英國回到打狗6個月，霍必瀾就再度被升職，這次是到羅星塔島〔Pagoda Island〕當副領事官。不過他選擇留在打狗，而沒有馬上過海到羅星塔島就任，這個島是一個在福州下游數哩處供船隻下錨的地方。他延宕的原因可能是考慮到夫人瑪麗・唐娜桑・霍必瀾的健康，她自夏天開始以來，就一直被某種奇怪而無法判斷的病痛所困擾。[25]

1883年夏天，她和嬰兒桃樂西由英國返回打狗才幾個月，瑪麗・霍必瀾開始苦於一般無特殊原因的身體不適，因而尋求買醫師的醫療建議。

在買醫師的記錄中顯示，瑪麗抱怨身上出現一些「無以名狀的症狀，一般性的倦怠，體重減輕，早晨醒來覺得很疲累，有時會腹瀉和發燒。」官邸中其他的人也有相類似的症狀，不過其中有些人較多的時間是不在官邸屋子裡的，他們的症狀就不會像每天多數時間都待在官邸屋內的奶媽那麼嚴重。買醫師懷疑這些人的不適與排水溝的污穢臭氣有關，這在濕熱氣候下是很尋常的致病因素，可是由於領事官邸位置遠離擁擠的聚落而且通風良好，所以他排除了這個因素；此外，他的報告中提到霍必瀾極度勤快地檢查與清洗讓洗澡水流出屋子的排水管，這更讓原因撲朔迷離。[26]

1884年1月1日當怡記洋行終止租給赫思義的房子合約時，關於健康與住處的問題變得更加複雜，怡記終止合約的原因是他們必須收回那一半的房屋來自用。幸運地，在打狗居留一段時間後，赫思義的健康狀況已顯著地改善，這讓買醫師肯批准他回到臺灣府直到3月底，當雨季又將使臺灣府領事館變得對健康有極度不良的影響為止。[27]

買醫生給瑪麗的所有的治療與預防措施到最後都證明無效。當1884年新的一年開始時，瑪麗遭到一波更為嚴重的症狀與病痛的襲擊，沒有任何方法可以阻止這個病痛殘酷無情的進展。機會使然，在新年到來的第8天有人發現了一個之前無人知曉的堵塞陰溝，位

圖 5-5：瑪麗‧霍必瀾在打狗的墓碑
瑪麗‧唐納桑‧霍必瀾位於打狗墓園的墓石。
〔來自霍必瀾家族慷慨的授權許可，版權所有，翻印必究〕

Image 5-5： Mary Warren's gravestone at Takow
Mary Donnithorne Warren's gravestone at the Takow Foreign Cemetery.
(By kind permission of the Warren family. All rights reserved)

於山丘旁官邸下方。這陰溝發散出令人作嘔的極端惡臭，極有可能是瑪麗致病的原因。眾人追溯這溝渠，發現它通到山上官邸後方的廚房，在廚房裡發現家中不知情的僕役把廚房廢水全排到本來要排放雨水的溝渠。[28]

這個發現對可憐的瑪麗‧唐娜桑‧霍必瀾來說是太遲了，她死於1884年1月14日，在第二波病情開始惡化之後的第十天。[29]

瑪麗‧唐娜桑‧霍必瀾被葬在打狗的外國人墓園〔見圖5-5〕，這處墓園位於領事邸和20年前，即1864年曾簽下永久租約，準備當作英國領事館預定地的那塊地。[30]

地方上的外國社群得知這個消息後非常地震驚。霍必瀾發現他自己才38歲就已成為鰥夫，身邊還帶著一個不到兩歲的小女兒。出乎意料地，額勒格里及時來到，接手他在福爾摩沙南部的位置，於是在1884年2月1日，他的夫人過世一個月後，霍必瀾離開打狗轉赴羅星塔島擔任副領事官。我們並沒有確切的紀錄可以知道接下來桃樂西的人生旅程；然而，我們知道霍必瀾於1888年6月4日到1889年7月27日間再次請假離開職位，而1891年英國的戶口普查資料顯示，桃樂西與她的姊姊瑪麗一起在英格蘭上學。[31]當霍必瀾在羅星塔島的副領事館任職時（這是福州領事館的副館），他在1884年8月親眼目睹了法國海軍上將孤拔〔Amédée Anatole Prosper Courbet〕率領的艦隊炮擊閩江口的清軍砲臺（譯注：即中法戰爭中的馬尾海戰）。多年以後，當他退休蟄居於英國德本郡的Sidmouth時，曾告訴前來採訪的喬治‧恩尼斯‧莫理森〔George Ernest Morrison〕（他曾擔任時代雜誌駐北京記者多年），親眼看到法國海軍的炮擊行動是他整個派駐中國的時間裡，最有趣的經歷。

當打狗的外國人墓園在1871年移交給地方的外國社群使用時，原先附帶的前提條件是要在此處蓋一個小型的追思禮拜堂。一開始時因為缺乏足夠的捐款，這個附帶條件從未被達成。於是乎，打狗外國人社群把瑪麗‧唐娜桑悲劇性的死亡當作一個令人哀傷的轉機，以好好彌補這個尚未完成追思禮拜堂的缺憾。由於過去與現在打狗居民的慷慨解囊，充裕的捐款源源不絕的湧至，很快地就募集了足夠經費來建造一棟紀念她的追思堂。紀念瑪麗‧唐娜桑‧霍必瀾的追思堂如期完工，並於1886年1月14日在眾人追思的儀式後啟用〔見圖5-7〕。[32]

§

In September 1883, just six months after his return to Takow, Warren was again promoted. He was now appointed to be the Vice-Consul at Pagoda Island [羅星塔]. Yet Warren chose to remain at Takow and not to proceed immediately across to Pagoda Island, which was an anchorage that lay a few miles downstream from Foochow. The reason for his delay was probably his concern for his wife, Mary Donnithorne Warren, who had been suffering from a strange, unidentified illness since the summer began. [25]

During the summer of 1883, just a few months after her arrival with the baby Dorothy, Mary Warren began to suffer from a general malaise and sought the advice of Dr. Myers.

Myers records that she complained "of obscure symptoms, general languor, loss of flesh, rising unrefreshed in the morning, with occasional attacks of diarrhoea and fever." Others in the house suffered from similar symptoms, but as they spent more time away from the building, their effects were not so severe as those suffered by the nursing mother who was spending most of the day indoors. Dr. Myers suspected foul air from the drains, a common cause of illness in hot humid climes, but discounted this due to the isolated and airy position of the Consular Residence; moreover, he reported that Warren was extremely diligent in examining and flushing out the pipes for carrying away the bath water from the house. [26]

More complications regarding health and accommodation were to arrive on 1 January 1884, when Bain & Co terminated the rental agreement for the part of their house that Hausser was living in, as they needed the premises for their own use. Fortunately, Hausser's health had improved sufficiently during his residence at Takow for Dr. Myers to permit him to return to Taiwan-foo until the end of March, when the rains would again make the Taiwan-foo Consulate extremely unhealthy. [27]

The treatments and preventative measures prescribed to Mary Warren by Dr. Myers were all to no avail. As the New Year of 1884 began, Mary suffered a much more severe attack and nothing could stop its remorseless progress. By chance, on the eighth day an unknown blocked drain was discovered on the hillside just below the Residence. From this drain was emanating the foulest air, such as would cause Mary's illness. The drain was traced up to the kitchen behind the Residence, where the household staff had unknowingly been washing kitchen waste down a drain intended only for rainwater. [28]

The discovery came too late for poor Mary Donnithorne Warren, who died on 14 January 1884, the tenth day of the attack. [29]

Mary Donnithorne Warren was buried (see Image 5-5) in the Foreign Cemetery at Takow, which was located on the land that Consul Swinhoe had permanently leased 20 years previously in 1864 as the intended site for the British Consulate. [30]

The local foreign community was in shock. Warren now found himself a widower at the age of just 38, with a young daughter under 2 years old. Fortuitously, William Gregory arrived to take over Warren's position in South Formosa, and on 15 February 1884, one month after his wife's death, Warren departed to Pagoda Anchorage as Vice-Consul. Exactly what happened to Dorothy next is not known; however, Warren took another Leave of Absence from 4 June 1888 to 27 July 1889, and the 1891 British census records show Dorothy at school with her elder sister Mary in England. While at the Pagoda Island Vice-Consulate [大英國副領事館], a sub-Consulate of the Foochow Consulate, in August 1884 Warren was witness to the bombardment of the Min Forts [閩江砲臺], by the French fleet under Admiral Amédée Anatole Prosper Courbet [孤拔]. Years later in retirement at Sidmouth, Devon, Pelham Warren was to tell George Ernest Morrison [莫理循], who had been for many years The Times correspondent in Peking that watching the French naval bombardment had been his most interesting experience of all while in China. [31]

When the Takow Foreign Cemetery had originally been ceded to the local foreign community in 1871, it was done so on the condition that a small mortuary chapel be built upon the site. Due to a lack of funds in the original subscription, this condition had never been met. Thus, the foreign community saw the tragic death of Mary Donnithorne Warren as a sad opportunity to make good this deficiency. Sufficient funds were speedily forthcoming, from past and present residents of Takow, to erect a mortuary chapel in her memory. The construction of the Memorial Mortuary Chapel for Mary Donnithorne Warren was duly completed and the Chapel dedicated on 14 January 1886 (see Image 5-7). [32]

Frederick Hausser and the French Blockade of 1884-1885

腓特烈·赫思義與法軍1884到1885年的封鎖

皮耶·腓特烈·赫思義於1856年10月23日出生在英格蘭的米德塞克斯郡。他的父親是一位來自Soultz, Bas-Rhin地區的音樂教授，那是一塊德國與法國輪流統治的領土。或許就是因為赫思義這種曖昧的出身背景，解釋了為何一個如此有能力的領事官員從1878年到1886年都一直只能擔任實習翻譯官的職位。赫思義家是一個對音樂浸染很深的家庭，他的三個姊妹中至少有兩位成為音樂老師。1886年，在他終於獲得升職後，赫思義回到英格蘭，並在1888年5月2日與露薏莎·海倫·布蘭登〔Louisa Helen Brandon〕結婚，他們有三個孩子，都出生於中國。赫思義最後在中國的領事官僚系統中，晉升到總領事的位置，並於1911年退休，不過，他晚年的職務生涯因為健康不佳與罹患某種妄想症而蒙上陰霾。[33]

霍必瀾在1884年2月要離開福爾摩沙之前，也效法一年前倭妥瑪曾做過的事，寫信給巴夏禮爵士〔Sir Harry Parkes，又譯哈利·派克斯〕，亦即當時的駐北京大臣公使，讚許赫思義。霍必瀾在信中表示：

「我利用此機會向您推薦，赫思義先生，很長的一段時間裡，他在此地的領事館擔任助理領事官與翻譯官的職務，在處理公務上非常地有效率。他處理或指揮領事館辦公室的日常工作時，乾淨俐落，令人無從挑剔，而且他精通中文，不管是官方語言的寫或說，以及地方方言都很流利，對於我們領事館而言，他的這些能力與表現在任何時候都深具價值，無可取代。」[34]

1884年2月在霍必瀾離開之後，赫思義又重新回到打狗的領事館駐守（譯注：在這之前他派駐在臺灣府城的英國領事館）。

與此同時，在遠方的越南，1883年發生的一連串事件在事後看來，對福爾摩沙產生了意料之外的後果及影響。法國人就如同當時的其他西方強權一樣，正意圖侵占中國勢力影響所及的範圍，磨刀霍霍準備好要征服今天屬於越南的土地，包含名叫東京的越南北部省份，那裡於太平天國之亂後就陷入一片混亂。在越南的東京地區，許多中國人組成的非正規軍中，包括了劉永福〔Liu Yung-fu〕所領導的黑旗軍〔Black Flag Militia〕，他在1895年宛如曇花一現的臺灣民主國運動期間，趁勢崛起，成為知名人物。[35]

在越南，法軍打敗一支被送來阻止他們的中國軍隊，然後在1884年逼迫中國簽署了天津條約〔Convention of Tientsin〕，迫使中國完全退出越南。中國沒有信守承諾：於是，一支受命前去驅趕中國人離開的法國武力中了埋伏，被砍頭的法國士兵屍體隨河水漂流而下。得知消息後，法國大眾非常激憤，導致政府下臺。為了報復，法國海軍在海軍上將孤拔〔Amédée Anatole Prosper Courbet〕領導下集結，首先破壞了福州的中國海軍武力，被破壞的船隻中有很多是法國製造的，然後又派遣在他與薩巴斯丁·李士卑斯〔Sébastien Nicolas Joachim Lespes〕將軍指揮下的海軍在1884年8月攻擊福爾摩沙。雖然孤拔成功地帶領法軍登陸基隆，但李士卑斯帶領的部隊卻被拒於淡水一地。在此役，清廷派遣劉銘傳〔Liu Ming-ch'uan〕來負責統領福爾摩沙島上中國軍隊的防禦佈署，劉銘傳後來成為臺灣建省後的第一任巡撫。孤拔不滿意自己在島上攻擊的進展緩慢，於是1884年10月23日，他開始改採從海上封鎖臺灣島的策略。[36]

儘管當時只是區區一個實習翻譯官，赫思義在1884年7月到同年12月22日這段期間被正式領事官額勒格里單獨留下，在打狗處理領事事務。到了1884年12月他自己要離開打狗的前夕，額勒格里跟他的前任一樣，也曾寫信給巴夏禮爵士，讚賞赫思義，寫道：「所以赫思義身處於一個被隔絕的位置，負責打理……一個雖然獨立但其實卻是受命於他人的職務，而且經歷了一段棘手且令人煩憂的擾攘時期；我想他在工作上的表現真可說是異常優異」。[37]

195

孤拔在1884年10月24日所發動的海上封鎖行動，位於福爾摩沙西岸的封鎖線，其南端是由鹽水港〔Yenshui〕延伸到南岬〔South Cape，譯注：鵝鑾鼻〕。法國砲艦Lutin號封鎖打狗，而砲艦D'Estaing號巡航安平外海，除此之外，10月26日令人生畏的法國裝甲艦La Galissonniere號也加入戰局，上面有孤拔的副手李士卑斯親自坐陣指揮。[38]

顯然地，在這段時間，外國居民與懷疑他們會幫助法國侵略者的臺灣本地人之間的氣氛幾近劍拔弩張。不過，由報告得知，外國社群在行為上都非常謹慎小心，唯獨買醫師是個明顯的例外。李士卑斯到達封鎖線的次日，他就准許蒸汽拖船新臺灣號〔Sin Taiwan〕可以繼續每日往返打狗與安平的旅程。李士卑斯這個決定宛如一顆定心丸，促使買醫師隨即要求，並且成功獲得身在La Galissonniere艦上的李士卑斯的許可，讓他可以開自己的汽艇手術刀號〔Scalpel〕來往打狗安平兩地，他所提出的理由是在這兩個港口內他是唯一的一位醫師，就在取得許可後，他隨即開往安平。[39]

就在他剛從安平回到打狗時，買醫師馬上被中國士兵懷疑是叛徒，而且也開始傳出了要把通敵的外國居民全部槍決的聲音。雖然有中國的官員介入幹旋，但打狗的事態還是變得很嚴峻，情形惡劣到赫思義認為有必要把領事館的檔案移到一艘拖船上。買醫師身為道臺劉璈〔Liu Ao〕的顧問，並從他那兒得到汽艇行駛的許可，他並不為這些惡劣形勢所動。就在次日，他又準備要駕手術刀號到安平去，這使得赫思義寫了一張簡短的手寫便條要他打消主意，因為這會有引發打狗當地的士兵與在地人因仇視外國人而爆發暴力行為的危險。很幸運地，赫思義成功地勸阻買醫師不再做出鹵莽的舉動，雖然新臺灣號也在10月28日停駛，因為害怕會招惹上麻煩。[40]

1884年12月15日，南部各個港口的封鎖因法國船艦駛離，在實際上可以說是解除了。此外，從10月末買醫師引發的事件直到1884年底，中國人與外國居民間的關係總算是平平安安地渡過這段時期，這主要得感謝中國官員誠摯的努力。在12月22日由額勒格里手中接管領事館，擔任代理領事官的施本施〔William Donald Spence，又譯威廉·唐納德·史賓塞〕，曾描述此次的封鎖「是極端殘酷且令人感到噁心地野蠻」，這場封鎖造成中國人與外國居民之間極度的緊張。[41]

　　1885年的4月，施本施寫信給北京的代理公使尼可拉斯‧羅德瑞克‧歐格訥〔Nicholas Roderick O'Conor〕，讚揚赫思義，也推崇道臺劉璈。他在報告中說赫思義在主管打狗領事館業務與保護檔案的措施上，表現得可圈可點，由於他目前升職的機會不大，施本施建請上級贈予他100英鎊的獎金，以肯定他傑出的工作表現。這筆獎金後來很快地就被批准，理由是獎賞「一位冷靜、充滿勇氣與能力傑出的官員。」[42]

　　在中國的領事工作系統中，領事職位的數量有限，具實績與資格的官員有時要等很多年，領著一份通常很低的薪資，才有空缺的職位出現。施本施自己就感到很挫折，他當了超過十年的助理領事官，最後決定在1885年辭退領事工作進入商界；有人說服了他不要輕易地就辭職，不過他卻在1890年6月25日以42歲之齡過世，到最後都沒有再得到任何升遷機會。從1878年到1886年間，赫思義一直擔任實習翻譯官，領的是200英鎊的薪水；這份收入很難有足夠的錢可以儲蓄，當然也絕對不夠用來結婚，更別說要返鄉。[43]

　　因為在打狗領事館時期的經歷，赫思義的健康嚴重受損。上頭發放的100英鎊獎金使得施本施能夠從1885年7月起，放赫思義6個月的假，離開打狗到日本修養，為了恢復他的健康。我們無法確定赫思義是否曾經從在打狗歲月所經歷的壓力打擊中復原過來，因為他在1891年於羅星塔島任職時，曾經又受到幾次嚴重的疑似幻覺性妄想症的侵襲，而且在1898年，當他被派到緬甸與中國的邊境時，也曾有類似的病情發作。[44]

　　至於法國人，他們對越南的控制權，在1885年6月與清朝簽署了第二次天津條約之後，得到了確認及保障。然而他們在福爾摩沙留下了約700名的死者，其中超過半數死於疾病，被埋在基隆的一個墓園；至於孤拔上將本身，則被埋葬在多風的澎湖群島〔Pescadores〕上。[45]

§

Pierre Frederick Hausser [赫思義] was born in Middlesex, England, on 23 October 1856. His father, Frederic Hausser, was a Professor of Music from Soultz, Bas-Rhin, an area that had alternated between German and French control. It was perhaps this ambiguity in Hausser's background that explained why such a capable Consular officer was left holding the post of Student Interpreter from 1878 until 1886. The Haussers were a highly musical family, with at least two of his three sisters becoming music teachers. After finally obtaining his promotion to Second Assistant in 1886, a rank with a salary of £400, Hausser returned to England to marry Louisa Helen Brandon on 2 May 1888, and they had three children, all born in China. Hausser eventually rose to the rank of Consul-General in the China Consular Service and retired in 1911, though his later career was blighted by ill-health and a certain paranoia. [33]

Before leaving Formosa in February 1884, Pelham Warren, just as Thomas Watters had a year earlier, wrote to Sir Harry Parkes [巴夏禮], the British Minister at Peking, to praise Hausser. Warren declared that:

I avail myself of the opportunity to commend to your notice the very efficient manner in which Mr. Hausser has for a long period discharged the duties of Assistant and Interpreter at this Consulate. His conduct of the ordinary office work of the Consulate leaves nothing to be desired, whilst his proficiency in Chinese, both the written and spoken official language, and the local dialect spoken here, has rendered his services at all times most valuable. [34]

Meanwhile, in faraway Vietnam [越南], events were unfolding in 1883 that would have unexpected consequences in Formosa. The French, like other Western powers, were encroaching into areas of Chinese influence and set about subjugating all the present-day country of Vietnam, including the northern state of Tongking [東京], which had been in turmoil since the end of the Taiping Rebellion. Amongst the Chinese irregulars fighting in Tongking were the Black Flag Militia [黑旗軍], under Liu Yung-fu [劉永福], who would rise to great prominence at the time of the short-lived Formosan Republic of 1895. [35]

The French had defeated a Chinese army sent into Vietnam and in May 1884 forced

China to sign the Convention of Tientsin [天津條約], which committed the Chinese to withdraw entirely from Vietnam. This the Chinese failed to do: a French force sent to drive them out was ambushed and the decapitated bodies of the French soldiers were floated back down the river. The French public were outraged and the Government forced to resign. A naval force was assembled under Admiral Amédée Anatole Prosper Courbet, who first destroyed the Chinese naval forces at Foochow, many of which were French-built ships, and then despatched naval forces under himself and Admiral Sébastien Nicolas Joachim Lespes [李士卑斯] to attack Formosa in August 1884. Though Courbet was eventually successful in landing French troops at Keelung, the French force under Lespes was firmly repulsed at Tamsui. The Ching court sent Liu Ming-ch'uan [劉銘傳], who would later become the first Governor of Taiwan Province, to oversee the Chinese defence of the island. Courbet, dissatisfied by the slow progress of his assault on Formosa resorted to a blockade of the island on 23 October 1884. [36]

Despite being just a Student Interpreter, Hausser had been left alone and in charge at Takow from July 1884 until 22 December 1884 by the officiating Consul William Gregory at Taiwan-foo. Upon the eve of his own departure in December 1884, Gregory was again to write to Sir Harry Parkes praising Hausser and stating that "Hausser has therefore held an isolated position, amounting ⋯ to a separate though subordinate charge, during a troublous and most anxious time; and I think that he has acquitted himself exceedingly well therein." [37]

The southern section of Courbet's blockade of the West Coast of Formosa imposed, on 24 October 1884, stretched from Yenshui [鹽水港] to the South Cape [南岬]. The French gunboat Lutin blocked Takow, while the gunboat D'Estaing cruised off Anping; these were joined on 26 October by the formidable French ironclad, La Galissonniere, with Admiral Sébastien Nicolas Joachim Lespes [李士卑斯], Courbet's second-in-command, aboard. [38]

Clearly this was a period of considerable tension between the resident foreigners and the native population who suspected the resident foreigners of helping the French aggressors. However, the foreign community reportedly behaved with great caution, with the solitary exception of Dr. Myers. The day after his arrival, Lespes gave permission for the steam-tug Sin Taiwan to continue making its daily trips between Takow and Anping. Emboldened by Lespes' decision, Dr. Myers promptly sought and obtained permission from Lespes, on board the La Galissonniere, to run his own steam launch, the Scalpel, between Takow and Anping, on the grounds that he was the only medical man at the two ports, and set off for Anping. [39]

Upon his return to Takow, Myers was immediately suspected of treachery by the Chinese soldiers and there were calls for all the resident foreigners to be shot for communicating with the enemy. Despite the intervention of the Chinese officers, the situation became very critical at Takow, such that Hausser deemed it necessary to remove the Consulate Archives to a tug. Myers, who was acting as an adviser to Tao-t'ai Liu Ao [劉璈] and from whom he had permission to run his launch, was unperturbed. The very next day Myers again proposed to go to Anping on the Scalpel, eliciting a curt written warning from Hausser to desist due to the very real danger of an outbreak of violence by the soldiery and local people against all foreign residents at Takow. Fortunately Hausser was successful in dissuading Myers from his reckless behaviour, though the Sin Taiwan runs were also then discontinued on 28 October, lest trouble ensue. [40]

On 15 December 1884, the blockade of the southern ports was effectively lifted when the French ships sailed away. Moreover, from the time of the Myers incident in late October until the end of 1884, relations between the Chinese and the resident foreigners had been passably good, mainly thanks to sincere efforts by Chinese officials. William Donald Spence [施本施], who had taken over charge of the Consulate as Acting Consul from Gregory on 22 December, described the blockade, which caused much tension between the Chinese and foreign residents, as 'most cruel and revoltingly brutal'. [41]

In April 1885, Spence wrote to Nicholas Roderick O'Conor [歐格訥], the Chargé d'Affaires at Peking, to praise Hausser and to commend Tao-t'ai Liu Ao. Spence reported that Hausser had acquitted himself admirably while in charge of the Takow Consulate and its Archives, and, given his slender opportunity for promotion, requested that a gratuity of £100 be paid to Hausser in recognition of his outstanding service, a gratuity that was speedily approved for "a cool, courageous & able officer". [42]

Given the limited number of Consulships in the China Consular Services, deserving officers would sometimes wait years, on an often low salary, for any vacancy to emerge. Spence himself was frustrated to remain over 10 years as an Assistant and decided to resign from the Consular Service in 1885 to enter commerce; he was persuaded to refrain from outright resignation, but died, aged 42, on 25 June 1890 without ever gaining promotion. Hausser had remained on a salary of £200, as a Student Interpreter, from 1878 until 1886; scarcely enough to save anything and certainly not enough to marry, let alone return home. [43]

Hausser's health had been severely impaired by his experiences at Takow. The prospect of the gratuity enabled Spence to grant Hausser six months leave in Japan from July 1885 in order to recover his health. It is uncertain whether Hausser ever recovered from the stress of his Takow days, as he suffered severe bouts of possibly delusional paranoia while at Pagoda Island [羅星塔] in 1891, and again up on the Burma-China border in 1898. [44]

As for the French, their control over Vietnam was assured by a second Convention of Tientsin signed in June 1885. Yet they left nearly 700 dead, of which more than half had died of disease, at a cemetery at Keelung; and Admiral Courbet himself lying buried upon the windswept Pescadores [澎湖群島]. [45]

After the French Blockade
在法國的軍事封鎖之後

　　1885年5月，臺灣島上所有的外國居民聯名寫了封道謝函給道臺劉璈，感謝他在法國封鎖期間給予他們的保護。劉璈在1881年時曾被指派到福爾摩沙擔任巡撫，他像劉銘傳一樣，有軍事背景。但是這兩人在法國封鎖臺灣期間，馬上就變成政治上的競爭對手。[46]

　　施本施在他的報告中提到關於對道臺劉璈的正式感謝，他的記錄中寫著：「劉璈對劉銘傳這位欽差大臣感到非常地憤慨，他指責後者懦弱與無能」，劉璈還用「掩不住的欣喜」語氣說左宗棠〔Tso Tsung-t'ang〕將軍曾批評過劉銘傳。劉道臺的輕率言論事後證明使他付出很大的代價，因為1885年10月劉璈自己被控告有收賄以及侵占公款的罪行：他的財產被查封，他的妻妾與家人被流放街頭。在判決過後正好一周時，劉銘傳就被指派為臺灣省第一任巡撫。[47]

　　劉銘傳接任臺灣巡撫之後，將自己的權力重心設置在臺北這個新的北臺灣都城，歷經260年的風光歲月之後，權力的重心轉離福爾摩沙南部，更具體的說，是從道臺之前曾經在那裡行使過最高權威的臺灣府城轉移出去。當臺灣由府改制為省，並以北部的臺北為省城時，原臺灣府依然維持它府城的地位，不過它的名字現在改成臺南府。[48]

　　1885年7月送走赫思義到日本養病後，只剩下施本施一個人單獨留在福爾摩沙南部：因為他住在臺灣府城的領事館，所以暫時沒有任何領事官員駐守在打狗。1885年8月，英國的三桅船狄克遜號〔M A Dixon〕被潮流沖到打狗薩拉森山頭下方撞上那裡的岩石而沈沒。船員與大多數貨物被救了回來，施本施從臺南趕到打狗，提取存放在打狗領事館辦公室保險櫃內的領事館運作基金，以分發獎勵金給救難人員。在沒有領事官員駐守的辦公室內還存有金錢的這件事，並沒有逃過有心人士的注意，於是就在9月8日，盜賊破門進入領事辦公處內，偷走整個保險櫃。這些盜賊用暴力打不開保險櫃，為了不讓錢財被別人拿走，這些盜賊就把整個保險櫃丟入潟湖中，並以此為滿足。大約在兩周之後，保險櫃在落水處湊巧被捕蝦人所發現。令人難以置信地，保險櫃內許多在外國註冊的地契文件，仍舊非常的完

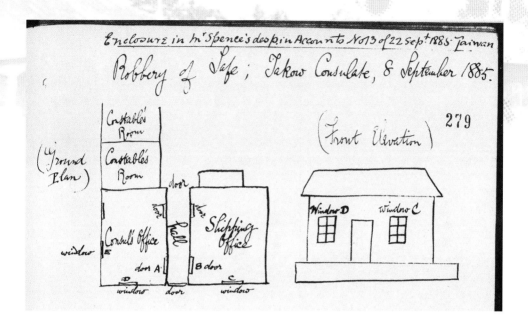

Image 5-6： 1885 Sketch Plan of Consular Offices
Sketch Plan of the British Consular Offices made by Acting Consul Spence at the time of the 1885 Burglary,
showing the then usage of the front rooms.

整。施本施提及這些文件如何「在陽光下小心地曬乾」，它們的內容「在經過長時間浸水後並沒有變得更糟。」[49]

在施本施對盜竊案所做的報告中，也包括了一張領事辦公處的配置圖，可以看出在1885年辦公處空間被使用的狀況〔見圖5-6〕，並且透露出一些關於安東尼·阿不拉多〔Antonio Alborado〕這位非常資深的領事館巡捕的稀有資訊。[50]

安東尼·阿不拉多在1822年左右生於馬尼拉，起先是在1865年時被郇和僱爲福爾摩沙南部領事館的巡捕。1869年，有一件事爲他贏得榮譽，那就是他走遍臺灣府街道去追捕威廉·畢格林〔William Pickering，又譯必麒麟〕，這個人因爲受到誘拐與非法侵佔財產的指控而被領事法庭傳喚。施本施在1885年有關盜竊案的報告中提到了阿不拉多巡捕與他的兒子，當時他們一般都是睡在領事辦公室隔壁的房間，雖然出事那晚是輪到守更夫輪值。施本施也順帶提到阿不拉多只會說「洋涇濱英語」〔pidgin English〕。此後阿不拉多也一直擔任領事館巡捕，至少到1896年，甚至有可能到1897年，那時照推算他應該已經75歲了。[51]

因爲打狗港現在一年之中只有幾個月的時間有船隻抵港進行糖的交易，再加上新改名的臺南城（譯注：臺灣建省後改臺灣府爲臺南府）不再是這個島嶼的權力中樞，於是在安平港這個幾乎所有南方外商都前來聚居的地方建一個新領事館的想法，又重新被提出來討論。早在1877年時，換句話說，甚至在打狗領事館都尚未建好之前，工部與大多數的領事官員都曾建議要把領事館蓋在安平：事實上，在所有曾在福爾摩沙工作過的領事官員中，只有有雅芝反對這個提議，雖然是少數派，但是他在領事官僚高層中有一個有力盟友，亦即威妥瑪爵士。跟環境衛生很不健康的臺南府城中「狀況糟糕的家屋」相比，安平被視爲是較爲適合的領事館設置地點，考量地點位置、方便性，特別是衛生條件。因爲傷寒、瘧疾等熱病經常在城市中傳染流行，所以在1886年2月，英國政府終於從安平的中國政府手中取得一塊地，如此一來施本施終於可以放心離開他的福爾摩沙南部代理領事官的職位。[52]

§

In May 1885 all the foreign residents drafted a letter of thanks to Tao-t'ai Liu Ao [劉璈] in appreciation of the protection that he had given them during the French Blockade. Liu Ao had been appointed as Circuit Intendant on Formosa in 1881, and, like Liu Ming-ch'uan, had a military background. Yet the two men were soon to become political rivals during the French blockade. [46]

In his report on officially thanking Tao-t'ai Liu Ao, Spence records that Liu Ao was 'in a high state of indignation with Liu Ming-ch'uan, the Imperial Commissioner, accusing him of cowardice and incapacity', adding 'with ill-concealed glee' that General Tso [Tso Tsung-t'ang, 左宗棠] had denounced Liu Ming-ch'uan. The Tao-t'ai's indiscretion was to prove costly, for in October 1885 Liu Ao himself was impeached on charges of bribery and embezzlement of public funds: his property was sealed up and his wives and families turned into the street. Precisely one week after the verdict, Liu Ming-ch'uan was appointed to be the first Governor of Taiwan Province. [47]

As Governor Liu Ming-ch'uan subsequently established himself at the new northern capital of Taipei [臺北], the power devolved away from South Formosa after a dominance of 260 years, and, in particular, from the Tao-t'ai who had previously exercised the highest authority from Taiwan-foo, the prefectural capital. When Taiwan changed from being a prefecture to being a province with its capital in the north at Taipei, Taiwan-foo remained a prefectural capital but its name was changed to Tainan-fu [臺南府]. [48]

Spence, after sending Hausser away to Japan in July 1885 on sick leave, was all alone in South Formosa: while he resided up at the Taiwan-foo consulate, there was temporarily no Consular officer stationed at Takow. In August 1885, the British Barque the M A Dixon had drifted on to the rocks below Saracen's Head at Takow and was wrecked. The crew and most of the cargo were saved and Spence came down from Taiwan-foo to distribute reward money from the Consular funds held in the safe at the Consular Offices at Takow. The fact that money was still being stored at the Offices at a time when there was no Consular officer in charge did not go unnoticed, and on 8 September 1885, burglars broke into the building and stole the whole safe. Unable to force entry into the safe, the burglars contented themselves with dumping it into the waters of the Lagoon, from where it was recovered by chance by shrimpers nearly two weeks later. Incredibly, the safe, containing many of the foreign-registered Title Deeds, remained intact and Spence relates how, "after a careful drying in the sun", the contents "were none the worse for their prolonged immersion". [49]

Spence's account of the burglary also includes a plan of the Consular Offices as they were used in 1885 (see Image 5-6), and gives some rare information about Antonio Alborado [阿不拉多], the long-serving Consular Constable. [50]

Antonio Alborado, who was born in Manila around 1822, was originally hired as Consular Constable in South Formosa by Robert Swinhoe in 1865. In 1869 Constable Alborado had the distinction of marching William Alexander Pickering [必麒麟], who had been summoned to appear before the Consular Court to face charges of abduction and illegal seizure, through the streets of Taiwan-foo. Spence's 1885 report on the burglary records that Constable Alborado and his son slept in the room next to the Consul's Office, though on the night in question the watchman was on duty. Spence also records that Alborado spoke only 'pidgin English' [洋涇濱英語]. Alborado continued as Consular Constable at least until 1896, and possibly until 1897, when he would have been 75 years old. [51]

With Takow port being only used for a few months a year for the sugar trade and the newly-named Tainan city no longer the island's centre of power, the idea of building a new British Consulate at the port of Anping, where nearly all the southern foreign merchants resided, was again pursued. As far back as 1877, in other words before the Takow Consulate had even been built, both the Office of Works and most of the Consular officers had proposed building a Consulate at Anping: indeed, of all the Consular officers who had served on Formosa, only Hewlett had been against this idea, but he had a powerful ally in Sir Thomas Wade . In contrast to the "wretched tenements" within the unhealthy city of Tainan-fu, Anping was regarded as the preferable place for a Consulate in terms of position, convenience and especially hygiene. With typho-malarial fever prevalent within Tainan city, a site was secured from the Chinese government at Anping in February 1886, allowing Spence to at last depart from his post as Acting Consul for South Formosa. [52]

Return of Consul Warren
霍必瀾領事的歸來

1886年4月，霍必瀾回到福爾摩沙南部，讓他有機會可以一窺剛建好不久，獻給他已故夫人瑪麗‧唐娜桑，一座小巧優雅的追思禮拜堂〔見圖5-7〕。剛回到福爾摩沙時，他的職位仍然是副領事官，一直要等到1886年7月19日，他正式的領事派任才公告。[53]

實際上，在他離開的這段期間，福爾摩沙南部幾乎沒有什麼改變。雖然那塊建造安平領事館的土地終於已成功的取得，但是證據顯示建造工程最快也要到1889年左右才完成。當福爾摩沙本身成為清帝國的一個正式的省份後，照道理來說它現在應該具有更重要的地位；不過，在新巡撫劉銘傳的統治下，權力重心已經漸漸轉移到島嶼的北部，臺南正在快速地成為一處崩塌停滯的落後地方。[54]

霍必瀾對於中國官方往往不追究積欠外商債務的中國商人這件事，感到特別地憤怒。只要當外商到法庭申告中國商人欠款，過了不多久這些中國商人就會宣告破產或死亡，或者是人已經離開臺灣島。劉銘傳本人很快地就對霍必瀾他全心全力地追究這些債務案件一事感到厭惡，因而開始極度地厭惡他。[55]

很顯然地，在南部霍必瀾並非是唯一對劉銘傳起反感的人。當劉銘傳後來在1889年5月訪問臺南時，地方上那些被他的糖稅與其他稅賦激怒的居民，把他圍困在自己的衙門內，因為如此，劉銘傳從未再訪問過南部。[56]

1891年6月，劉銘傳因為健康情況不佳而離開臺灣。他的離開似乎為福爾摩沙南部開啟了一個較少衝突對立的時期，以至於霍必瀾很快地就能向上頭報告說現在與中國官方間已經有較為友善的關係。[57]

不過，官方對打狗港的忽視卻仍然不變，而且在打狗的領事館建築物自然無法避免地會受到天氣的影響，也因缺乏使用而比較容易頹圮。雖然沒有人對官邸的保養維護持有異議，但1892年2月馬歇爾發現領事辦公處與牢房的建築已經有點殘破，並且受到嚴重的白蟻

圖 5-7：打狗外國人墓園的葬儀追思禮拜堂
由外國人社區於1886年發起建造打狗墓園葬儀追思堂紀念瑪麗‧霍必瀾。
〔來自Logie收藏之慷慨許可，版權所有，翻印必究〕

Image 5-7： Mortuary Chapel at Takow Foreign Cemetery
The Mortuary Chapel built by the Foreign Community at the Takow Cemetery in about 1886 in memory of Mary Donnithorne Warren.

侵蝕，於是馬歇爾計劃賣掉它們，估計價值約9000墨西哥銀元〔換算當時的英鎊約為1692鎊〕。雖然霍必瀾對於變賣掉辦公室與牢房持著非常保留謹慎的態度，但他承認這裏的牢房很多年來都沒有再拘留過犯人，而且現在也很少有船運商務會在打狗進行。即使如此，他仍然相信打狗是福爾摩沙南部的天然良港，只要港口能疏濬，將會再度繁榮起來。[58]

假如早前的那些年，打狗的領事館建築因為天氣與缺乏使用而屋況變差，那麼1892年，這地震與颱風次數異常多的一年，對領事館建築的傷害更具有毀滅性。1892年4月22日就發生了一次非常嚴重的地震，它接下來的餘震甚至持續了整個夏天。記錄中福爾摩沙南部曾遭遇過最嚴重的颱風之一，就發生在1892年7月21日，整個村落被風吹走，大帆船被吹到海上漂流，數百名的死者曝屍於海岸邊。霍必瀾在報告中提到所有外國人蓋的建築物都受到嚴重的破壞，而打狗的領事官邸由於它暴露在山丘上，毫無遮蔽，其受損狀況可說更加嚴重。[59]

就在9月份當更多的颱風掃過臺灣島之後，馬歇爾在1892年11月急忙趕過來臺灣，評估各地領事館財產的受損狀況。有關打狗領事館建築，馬歇爾勘查之後報告的結果如下：

領事官邸：屋頂瓦片好幾處剝落〔設計上有兩層平瓦，較低的一層鎖到屋頂緣木上〕，有五處天花板被完全破壞，一個磚砌煙囪被吹倒，窗戶玻璃被吹掉，門窗被吹入屋內且有多處破損，界牆與牆上開的門有部份被破壞，建築物本身有很多小的損害。

辦公室，牢房和巡捕居所：這裡的屋頂也有部份剝落，但天花板完全不見了；牢房院子的牆被吹倒，以及領事辦公處庭院的前牆，獨立辦公室的門窗與圍牆門，以及領事辦公處庭院入口都被破壞〔見圖5-8〕。

建築結構的穩定性沒有受損；沒有發生下陷或斷裂，主要的屋頂木樑健全完好，沒有被風吹走，不過白蟻侵蝕了好幾處的平行桁條與領事辦公室的木板部份⋯⋯

圖 5-8：1899年所拍攝的打狗領事辦公處照片，顯示了1892年的颱風如何吹垮了牢房院子的圍牆。
〔來自Edinger收藏之慷慨許可，版權所有，翻印必究〕

Image 5-8：Takow Consular Offices circa 1899
The Takow Consular Offices photographed circa 1899,
showing how the 1892 typhoon had blown down the Gaol Yard wall.
(Courtesy The Edinger Collection. All rights reserved)

我正著手拆除牢房院子的圍牆，因為這棟建築裡將不會再關犯人；而且因為白蟻
啃蝕了巡捕住所的木頭地板，所以我更換了新的地板。[60]

針對需要之處進行修繕的總經費為1400墨西哥銀元。在向倫敦請求許可的經費總額
中，馬歇爾還加進了一筆興建280英呎長的碎石牆之經費，這道牆的目的是用來界定領事官
邸東北方與清政府財產之間的界線，以防止對方更進一步的侵占。我們由證據中知道1892
年夏天，在颱風季時居住在打狗的是一位二等助理領事官，額必廉〔Pierce Essex O'Brien-
Butler〕，因為在留下的資料中，馬歇爾曾申請75英鎊給他，以鼓勵他在毀滅性的颱風來臨
時為了保護領事館建築所作的努力。[61]

1892年10月，有兩起船難發生在臺灣海峽的澎湖群島〔Pescadores〕附近：其中一起
是半島東方汽船公司〔the Peninsular and Oriental〕的蒸汽船Bokhara號，上面載著香港
板球隊，這支隊伍可以說是英國通商口岸生活的重心。在非貿易季節時，英國通商口岸的
生活可以說是沒有什麼休閒放鬆的活動。在幾個受歡迎的休閒活動中，香港板球俱樂部可
能是當中最早成立的一個，在1851年組成，它們不只推廣板球，也致力於草地網球與槌球
的推展〔見圖5-9〕。Bokhara號在1892年10月8日離開上海開往香港，但在靠近澎湖群島
海域時意外地遇到颱風而偏離預定航道，於1892年10月10日夜晚在沙島失事沉沒。英國領
事霍必瀾，與買醫師以及羅伯·海斯汀由安平出發去調查情況。搭乘此船的123名船員與25
位旅客當中，僅有23名被救生還：25位旅客中，僅有二名被救回，這兩位都是香港板球隊
成員。1893年，就在霍必瀾最後一次離開福爾摩沙前不久，在沙島上設立了一座紀念碑。
於是，霍必瀾在福爾摩沙的工作生涯開始於1870年Loudoun Castle號的船難，而結束於
1893年建造一座紀念碑來紀念Bokhara號的悲劇。[62]

霍必瀾在1893年8月離開臺灣，把福爾摩沙南部領事館的業務交給安布羅斯·約翰·孫
德雅〔Ambrose John Sundius〕。當他要離開打狗時，「外國人社群知道他喜好狩獵，以
大家所有人的名義送給他一把槍作為離別贈禮，並且愉快地說，在霍必瀾身上他們看到他
一生做人處事的宗旨是自我要求的責任，而非野心」〔見圖5-10〕。[63]

圖 5-9：1892年香港板球俱樂部隊伍
1892年香港板球俱樂部隊伍，除了2人生還，全都在1892年澎湖群島附近的砂島，因船難喪生。來自1892年倫敦畫報。
〔來自香港板球俱樂部之慷慨許可〕

Image 5-9 : Hong Kong Cricket Club team, 1892
The 1892 Hong Kong Cricket Club team who were all, save two, lost in the shipwreck of the Bokhara, off the Pescadores, in 1892. From the Illustrated London News of 3 December 1892.
(Courtesy of the Hong Kong Cricket Club. All rights reserved)

圖 5-10：1890年代在福爾摩沙南部的一場打獵聚會
一個幾乎全部的安平與打狗之外國人社群都參加的南福爾摩沙打獵聚會。
霍必瀾被認爲是，從左邊算過來，戴著硬草帽的第四位男士。
〔來自Logie收藏之慷慨許可，版權所有，翻印必究〕

Image 5-10 : 1890s Shooting Party in South Formosa
An 1890s shooting party in south Formosa showing almost the whole foreign community from Anping and Takow.
Consul Warren is believed to be the fourth man from the left wearing the straw boater.
(Courtesy of the Logie Collection. All rights reserved)

霍必瀾在1893年被任命爲漢口領事，並在1899年10月在名義上成爲當地的總領事。不過實際上，在1899年5月時，他由漢口被調到上海擔任代理總領事，他開始負責業務時正值義和團運動〔Boxer Rebellion〕嚴重威脅到北京的公使館以及全中國的安危。霍必瀾在這個危機關頭的行事處置穩定了中國東南部的情勢，幫他贏得騎士的爵位，於1901年7月並正式被派爲上海的總領事。佩翰‧霍必瀾爵士於1911年1月20日從中國領事工作的崗位中退休。退休後的餘生，他由女兒瑪麗‧艾琳納‧霍必瀾所照料，住在英國德本郡Sidmouth地方的「The Moorings」宅邸，也就是他兒子理查‧萊爾德‧霍必瀾（曾任職於中國海關）的宅邸。1923年11月21日華倫爵士在上面所提到的宅邸中與世長辭，安息於Sidmouth的天普街墓園裡。

§

Pelham Laird Warren returned to South Formosa in April 1886, allowing him to see the ethereal Memorial Chapel to his late wife, Mary Donnithorne Warren, that had been newly erected (see Image 5-7). Upon his return to Formosa, Warren still held the rank of Vice-Consul, and his appointment to Consul was not gazetted until 19 July 1886. [53]

In fact, little had changed in South Formosa during the period that Warren had been away. While a site had finally been secured for the Anping Consulate, it appears that the construction was not completed until about 1889, at the earliest. Formosa itself had supposedly assumed greater importance as a Province within the Chinese Empire; yet the power, under the new Governor Liu Ming-ch'uan, had slipped away to the north of the island and Tainan was fast becoming a corrupt backwater. [54]

Warren was particularly outraged at the lack of prosecution by the Chinese authorities of those Chinese merchants indebted to foreign traders. No sooner did the foreigner merchant apply to the courts, than the Chinese merchant was declared bankrupt, or deceased, or to have left the island. Liu Ming-ch'uan for his part soon tired of Warren's energetic pursuit of these debts, and developed a strong dislike of Warren. [55]

Warren was apparently not the only one in the south to develop a strong antipathy towards Liu Ming-ch'uan. When Liu subsequently visited Tainan in May 1889, the local inhabitants, incensed by Liu's sugar taxes and other imposts, besieged him within his own yamen, such that Liu never visited the south again. [56]

Liu Ming-ch'uan withdrew from the island on account of ill-health in June 1891. His departure seemed to herald a less confrontational period in South Formosa, as Warren was soon able to report cordial relations with the Chinese authorities. [57]

The official neglect of the harbour at Takow continued, and the Consular buildings there duly suffered from the climate and the lack of use. While the retention of the Consular Residence was beyond dispute, in February 1892 Marshall found the buildings of the Consular Offices and Gaol to be generally dilapidated and suffering from the ravages of the white ants, and proposed their sale, estimating their value at 9,000 Mexican dollars (equivalent then to about £1,692). Warren had strong reservations about endorsing the sale of the Consular Offices and Gaol, although he conceded that there had been no prisoners held at the gaol for some years and that little shipping business was now being carried out at Takow. Nevertheless, Warren remained convinced that Takow was the natural port for southern Formosa, and would rise once again if only the harbour were dredged. [58]

If the Consular buildings at Takow had suffered from the weather and lack of use in previous years, 1892, a year of an exceptional number of earthquakes and typhoons, was to prove destructive. A severe earthquake, with aftershocks lasting throughout the summer, occurred on 22 April 1892. One of the most severe typhoons ever to strike south Formosa was recorded on 21 July 1892, with entire villages being swept away, junks driven out to sea, and hundreds dead along the coast. Warren relates that all the foreign buildings were extensively damaged, and that the Consular Residence at Takow, from its exposed position on the hill, suffered very severely. [59]

After further typhoons had swept the island in September, Marshall hurried across in

November 1892 to assess the damage to the Consular properties. Marshall reported on the result of his examination of the Takow buildings as follows:

Consular Residence: The roof tiling (two courses of flat tiles, the lower one screwed to the boarding) was stripped in several places, five of the ceilings were completely destroyed, a brick chimney was blown down, window glass blown out, doors and windows also blown in and destroyed in places, boundary wall and gate partially destroyed, and a great deal of minor damage done to the building.

Offices, Gaol, & Constable's Qtrs [Quarters]: Here also the roof was partially stripped and all the ceilings washed down, the Gaol Yard wall was blown down, also the front wall of the Compound, doors, windows, and gates of Out Offices, and entrance to Compound were destroyed. [see Image 5-8]

The stability of the buildings remains unimpaired; there are no settlements or fractures, the main roof timbers are sound and have not been displaced. White ants have however shewn themselves in some of the purlins and boarding of the Consul's house. …

I am abolishing the Yard Wall of the Gaol, for there are never any prisoners in the building; and as the wood floors of the Constable's [Quarters] become eaten up by the white ants, tile floors are substituted. [60]

The total cost of carrying out the necessary repairs would be 1,400 Mexican dollars. Marshall also inserted for London's approval the cost of building a 280-foot rubble stone wall to define the limit of the Government property to the north-east of the Consul's Residence, to prevent any further encroachments. During the summer of 1892, it is clear that Pierce Essex O'Brien-Butler [額必廉], the Second Assistant, was residing at Takow during the typhoons as Marshall requests a payment of $75 for his good work in protecting the Consular buildings during these disastrous typhoons. [61]

In October 1892, two wrecks occurred at the Pescadores [澎湖群島] in the Taiwan Strait; of these, the wreck of the Peninsular and Oriental [半島東方汽船公司] steamer Bokhara, carrying the Hongkong Cricket team struck at the very heart of British Treaty Port life. The Treaty Port life was one with few distractions during the non-trading months. The Hongkong Cricket Club was probably the earliest of these welcome distractions, having been formed in 1851, to promote not only cricket, but also lawn tennis and croquet (see Image 5-9). The Bokhara had left Shanghai on the 8 October 1892 bound for Hongkong, but, falling foul of an unexpected typhoon near the Pescadores, was wrecked off Sand Island [沙島] on the night of 10 October 1892. Consul Warren set out from Anping with Dr. Myers, and Robert Hastings to investigate. Of the 123 crew and 25 passengers on board, only 23 had been saved: of the twenty-five passengers, only two, both members of the Hongkong cricket team, were saved. A monument was erected on Sand Island in 1893, shortly before Warren's final departure from Formosa. Thus Warren's career on Formosa had begun with the wreck of the Loudoun Castle in 1870 and ended with the erection of a monument to tragic loss of the Bokhara. [62]

Warren departed from Taiwan in August 1893, and handed over charge of the South Formosa Consulate to Ambrose John Sundius [孫德雅]. Upon the departure of Consul Pelham Laird Warren, "the foreign community as a whole, knowing him to be a keen shot, gave him a gun as a parting present and pleasingly said that they had been able to see that duty, not ambition, had ever been the guiding influence on his life" (see Image 5-10). [63]

Pelham Warren in 1893 was appointed Consul at Hankow [漢口], where he nominally became Consul-General in October 1899. In fact, Warren had been brought down from Hankow to Shanghai in May 1899 to officiate as Acting Consul-General, and so was in charge when the Boxer Rebellion [義和團運動] posed its greatest threat to the Peking Legations and the whole of China. Warren's handling of the situation, which ensured that peace prevailed in southeast China, earned him a knighthood and official appointment as Consul-General at Shanghai in July 1901. Sir Pelham Warren retired from the China Consular Service on 20 January 1911. Warren spent his last years being cared for by his daughter, Mary Eleanor Warren, living at

'The Moorings', Sidmouth, Devon, the house of his son, Richard Laird Warren, who was in the Chinese Maritime Customs. Sir Pelham Laird Warren, K.C.M.G., died on 21 November 1923 at The Moorings in Sidmouth, Devon, and was buried at the Temple Street Cemetery, Sidmouth, Devon. [64]

Last Days of Ching Rule over Formosa
清朝統治臺灣的最後時光

1893年10月，新任的領事胡力檔〔Richard Willett Hurst，又譯理查・威勒特・赫斯特〕抵達福爾摩沙南部，由孫德雅手中接管領事館。在胡力檔到來的前幾個月，打狗又受到三個更嚴重颱風的侵襲，導致位於打狗港的領事館建築遭到大規模的損壞。此外，1893年12月馬歇爾又進行了另一次的勘查，他發現兩棟建築的屋頂木材都有被白蟻感染蛀食，不過經評量後，他認為這些建築還能再使用四年。往好的方向看，馬歇爾發現這些建築與地板都被維護得乾淨整齊。[65]

領事館的外表似乎也欺騙了胡力檔領事，因為1894年夏天他放心地決定與他的家人，包括夫人瑪格麗特〔Margaret〕與兒子傑佛瑞・威勒特・胡力檔〔Geoffrey Willett Hurst〕一起住在打狗領事官邸。他之後發現這個家又冷又不舒服，但至少在雨季來臨以前尚可忍受，不過一到了雨季，雨水會像瀑布般穿越屋頂而下。他描述「在溼漉漉的天氣中毫無例外地必須套上膠鞋，從一個房屋移動到另一個房間時必須打傘，通道上必須放著許多踏腳石以免地上形成一灘灘的積水」。[66]

劉銘傳離開後，新的巡撫邵友濂〔Shao Yu-lien〕放任整個島的事務到幾乎停滯的狀態。因為這樣，對逐漸逼近野心勃勃的日本，福爾摩沙缺乏防備的能力，雖然因為邵友濂的要求，清廷派中法戰爭的老將劉永福〔Liu Yung-fu〕以及他麾下的黑旗軍，渡海來防禦臺灣南部。1894年，日本與中國的軍隊競相要去鎮壓在朝鮮的一場叛亂，兩方皆聲稱朝鮮是自己的領土。當發現朝鮮反叛軍潰敗後，中國與日本軍隊開始把矛頭指向彼此，結果就引發了1894－1895年的甲午〔第一次中日〕戰爭〔Sino-Japanese War〕。劉永福派遣他的三子劉成良〔Liu Ch'eng-liang〕擔任福爾摩沙南部防衛線的一環，他於1895年2月時駐紮在薩拉森山頭（譯注：即旗後山），負責打狗碉堡（譯注：即旗後砲臺）的防守。[67]

在劉成良所部接管碉堡之前，1895年2月1日當天先進行一次軍火的清點。就在清點存貨的過程中，一個存放一噸重槍用火藥的火藥庫爆炸，殺死了70個人，幾乎包括了碉堡

圖 5-11：1895年英國皇家海軍水星號在打狗港外。
1895年版畫，英國皇家海軍巡洋艦水星號停靠在打狗港外， 來自1895年4月20日之倫敦畫報。
〔來自羅榮文之慷慨許可，版權所有，翻印必究〕

Image 5-11 : H.M.S. Mercury outside Takow Harbour in 1895
1895 Engraving of the British cruiser H.M.S. Mercury stationed outside Takow Harbour in 1895
from the Illustrated London News of 20 April 1895.
(By kind permission of Lo Rong-Wen [羅榮文]. All rights reserved)

內所有的士兵。碉堡其他的部份也受到嚴重損害。就在港口入口處對面的領事官邸內，胡力檔與家人仍住在裡面，爆炸造成許多灰泥由天花板掉下來，大部份窗戶上的玻璃都破裂了。然而，遭受最嚴重毀損的，要算是距離爆炸地點只有數百碼的買醫師屋邸：大約一百片玻璃窗成為碎屑，屋頂受創，門被震離門框上的樞紐。萬大衛紀念醫院因為地處薩拉森山頭斜坡的下坡處，所以沒有受到甚麼傷害，因為如此，當劉成良稍後在2月抵達後，才能夠使用與醫院相鄰的藥劑師的房子作為總部。[68]

大陸來的中國軍隊在福爾摩沙等待日本來襲的這段時間，他們漸漸變得躁動不安，以至開始有一些意外狀況發生。1895年2月18日，有些外國女人被調戲騷擾，甚至連胡力檔領事都不能倖免，當他沿著潟湖北岸進行他的例行散步，經過外國人墓園，往上進入他們在柴山的營帳時，也受到廣東籍士兵的騷擾。幸運地是，英國皇家軍艦水星號〔H.M.S. Mercury〕在霍克斯〔Fawkes〕艦長指揮下，於2月19日到達打狗，使情勢平靜了下來〔見圖5-11〕。考慮到中國官員現在已經控制住他們的軍隊，胡力檔在不情願的情況下勉強答應讓皇家軍艦響尾蛇號〔H.M.S. Rattler〕在替代它的軍艦尚未到達前，就於次日開往香港，只留下水星號單獨在打狗。沒多久，又有一個更嚴重的意外發生，這次肇事的是湖南〔Hunan〕的軍隊，他們騷擾了一位海關官員的外國妻子。胡力檔當機立斷地將這位憤慨的海關官員夫人與他自己的夫人瑪格麗特，送往安平，而且請求要分派哨兵到所有外國人的物業巡守。[69]

由於日本軍隊的勝利，第一次中日戰爭（甲午戰爭）落幕，在1895年4月17日，雙方簽署了馬關條約〔Treaty of Shimonoseki〕。這份條約中，有許多加諸於中國的殘酷嚴厲處置，其中之一就是把臺灣與澎湖群島割讓給日本。然而，臺灣人決定要反抗這個把臺灣割讓給日本的條款，於是大約在1895年8月時，清朝派來的劉永福最後居然成為臺灣民主國名義上的領袖，並把根據地設於臺南。[70]

1895年3月26日，入侵臺灣的關鍵，也就是澎湖群島落入日本軍隊之手，於是整個臺灣島陷入恐慌。當臺灣島上的形勢變得更為嚴峻且難以控制時，大部份外國女人與小孩都被送到安平，因為那裡被認為是較好的撤退地點。胡力檔自己在4月初期就遷至安平，但買醫師堅持他的家人，包括夫人和兩個女兒，要留在打狗。除買醫師一家外，只有領事館助理領事官伯崇‧馬克‧納維爾‧柏金斯〔Bertram Mark Nevill Perkins〕，以及一個海關官員，麥理惠先生〔Mr. McLavy〕與他的夫人選擇留在打狗港。[71]

在1895年5月29日，臺灣民主國的旗幟在打狗碉堡升起。胡力檔本來已經遷到相對上比較安全的安平，但在6月份時在英國皇家砲艦蘇格蘭呢號〔H.M.S. Tweed〕上有一位年輕外科醫師死亡，這件事迫使他在1895年6月9日再度回打狗。這位外科醫師，波西‧洛德〔Dr. Percy Lord〕，死於肺炎，而且被埋在打狗的外國人墓園。葬禮當天黃昏的朦朧中，日本巡洋艦秋津洲〔I.J.N. Akitsushima〕被瞥見在打狗北方6哩處下錨，次日清晨它以不慌不忙的姿態，維持在中國砲手可射擊到的範圍之外，偵查打狗的形勢，之後才向南方駛去。[72]

日本武裝部隊對臺灣發動攻擊的時機已經迫在眉睫。胡力檔很快地勸導所有的女人與小孩們登上港口內的船開往大陸，他自己則在安平領事館的上層走廊安裝一挺格林機關槍作為防禦，讓自己能稍微安心一點。這些齊聚在安平的外國居民，僅僅擁有58名英國海軍陸戰隊員所能提供的微弱保護，現在發現自己身處於3500名情緒不穩的中國士兵與在臺灣海峽某處虎視耽耽的可怕日本軍隊之間。[73]

整個夏天，可怕的日本軍艦不定時地出現在打狗港外海的臺灣海峽，然後在1895年的10月，日本軍隊終於決定奮力一擊。日本方面在10月14日預先告知英國他們計劃攻擊打狗，知道這個消息後，所有仍留在打狗的外國居民（現在僅剩下買醫師一家人與阿不拉多巡捕）都安全地由海岸邊登上皇家海軍蘇格蘭呢號〔H.M.S. Tweed〕，然後撤離。然而，英國領事館裡的中國僕役拒絕離開領事館建築，他們反而選擇帶著家人躲在打狗領事館官邸避難。[74]

日本軍隊最後決定在次日（譯注:即10月15日）清晨7點鐘對打狗發動攻擊，到下午4點鐘時，日本旗幟已經升起，高掛在柴山碉堡上。日本人在潟湖南邊買醫師的中國藥劑師家中建立他們的指揮總部，這個房子就是近期內才被劉永福之子劉成良撤空當成住處的地方。這段時間針對歐洲人的住處雖然有些小規模的搶劫發生，不過英國領事館的中國僕役被發現時都安然無恙。領事官邸被大約20名日本士兵占領，他們毫不客氣地享用了好幾瓶胡力檔領事珍藏的酒。[75]

1895年10月20日，劉永福逃離臺灣，而到了10月21日，安平與臺南府城就已經對日本人投降，他們把日本旗幟升上安平砲臺〔Anping Fort〕，今天的億載金城〔Eternal Golden Castle〕。[76]

1895年11月30日，胡力檔領事得到英國外交國務卿的指示，從此以後臺灣的領事官員就成為英國駐東京公使的下屬，而不再由駐北京公使管轄。因為如此，派駐東京的英國公使大臣恩尼斯特‧梅森‧薩道義爵士〔Sir Ernest Mason Satow〕，接手管理臺灣的領事館，臺灣從此成為日本的領土，此後領事官員將會被要求能說日文。[77]

§

The newly appointed Consul, Richard Willett Hurst [胡力檔], reached South Formosa in October 1893 and took over charge of the Consulate from Sundius. In the months preceding Hurst's arrival, Takow was struck by three more severe typhoons, which caused a vast amount of damage to the Consular buildings at the port. Moreover, another inspection by Marshall in December 1893 found that the roof timbers in both buildings were again infested with white ants, but considered that the buildings could continue to stand for another four years. On a more positive note, Marshall also found that the buildings and grounds were being maintained in a clean and neat condition. [65]

Appearances probably seemed deceptive to Consul Hurst too, for in the summer of 1894 he chose to live with his family, comprising his wife Margaret and son Geoffrey Willett Hurst, at the Takow Consular Residence. The home proved cold and uncomfortable, which could be tolerated at least until the rainy season began and the rain cascaded through the roof. Hurst relates how "it was always necessary in wet weather to put on galoshes and carry umbrellas to pass from one room to another, while stepping stones had to be placed in the passages to keep clear of the pools of water". [66]

After the departure of Liu Ming-ch'uan, the new Governor, Shao Yu-lien [邵友濂], allowed the island to fall back into near inertia. As such, Formosa was ill-prepared to meet the looming threat of an assertive Japan, though at Shao's request, the Ching court sent across Liu Yung-fu [劉永福], the veteran of the Sino-French War, and his Black Flag Militia [黑旗軍] to defend the south of the island. In 1894, the Japanese and Chinese armies found themselves both racing to quell an insurrection in Korea, which both claimed as their territory. Finding that the Korean rebellion had collapsed, the troops from China and Japan fell upon each other, thus sparking the First Sino-Japanese War of 1894–1895. As part of the defence of South Formosa Liu Yung-fu placed his third son, Liu Ch'eng-liang [劉成良], in charge of the Takow Fort on Saracen's Head in February 1895. [67]

Prior to the handover of the fort to Liu Ch'eng-liang, an inventory of munitions was carried out on 1 February 1895. During the inventory-taking a powder magazine, containing about one ton of gunpowder, exploded killing over 70 people, including virtually all the soldiers in the fort. Other property was also severely damaged. Across the harbour mouth at the Consular Residence, where Hurst and his family were still living, much of the plaster fell from the ceilings, and most of the panes of glass were broken. However, far greater damage was sustained at the properties of Dr. Myers, which lay just a few hundred yards from the scene of the explosion: about one hundred panes of glass were smashed, the roof was damaged, and doors were wrenched off their hinges. The David Manson Memorial Hospital was relatively unscathed, being lower down the slope of Saracen's Head, and Liu Ch'eng-liang was able to take up quarters there at the adjacent Dispenser's House upon his arrival later in February. [68]

As the mainland Chinese troops awaited a Japanese attack on Formosa, they became restive and various incidents occurred. On 18 February 1895, some of the foreign women were molested, and even Consul Hurst was harassed by Cantonese soldiers when taking his regular walk along the northern shore of the Lagoon, past the Foreign Cemetery, and up towards their camp on Ape's Hill [猴山]. Fortunately, on 19 February, H.M.S. Mercury, under Captain Fawkes, arrived at Takow, which calmed things down (see Image 5-11). Thinking that the Chinese officers now had their troops under control, Hurst reluctantly agreed to the H.M.S. Rattler departing the next day for Hongkong before her replacement arrived, and thus leaving H.M.S. Mercury alone at Takow. Immediately there was a further serious incident, this time involving Hunan [湖南] troops, who had molested the foreign wife of a Customs official. Hurst promptly sent the aggrieved Customs official's wife and his own wife, Margaret up to Anping, and requested that sentries to be assigned to all foreign premises. [69]

With the Japanese forces victorious, the First Sino-Japanese War was ended by the Treaty of Shimonoseki [馬關條約], signed on 17 April 1895. Amongst the many harsh terms imposed on China by the Treaty, Formosa and the Pescadores were ceded to Japan. Yet Formosa decided to resist the transfer to Japanese rule, with Liu Yung-fu ultimately becoming the nominal head of the Republic of Taiwan, based at Tainan, in around August 1895. [70]

On 26 March 1895, the Pescadores, the key to Formosa, fell to the Japanese forces and the whole of Formosa was thrown into a panic. As the situation became even more tense and ill-disciplined, most of the foreign women and children were moved to Anping, which was considered a good evacuation point. Hurst himself moved up to Anping in early April, but Dr. Myers insisted that his family, his wife and two daughters, remain at Takow. Apart from Myers, only the Consular Assistant, Bertram Mark Nevill Perkins, and a Customs officer, Mr. McLavy [麥理惠], and his wife remained at the port. [71]

On the 29 May 1895 the flag of the Republic of Taiwan was hoisted at Takow Fort. In June, Hurst himself moved up to the comparative safety of Anping, but the death of a young British surgeon, of the Royal Naval gunboat H.M.S. Tweed , obliged him to return again on 9 June 1895. The surgeon, Dr. Percy Lord, had died of pneumonia and was buried at the Foreign Cemetery at Takow. At dusk on the evening of the burial, the Japanese cruiser I.J.N. Akitsushima [秋津洲] was sighted at anchor about 6 miles north Takow, and the following morning she made a leisurely reconnaissance of Takow, slightly out of range of the Chinese gunners, before steaming on to the south. [72]

An attack on South Formosa by the Japanese forces was clearly imminent. Hurst promptly advised all women and children to leave for the mainland aboard the ships in port, and contented himself with mounting a Gatling machine-gun on the upper verandah of the Anping Consulate. The foreign residents that huddled at Anping, with the meagre protection of 58 British Marines, were now caught between 3500 restive Chinese troops on the land and a formidable force of Japanese troops somewhere out in the Taiwan Strait. [73]

Throughout the summer the formidable Japanese warships appeared from time to time out in the Taiwan Strait off Takow, and in October 1895 the Japanese forces pounced. The Japanese advised the British of their intention to attack Takow on 14 October, whereupon all the foreign residents at Takow, by now consisting only of the Myers family and Constable Alborado, were safely evacuated from the shore by H.M.S. Tweed. The Chinese servants of the British Consulate, however, refused to leave the Consular buildings instead choosing to take refuge with their families inside the Consular Residence at Takow. [74]

The attack on Takow by the Japanese forces began at 7 a.m. on the following day, and by 4 p.m. the Japanese flag was hoisted over the Ape's Hill Fort. The Japanese established their headquarters on the south side of the Lagoon, in the house of Dr. Myers' Chinese dispenser, that had lately been vacated by Liu Yung-fu's son, Liu Cheng-liang. Although some minor looting of European houses had taken place, the British Consular servants were all discovered to be safe. The Consular Residence was found to be occupied by some 20 Japanese troops, who had helped themselves to several bottles of Hurst's wine. [75]

On 20 October 1895, Liu Yung-fu fled from Formosa, and on 21 October Anping and Tainan surrendered to the Japanese who hoisted their flag over the Anping Fort (Eternal Golden Castle) [億載金城]. [76]

On 30 November 1895 Consul Hurst was instructed by the British Secretary of State for Foreign Affairs that Consular officers in Formosa were henceforth under H.M.'s Minister at Tokyo and no longer under the British Minister at Peking. Thus, Sir Ernest Mason Satow [薩道義], the British Minister at Tokyo, took over control of the Consulates on Formosa, which was now a Japanese possession where the Consular officers would be required to speak Japanese. [77]

Notes to Chapter Five
第五章註解

1. Private correspondence, Warren family; Lo &
   Bryant, p. 631; 1851 England Census for Pubrook,
   Hampshire, HO 107/1656, Page 3, Warren; 1875
   Death Certificate, Portsea Island, No. 67, Admiral
   Richard Laird Warren; Obituary in The Times of
   22 November 1923; and Victoria College records,
   Entry No 494; 1861 Channel Islands Census returns
   for St. Saviour, Jersey, RG 9/4407, Page 2, Warren.

2. Coates, pp. 85-87, and p. 511; FO 17/486.

3. Coates, p. 505, pp. 85-87, and
   Appendix II (pp. 491-511).

4. FO 228/495, StJohn to Hewlett, 4 April
   1870; Lo & Bryant, pp. 430-431.

5. FO 228/505, Taiwan 21, 9 December 1871.
   Matsu is the Goddess, or Patron Saint, of
   fishermen and all connected with the sea.

6. China Directories 1870-1873, Formosa; Lo
   & Bryant, pp. 430-31; Coates, p. 212; and
   China Directory for 1874, Foochow.

7. Coates, p. 89; Death Certificate for Admiral
   Richard Laird Warren, died 29 July 1875 at
   Kirkstall Lodge, Southsea, Portsea Island
   Registration District; London Marriages 1875, St
   Mary's Church, St Marylebone, Middlesex, Page
   92, No 183, 9 September 1875, Pelham Laird
   Warren and Mary Donnithorne Humpage.

8. FO 228/570, Intelligence Report for Ningpo, 1
   January to 30 April 1876; Lo & Bryant, p. 305; G.R.O.
   Consular Births 1876-1880; Warren family records.

9. Lo & Bryant, p. 305; FO 228/570, Intelligence
   Report for Ningpo, 1 August to 31 October
   1876; Lo & Bryant, pp. 537-539.

10. Warren family records; 1977 G.R.O. Deaths, North

Dorset, Volume 23, Page 502, Richard Laird Warren,
born; China Directories for 1878 & 1879, Wenchow
data; Charlotte Myers married Percy Romilly
Walsham [華善], the son of Sir John Walsham
[華爾身], British Minister at Peking; Charlotte
Cunningham Scott Myers' Birth Certificate,
registered 16 October 1878 at British Consulate
Wenchow, born 3 October 1878 at Wenchow; Hoe,
Susannah, Women at the Siege, Peking 1900, The
Women's History Press, Oxford, 2000, p. 36; Lucy
Soothill's Obituary for James Russell Brazier, 1926.

11. Imperial Maritime Customs, Medical Reports,
    21st Issue, Filaria Disease in South Formosa, Dr
    W. W. Myers, p. 1, and Dr W. W. Myers' Report
    on the Health of Takow for the Two Years ended
    31st March 1881, pp.59-60; Imperial Maritime
    Customs, Medical Reports, 2nd-5th Issues, Dr
    D Manson's Reports on the Health of Takow;
    Landsborough, David, The Development of
    Scientific Medicine and its Impact on Society
    in Taiwan, 1865 to 1945, unpubl. paper.

12. FO 228/661, Intelligence Report for First Quarter
    of 1880; FO 228/974, Warren to Wade, 2 January
    1880; Birth Certificate of Ethel Marion Warren,
    registered at British Consulate at Taiwan on 12 May
    1880, born 18 March 1880 Ningpo; G.R.O. Consular
    Births, 1876-1880, Taiwan, Volume 6, Page 373;
    FO 228/974, Warren to Wade, 29 March 1880.

13. The term "Bund", which means an embankment
    or an embanked quay, comes, like the word
    "Bungalow", from India; FO 678/3039.

14. FO 228/892, Warren to Walsham, 13 September
    1890; Godown, from the Malay word 'godon',
    means a warehouse and was commonly used
    in India and China; FO 228/685, Intelligence
    Report for 3 months to 31 July 1881, Phillips.

15. FO 228/661, Political Summary for 1879, 5 April 1880, Warren.

16. FO 228/974, Warren to Wade, 11 November 1880, and Warren to Wade, 15 November 1880; Coates, p. 517; 1861 England Census Returns, Hausser, RG 9/119, Folio 102, Page 12.

17. FO 228/974, Myers Memo, December 1881; FO 678/3186, Lease agreement for premises occupied [by British Consulate] at Taiwanfoo 1872; Hewlett's Gravestone at St Mary's Churchyard, Harrow-on-the-Hill reads, "In Memory of Rose Wife of Archer Rotch Hewlett of this Parish. Born Advent Sunday [29 November] 1840, Died on 9th December 1868 at Foochow, China, aged 28 years. Also Archer Rotch Hewlett, born May 15th 1838, Died February 9th 1902."; 1867 London Marriages and Banns, Harrow, St Mary, page 88, No. 242, Banns of Marriage between Archer Rotch Hewlett, Bachelor of this Parish, and Rose Whitfield, Spinster of the Parish of St Paul's, Newington, were published, as follows: 1st, on Sunday December 15; 2nd on Sunday December 22; and 3rd on Sunday 29 December. (Married at St. Paul's Church, Newington, Page 198, No. 395, on 18 January 1868); see Coates, p. 450, on Holland.

18. FO 228/685, Intelligence Report for 3 months to 30 April 1881, Phillips; Coates, p. 89.

19. Coates, p. 342.

20. FO 228/974, Phillips to Wade, 2 July 1882; FO 228/712, Intelligence Report, 1 May to 31 October 1882, Watters; FO 228/999, Warren to Grosvenor, 6 April 1883, and Watters to Grosvenor, 2 April 1883.

21. FO 678/3044, Certificate of measurement of SS Scalpel, Dr Myers' steam launch, 1884; FO 228/1089, Steam Launch Certificate issued by I.M.C., 1891; FO 228/685, Trade Report for 1880, Phillips; FO 228/712, Intelligence Report for 3 months ended 31 January 1882, Phillips; FO 228/881, Intelligence Report, 3 months to 30 June 1889, Playfair.

22. I.M.C. Medical Reports, No. 28, Dr W. W. Myers' Report on the Health of Takow, for the Two Years ended 31st March 1884.

23. FO 228/374, Encl. 4, Swinhoe to Wade, 21 November 1864; FO 228/999, Warren to Grosvenor, 5 July 1883.

24. FO 228/999, Warren to Grosvenor, 28 July 1883.

25. FO 228/999, Warren to Parkes, 25 September 1883.

26. I.M.C. Medical Reports, No. 28, Dr W. W. Myers' Report on the Health of Takow, for the Two Years ended 31st March 1884.

27. FO 228/999, Warren to Parkes, 2 January 1884.

28. I.M.C. Medical Reports, No. 28, Dr W. W. Myers' Report on the Health of Takow, for the Two Years ended 31st March 1884.

29. I.M.C. Medical Reports, No. 28, Dr W. W. Myers' Report on the Health of Takow, for the Two Years ended 31st March 1884.

30. Oakley, David C., The Foreign Cemetery at Kaohsiung, Taiwan Historica [臺灣文獻館], Vol. 56, Issue 3, 2005, pp. 265-295.

31. Lo & Bryant, pp. 315-316, pp. 432-33; FO 228/999, Gregory to Parkes, 21 February 1884; 1891 England Census Returns for Winchester, RG 12/936, Folio 124, Page 5; Lo Hui-min [ed.], The Correspondence of G. E. Morrison, Vol. 2, 1912-1920, Cambridge University Press, Cambridge, England, 1978, p. 817, Morrison to Jordan, Sidmouth, 6 May 1920.

32. FO 228/505, Hewlett to Wade, 16 May

1871; Warren family records.

33. Coates, pp. 210-11, and pp. 251-52; Lo & Bryant, p. 616; 1861 England Census Return, RG 9/119, Folio 102, Page 12, Hausser; 1871 England Census Return, RG 10/1082, Folio 42, Page 27, Hausser; London Marriages, 1888, St Jude's Church, South Kensington, Middlesex, Page 171, No. 341, Hausser – Brandon; 1911 England Census, RG 14/8846, Schedule No. 156, Hausser.

34. FO 228/999, Warren to Parkes, 15 February 1884.

35. Rouil, Christophe, Formose, Des Batailles Presque Oubliees ⋯, Les Editions du Pigeonnier, Taiwan, 2001, pp. 11-13.

36. Hibbert, pp. 315-317; Fairbank, John K., and Reischauer, Edwin O., China: Tradition & Transformation, Houghton Mifflin Company, Boston, 1989, pp. 352-355; Hung, Chien-chao, A History of Taiwan, Il Cerchio Iniziative Editoriali, Rimini, 2000, pp. 151-153; Dodd, John, Journal of a Blockaded Resident in North Formosa 1884-1885, Daily Press Office, Hongkong, 1888, pp. 63-64 [Reprinted by Ch'eng Wen Publishing, Taipei, 1972].

37. Lo & Bryant, p. 432; FO 228/999, Gregory to Parkes, 22 December 1884.

38. Beazeley states that South Cape [南岬], as shown on the charts was unknown in Formosa, but was referred to as Wo-lan-pi (Oluanpi) [鵝鑾鼻]. See Beazeley, M., Notes of an overland journey through the southern part of Formosa in 1875, from Takow to the South Cape, with sketch map, in Proceedings of the Royal Geographical Society and Monthly Record of Geography, New Monthly Series, Vol. 7 (January 1885), pp. 1-22, p. 14; FO 228/807, Spence to Parkes, 26 January 1885; FO 228/807, Spence to Parkes, 1 January 1885.

39. FO 228/807, Spence to Parkes, 1 January 1885.

40. FO 228/807, Spence to Parkes, 1 January 1885.

41. FO 228/807, Spence to Parkes, 1 January 1885; FO 228/999, Spence to Parkes, 22 December 1884; Coates, p. 329.

42. FO 228/807, Spence to O'Conor, 20 April 1885; FO 228/1020, Spence to O'Conor, 20 April 1885; FO 228/807, O'Conor to Spence, 25 August 1885.

43. FO 228/1018, O'Conor to Spence, 18 January 1886; Coates, p. 344; Lo & Bryant, p. 628; 1891 National Probate Calendar, Page 324, William Donald Spence, late of Shanghai of H.B.M. Consular Service, died on 25 June 1890 at 152 Harley Street, Middlesex; Hong Kong Daily Press, 20 August 1890, Page 2, Obituary for W. D. Spence.

44. FO 228/1020, Spence to O'Conor, 20 April 1885; Lo & Bryant, p. 432; Coates, pp. 210-11, and pp. 251-2.

45. Hibbert, p. 317; Rouil, pp. 149-150.

46. FO 228/807, Spence to O'Conor, 20 April 1885, Enclosure dated 4 May 1885; Dudbridge, Glen [ed.], Aborigines of South Taiwan in the 1880s: Papers by the South Cape Lightkeeper George Taylor, SMC Publishing Inc., Taipei, 1999, p. 6.

47. FO 228/807, Spence to O'Conor, 20 April 1885; FO 228/807, Spence to O'Conor, 5 October 1885; FO 228/807, O'Conor to Spence, 29 October 1885. Tso Tsung-t'ang [左宗棠] was the Imperial Commissioner in charge of military affairs in Fuchien Province, of which Taiwan was still a part, during the Sino-French War; while Liu Ao was the protégé of Tso, Liu Ming-ch'uan was the the protégé of Li Hung-chang [李鴻章]. See Huang Hsiao-ping, The Conflict between Liu Ao & Liu Ming-ch'uan and the Sino-French War in Taiwan, pp. 288-276, Bulletin

of Historical Research, No 1. January, 1973.

48. Coates, p. 330.

49. Davidson, p. 218; FO 228/1020, Spence to O'Conor, 22 September 1885.

50. FO 228/1020, Spence to O'Conor, 22 September 1885.

51. FO 228/974, Hewlett to Wade, 20 October 1879; FO 228/1020, Spence to Parkes, 8 January 1885 (Encl. 1, Alborado to Gregory, 20 December 1884); Pickering, pp. 236-7; Pidgin English was the name given to a Chinese-English-Portuguese pidgin [洋涇濱] used for commerce in Canton during the 18th and 19th centuries; FO 228/1020, Spence to O'Conor, 22 September 1885; FO 262/735, Hurst to Satow, 1 January 1896; China Directory, 1897.

52. FO 228/596, Frater to Fraser, 1 May 1877; Peking to Frater, 20 July 1877; FO 228/1022, Marshall to O'Conor, 10 November 1885; FO 228/1028, Spence to O'Conor, 23 February 1886.

53. FO 228/1028, Warren to O'Conor, 21 April 1886; London Gazette, 3 August 1886.

54. FO 678/3186; FO 228/867, Warren to Walsham, 18 February 1888; Coates, pp. 330-31.

55. FO 228/867, Warren to Walsham, 18 February 1888; Coates, pp. 330-31; FO 228/881, Intelligence Report for 3 months ended 30 June 1889.

56. FO 228/881, Intelligence Report for 3 months ended 30 June 1889; Davidson, pp. 245-24.

57. Davidson, p. 253; FO 228/1089, Warren to Beauclerk, 17 November 1892.

58. £1,692 is equivalent to about £170,000 in 2012 money. WORK 10/33/10, O.W.L. to Foreign Office, 24 February 1892; WORK 10/33/10, Warren to Walsham, 10 May 1892; WORK 10/33/10, Walsham to Salisbury, 31 May 1892.

59. FO 228/1089, Intelligence Report for 3 months ended 31 July 1892; The Government-General of Formosa Bureau of Communications, The Climate, Typhoons, and Earthquakes of the Island of Formosa (Taiwan), Taihoku Meteorological Observatory, Taihoku, 1914, p. 74.

60. WORK 10/33/10, pp. 67-69, Marshall to O.W.L., 22 November 1892.

61. WORK 10/33/10, pp. 67-69, Marshall to O.W.L., 22 November 1892.

62. I.M.C. Tainan Trade Report for the Year 1892; Information from Hong Kong Cricket Club; see also Hall, Peter, 150 Years of Cricket in Hong Kong, The Book Guild Ltd, Lewes, Sussex, 1999; FO 228/1089, Warren to Beauclerk, 25 October 1892.

63. Warren departed between 9 and 31 August 1893 (see FO 228/1125, Tainan 21 & 22); Coates, pp. 330-31.

64. The Edinburgh Gazette, 15 December 1893, Foreign Office, 1 December 1893; The London Gazette, 7 November 1899, Foreign Office, 12 October 1899; Coates, pp. 224-5; Lo & Bryant, pp. 362-366, p. 631; R. J. Adams, the Sampson Society, Sidmouth; 1923 National Probate Calendar, Page 206, Warren, Sir Pelham Laird; Potsbury's Funeral Directors, Sidmouth.

65. FO 228/1125, Telegram from Holland to O'Conor, 18 October 1893; FO 228/1125, O'Conor to Sundius, 23 September 1893; WORK 10/33/10, Marshall to O.W.L., 5 December 1893.

66. FO 262/735, Hurst to Satow, 28 April 1896, encl. Hurst to Marshall, 7 February 1895.

67. Hung Chien-chao, p. 158; Hibbert, p. 317; FO
    228/1199, Hurst to O'Conor, 23 February 1895.

68. FO 228/1199, Hurst to O'Conor 6 February 1895;
    FO 228/1199, Hurst to O'Conor, 23 February 1895.

69. FO 228/1199, Hurst to O'Conor, 23 February 1895.

70. Hibbert, p. 317; Hung Chien-chao, pp. 166-188;
    Davidson, pp. 351-353; see also Lamley, Harry
    J., The 1895 Taiwan Republic: A Significant
    Episode in Modern Chinese History, Journal of
    Asian Studies, 27:4 (August 1968), pp. 739-762.

71. Davidson, pp. 266-268; FO 228/1199,
    Hurst to O'Conor, 4 April 1895.

72. FO 228/1199, Decipher of Telegram from
    Hurst to O'Conor, 29 May 1895; FO 228/1199,
    Hurst to O'Conor, 14 June 1895.

73. FO 228/1199, Hurst to O'Conor, 14 June 1895;
    FO 228/1199, Hurst to O'Conor, 17 June 1895.

74. FO 228/1199, Intelligence Report for Quarter
    ended 30 September 1895; FO 262/735,
    Hurst to O'Conor, 19 October 1895.

75. FO 262/735, Hurst to O'Conor, 19 October 1895.

76. FO 262/735, Hurst to O'Conor, 23 October 1895.

77. FO 228/1199, Beauclerk to Hurst,
    telegram, 30 November 1895.

日本統治臺灣時期的
打狗領事館

The Takow Consulate
under the Japanese Rule of Formosa

British Japan Consular Service
在日本的英國領事服務工作

自從1858年簽署日英修好通商條約〔Anglo-Japanese Treaty of Amity and Commerce〕之後，從1859年開始，英國就在日本建立了領事服務制度。恩尼斯特‧梅森‧薩道義爵士〔Sir Ernest Mason Satow〕於1862年開始他在日本的外交官生涯，之後在1895年6月時更以英國女王派駐東京的全權特命大使〔Her Majesty's Envoy Extraordinary and Minister Plenipotentiary at Tokyo〕身份回到日本。因此，他甫一接手日本的領事工作後，就不得不應付日本這個新崛起的強權，而且對日本剛得到的福爾摩沙與該地的南方港口投注以最大的關切重視。[1]

第一位被派到福爾摩沙南部且能說日文的領事是喬瑟夫‧亨利‧朗福〔Joseph Henry Longford〕，到任時大約是47歲。他已婚，有四個年齡大致由6到12歲之間的孩子。在他被指派到福爾摩沙南部之前，他與家人住在東京公使館內副領事居住的房子，而且還額外地被分配到實習生居所的兩個房間。因此朗福對打狗官邸有著很高的期待，他將以領事的身份入住打狗領事官邸，而且還計畫延聘一位家庭教師來教育及照顧他的四個孩子。[2]

朗福與恩尼斯特‧阿弗列‧葛里菲斯〔Ernest Alfred Griffiths〕於1896年4月23日抵達安平。葛里菲斯留在安平，而朗福則是馬上南下到打狗，於4月30日由胡力檣〔Richard Willett Hurst〕手中接下打狗領事館的管轄權。[3]

當領事工作由中國領事體系移交給日本領事體系時，首先要作的就是由要離開的領事胡力檣，與剛要上任的領事朗福，雙雙針對領事館內各棟建築的狀態準備書面報告。

朗福與胡力檣針對打狗領事官邸所寫的報告幾乎大同小異。他們詳細地指出好幾處木造走廊的柱子已經被白蟻蛀蝕腐壞，不過沿著走廊設置的窗櫺狀態大致上還算不錯。門窗周圍的灰泥塗料有很多地方都有龜裂，但這只是表面上的情形而非結構上的問題。但是比較令人擔心的是，幾乎所有的牆壁與天花板都因雨淋與潮濕而褪色。[4]

　　胡力檔報告中提到，官邸最後一次進行牆壁與天花板塗色或刷白已經是三年前的事了，他並且在報告中附帶一份書信，那是他在1895年2月寄給馬歇爾的，信中提及建築物的狀況。在給馬歇爾的信中，胡力檔向他報告「我在打狗的居所危險與不適合人居住的狀態，天花板灰泥常常會掉下來，造成我自己與家人很大的危險」。他繼續說明這房子不僅常因附近碉堡發射大砲而被搖撼震動，而且也常有暴風雨襲擊；更糟糕的是，薩拉森山頭碉堡的那次大爆炸使這房子變得更加脆弱。他對這些危害非常地關切擔憂，深怕屋頂的沉重樑木與屋瓦很快地就會崩塌，落在他的家人頭上，於是他極力建議改用輕巧防水的瀝青屋頂毛氈〔Asphalt Roofing Felt〕。[5]

　　過了一個月多之後，朗福才自己發現胡力檔會如此緊張的原因。1896年6月8日的夜晚，強烈颱風侵襲打狗。到了晚上11點，雨水從屋頂傾瀉到領事官邸的每一個房間內，由天花板沖下很多塊狀的灰泥，整個房子淹大水。整個大廳如同一條河水，而就像胡力檔在1894年的經驗，朗福必須捲起褲管，赤著腳、撐著傘才能走過門廳走廊。經過整整一夜不眠不休地與三個僕役一起搶救他的財物，以免它們被大雨毀損，朗福別無選擇，還是得留在這個到處都是水的官邸，因為打狗所有的其他建築物都擠滿了日本人。[6]

　　甚至早在還沒來到福爾摩沙南部之前，朗福就已經研究過打狗領事官邸的平面設計圖，而且認定了在當地的氣候下，這棟建築物對他自己、夫人與四個孩子而言，實在不夠大。此外，由於打狗沒有任何的教育設施，朗福進一步強調他將需要一個安頓家庭教師的房間與一個學習用的教室。馬歇爾非常地不能接受朗福的要求，要在打狗官邸額外多加三個房間，他認為這建築物完全符合一般辦理領事業務的需求。[7]

　　然而，外交部對朗福要在打狗領事官邸增加額外房間的需求非常地堅持，不放棄向位於倫敦的工部辦事處提出申請。不過輪到伯斯決定時，他駁回了這個增加房間的想法，工部覺得不能只是為了要滿足他們認為例外的一個案例，就因此核准增加房間的計畫。然而上面提到的1896年6月颱風淹沒官邸以及朗福領事的事情，似乎讓增加新房間的爭論起死回生，因為在1896年7月，薩道義重新針對這項爭議質問馬歇爾，雖然現在他已經願意接受只增加兩個房間。朗福後來成功地避免了正面處理這個議題，因為1896年12月，他回到日本擔任長崎〔Nagasaki〕的領事，留下葛里菲斯管理福爾摩沙南部事務。[8]

　　值得注意的是，在日本人登陸福爾摩沙南部後的起先幾個月，他們就已經戮力改善島嶼內部的交通運輸。日本人最早的施政措施之一是在1895年底前建造完成的安平與打狗間臺車軌道〔Decauville tramway，臺車〕。雖然一開始是做為軍事用途，但很快地它就開放給非軍事單位的個人所使用，因此大大地便利了領事館官員在安平與打狗之間的往返。[9]

　　雖然不願意為打狗領事官邸再增加任何房間，馬歇爾卻承認官邸已變得不適合居住。由於恩尼斯特·薩道義爵士考慮後覺得打狗領事館建築物應該被保留，於是乎馬歇爾乃建議打狗的兩棟領事館建築物應該在1897/98這段時間重建，在此同時，領事可以住在安平，而助理官則使用仍然堪用的打狗領事辦公室與巡捕住所。就在他剛啟動了這個整修打狗領事官邸的行政程序後，馬歇爾就由上海工部辦事處的職位上退休，返回英格蘭。[10]

　　馬歇爾的第一位夫人，瑪格麗特·內·希德，於1881年逝世於英格蘭，之後1888年左右他在上海與愛芙琳·霍根〔Evelyn Hogan〕再婚，對方小他20多歲。1914年12月16日，法蘭西斯·朱利安·馬歇爾以81歲高齡在倫敦南肯辛頓區的一間長住旅館，名叫波頓公寓旅館，與世長辭。[11]

§

Britain had established a Consular service in Japan from 1859, after the signing in 1858 of the Anglo-Japanese Treaty of Amity and Commerce [日英修好通商條約]. Sir Ernest Mason Satow [薩道義] had begun his diplomatic career in Japan in 1862, and had returned as Her Majesty's Envoy Extraordinary and Minister Plenipotentiary at Tokyo in June 1895. Thus, as soon as Satow took charge he was obliged to deal with the emerging power of Japan, and attached the greatest importance to Japan's new possession of Formosa and its southern ports. [1]

The first Japanese-speaking Consul to be placed in charge of South Formosa was Joseph Henry Longford, then aged about 47. Longford was married, with four children between the ages of 6 and 12. Prior to his appointment to South Formosa, he and his family had been accommodated at the Tokyo Legation in the Vice-Consul's house and permitted the use of two additional rooms in the Students' Quarters. Longford thus had high expectations of Takow, where he was to be housed as Consul, and planned to install a Governess to teach and help care for his four children. [2]

Longford and Ernest Alfred Griffiths arrived at Anping on 23 April 1896. While Griffiths remained at Anping, Longford immediately came down to Takow to take over charge of the Takow Consulate from Richard Willett Hurst on 30 April. [3]

The first task in the handover from the Chinese Consular Service to the Japanese Consular Service was for the outgoing Consul, Hurst, and the incoming Consul, Longford, to prepare reports on the condition of the various Consular buildings.

The reports of Hurst and Longford for the Takow Consular Residence are largely the same. They detail several of the wooden verandah pillars as being rotten from attacks by white ants, though the lattice work over the verandah was in generally good condition. There were many cracks that could be found in the plasterwork around the doors and windows, but this was of a superficial nature only. However, almost all the walls and ceilings were discoloured from rainwater and damp. [4]

Hurst noted that it had been three years since any colouring or whitewashing of the walls and ceilings was last done at the Residence, and also enclosed a letter that he had sent to Marshall in February 1895, regarding the state of the building. In the letter to Marshall, Hurst had reported the 'dangerous and uninhabitable state of my house at Takow [with] ceiling plaster constantly falling down to the great danger of myself and family'. He goes on to say that the house was not only being constantly shaken by the firing of the big guns in the adjacent forts, but also by the violence of storms; moreover, the massive explosion at the Saracen's Head Fort had further weakened the house. Hurst was very concerned lest the heavy timbers and tiling of the roof would soon collapse upon his family, and strongly urged that light and waterproof Asphalt Roofing Felt be used. [5]

A little over a month later Longford was to find out the cause of Hurst's alarm. On the evening of 8 June 1896 a strong typhoon struck Takow. By 11 p.m. rainwater was cascading from the roof into every room of the Consular Residence, bringing down large patches of plaster from the ceilings and flooding the house. The hall became literally a river of water, and, as Hurst had experienced in 1894, Longford needed to pass along the hallway barefoot, with his trousers rolled up, and carrying an umbrella. After a sleepless night trying to save his belongings from utter ruin with the help of three servants, Longford had no option but to remain in the drenched Residence as all the other buildings at Takow were crowded with Japanese. [6]

Even before coming to South Formosa, Longford had studied the plans of the Takow Consular Residence and decided that the building was insufficiently large for himself, his wife, and four children in such a climate. Moreover, there being no educational facilities of any kind at Takow, Longford further declared that he would need accommodation for a resident Governess and a School Room. Marshall was singularly unimpressed with the demand for three extra rooms to be added to the Takow Residence, considering the building fully adequate for the general requirements of the Service. [7]

However, the Foreign Office persisted to the Office of Works in London on the need for the extra rooms for Longford at Takow. Boyce in turn resisted the idea and the Office of Works felt unable to authorise the addition of rooms merely to meet what they deemed to be an exceptional case. Yet the typhoon that drenched the Consular Residence, and Consul Longford, in June 1896, appears to have resurrected the debate over the new rooms, for in July 1896 Satow was again querying Marshall on this point, though by now he was willing to accept just two extra rooms. Longford managed to avoid the issue, for, in December 1896, he returned to Japan to take up the post as Consul at Nagasaki [長崎], leaving Griffiths in charge of South Formosa. [8]

It should be noted that in the first few months after they landed in South Formosa, the Japanese had set about improving internal communications. One of their first undertakings was the construction of a Decauville tramway [臺車] between Anping and Takow before the end of 1895. Though this was initially for military use, it soon became available to certain non-military personnel, thus greatly facilitating the journey between Anping and Takow for Consular officers. [9]

Despite being unwilling to add any more rooms to the Takow Consular Residence, Marshall conceded that the Residence had become uninhabitable. As Sir Ernest Satow considered that the Takow Consular buildings should be kept, Marshall proposed that the two Consular buildings at Takow should be reconstructed in 1897/98, and that, in the meantime, the Consul reside at Anping and the Assistant use the still serviceable Consular Offices and Constable's Quarters at Takow. Having initiated the procedure for the restoration of the Takow Consular Residence, Marshall retired from the Office of Works at Shanghai and returned to England. [10]

His first wife, Margaret née Hider, having died in England in 1881, Marshall had married for a second time to Evelyn Hogan, some 20 years his junior, in Shanghai around 1888. Francis Julian Marshall died at The Bolton Mansions Hotel, a residential hotel, in South Kensington, London, on 16 December 1914 aged 81. [11]

The 1900 Restoration at Takow
1900年打狗的重建工程

　　1897年2月，新任領事威廉‧喬瑟夫‧肯尼〔William Joseph Kenny〕抵達，從葛里菲斯手中接過福爾摩沙南部的主導權。他聽從別人的建議，認為領事可以由安平輕易地管理福爾摩沙南部的業務，於是他一到達後，就馬上與葛里菲斯出發到打狗，在那裡他們花了三天，將領事館物業上的每樣物件做了一次鉅細靡遺的清點，然後帶著領事館檔案櫃回到安平。在外國商人眼中，以為英國政府正要由打狗撤離，所以德記洋行很快地就開出6000銀元的價格想要收購領事辦公處與該筆土地的永久租賃權。然而，肯尼告訴東京方面不要答應，一方面這個出價非常低，再者，他認為日本人管理下的打狗港會有好的遠景。[12]

　　1897年1月，剛由馬歇爾手中接任上海工部辦事處代理量地官的威廉‧庫望〔William Cowan〕，隨即得到身在倫敦的伯斯授權，要他重建打狗的領事官邸，而且指示他在1896/97年會計年度結束前開始工作。不幸地，當庫望收到授權令時，他人正在日本且有任務在身。當庫望終於回到上海時，已經沒有足夠的時間在會計年度結束的3月31日前開始這個工作，他被迫必須延宕重建工程，一直到他親自對這棟建築物進行測量後。[13]

　　1897年6月，庫望終於如期完成打狗領事官邸的測量工作，他建議要改變迴廊與屋頂的部分。關於迴廊，他建議用有女兒牆的磚造迴廊來代替木結構的迴廊，這將可以解決白蟻危害的問題，磚砌結構也可以保護屋頂不受颱風破壞。至於屋頂本身，庫望建議屋頂的木架必須用可以抗白蟻的香坡壘木，再以兩層厚的廈門瓦鋪設其上。至於整棟建築物其餘的部份，庫望則認為尚稱健全，無須改動。[14]

　　倫敦的工部委員會批准了庫望重建打狗領事官邸迴廊以及改造新屋頂的計畫，也授權此工程在1897/8年度開始進行，不過必須遵從伯斯在設計上的意見。伯斯熟悉打狗常見的猛烈傾盆大雨，提醒庫望不可只依賴一條女兒牆上的排水溝來宣洩雨水，不妨使用女兒牆面的小洞，讓雨水直接從屋瓦經過小洞流瀉到女兒牆下。這一點在下面討論修建的具體面向時，將會做更充分的檢驗。[15]

　　雖然打狗領事官邸的迴廊與屋頂已經被授權可以在1897/98年度開始重建，但是由於招標上的問題導致一直沒被發包，而且庫望也沒有在1898/99年度再次呈報要求上級給予工程的授權。臺灣此時處在一個非常混亂的狀態，由於日本政府的第三任臺灣總督乃木希典〔Nogi Maresuke〕採行高壓統治，使抵抗與騷動達到最高峰，很多臺灣人選擇逃離此地，越過臺灣海峽避開這場混亂，這也許可以解釋庫望所遭遇到的困難。[16]

　　事實上，代理領事官葛里菲斯已經成功地爭取到在1898年春天進行打狗領事官邸重建工程的預算書，也將它交給了庫望。然而，庫望很顯然地沒有任何進一步的行動，於是伯斯命令他必須在1899/1900年度提出預算申請。這項重建工作將由庫望的助理量地官西索‧約翰‧威廉‧辛普森〔Cecil John William Simpson〕來執行。[17]

　　1899年2月，伯斯由倫敦工部辦事處以外國工程總量地官的職位退休。他隨即被英國財政部送到遠東地區去視察領事館建築物，包括打狗與安平，這兩個地方他可能是在1899年末進行訪視的。伯斯估算打狗領事館建築約值5000英鎊。在打狗，他發現領事館的全部建築都沒有人使用，除了一位被請來照料領事館的當地看守者，正如同其他商人的房子一般：商人們都選擇住在北邊的安平，除了7到10月這幾個月，當船隻前來打狗載運蔗糖。伯斯對打狗貿易的前景持悲觀態度，然而他還是建議領事館建築應被保留個幾年再決定日本人是否將會改善港口，並且把南部鐵路終點站設在打狗，因為日本人很明顯地有這樣的計畫。唯一長住在打狗的外國居民是買醫師，他現在是在臺灣的日本政府的政治顧問，同時也是外科大夫以及萬大衛紀念醫院與醫學院的老師。[18]

　　1899年8月有一個強烈颱風橫掃過福爾摩沙南部，它對領事館造成的破壞確保了修復行動的必要性。恆春〔Hengch'un〕的氣壓降低到714.6毫米汞柱〔譯注：正常氣壓為760毫米汞柱〕，狂風吹走測量風速的風向球；在福爾摩沙南部，類似強度的劇烈颱風一直要等到1911年8月那次蹂躪大地的颱風才又再次出現。[19]

　　1899年10月，打狗官邸的屋頂又出現更多颱風帶來的傷害，不過重建所需的材料已經開始進場。工部辦事處購置了約40桶、每桶重400磅的水泥，由青洲水泥公司〔Green

Island Cement Company，即青洲英坭公司〕所生產，從香港的新旗昌洋行〔Shewan, Tomes & Co〕處購得，工部並且確定工程將在1900年春天開始。同時，代理領事官葛里菲斯報告道，打狗領事官邸因最近幾次的颱風而更加嚴重破損，許多屋瓦已被吹走，迴廊屋頂的緣木有多處裸露，這些情況使得重建工程顯得更為急迫〔見圖6- 1〕。[20]

　　1900年1月16日，工部終於與俊司〔Chun Sai〕這個包商簽了合約，內容是屋頂的更新，迴廊重建，加上打狗領事官邸內各種雜項修理與更新。依約這工程必須要馬上就動工，花費是6208金元〔Gold Yen〕，並要求必須在四個月內完工。俊司另外再同意這件他所承攬的合約項目在最後整個完工後，由他負責把工程成果維持在一個好的狀態，為期2年（譯注：換言之，即保固2年〕。[21]

　　打狗領事官邸的修復工作預定由羅伯·約翰·海斯汀〔Robert John Hastings，又譯希士頓〕監督，現有的紀錄將他描述為「一個有點地位名望的人，具備在地方上行走的知識，也能說當地方言；因此他能夠提供非常有價值的服務 。」因為擔任監工，海斯汀將可以賺得564金元〔相當於600墨西哥銀元〕的酬勞。[22]

　　羅伯·約翰·海斯汀〔見圖 6-2〕的父親是位英格蘭茶商，一般相信海斯汀在1860年代來到中國，曾於太平天國之亂時，參加上海附近，由查爾斯·喬治·戈登將軍〔General Charles George Gordon〕率領的常勝軍〔Ever-Victorious Army〕。海斯汀於1868年2月在上海進入清帝國海關服務，並在1869年被派到福爾摩沙的安平擔任負責登上商船監視卸貨以便於收取關稅的人員〔Tidewaiter，舊稱鈴字手]。1871年，他娶了安平海頭社〔Hai-tou-she〕人黃允官〔Huang Yun-kuan〕為妻。1882年當他升為海關三等驗貨官〔Assistant Examiner〕後，海斯汀選擇離開海關的崗位，進入安平的旗昌洋行〔Russell & Co〕工作，之後再加入唻記洋行〔Wright & Co〕。海斯汀於1912年12月11日卒於安平，在臺灣待了超過40年的歲月。[23]

　　在1900年打狗領事官邸整修重建的施工細節中，不僅詳細列出了使用的材料，也提供了一些線索，讓我們得以發現建築物原來設計上的一些問題。[24]

　　關於整修所用的材料，施工細節中載明，磚塊與屋頂鋪的瓦片都必須用是最好的，從

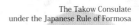

圖 6-1：打狗領事官邸，約在1899年拍攝
打狗領事官邸，大約在1899年之照片，顯示颱風剝離建築物前方屋瓦，暴露出迴廊的情況。
〔來自Edinger收藏慷慨授權，版權所有，翻印必究〕

Image 6-1：Takow Consular Residence circa 1899
The Takow Consular Residence photographed circa 1899,
showing how the wind had stripped tiles from the front of the building, leaving the verandah exposed.

圖 6-2：羅伯‧約翰‧海斯汀。
羅伯‧約翰‧海斯汀是一位英國商人，他從1867年至1912年過世前都居住在福爾摩沙，
他親眼見證打狗領事公館在1900年的整修。這是他在1900年前後，與他最小到最大的12個孩子之合照。
〔來自Arthur收藏的慷慨許可，版權所有，翻印必究〕

Image 6-2：Robert John Hastings
Robert John Hastings, a British merchant who lived on Formosa from 1867 until his death in 1912, and who oversaw the 1900 restoration of the Takow Consular Residence. Hastings is shown in about 1900 with the youngest and oldest of his 12 children. (By kind permission of the Arthur Collection. All rights reserved)

廈門買來的硬燒磚瓦。屋頂的樑木特別指定要用香坡疊木，一種抗白蟻的堅硬木材；大多數其餘的木料則須使用福州杉。一般的結構部分須使用品質最好的石質石灰，但用於內部牆壁與天花板灰泥塗層的，則應該是品質最好的貝殼石灰。施工細節中也提到一種高度耐用的土壤水泥石灰混合物，名為朱南〔Chunam〕，那是用來鋪設庭院的表面層，並用來完成入口石階的邊牆。[25]

如同伯斯原先於1897年所作的指示，在施工細節裡有很大的一部份放在如何在新砌的磚造柱子上方建構出女兒牆。磚造柱子的用意是用來避免白蟻侵蝕而弱化了迴廊構造之危險。一般認為在磚柱上方加砌女兒牆，是為了降低颱風直接吹到屋瓦底下，導致屋瓦由屋頂剝離的機會，這種情形曾發生在1899年8月的颱風。然而，使用女兒牆時通常也會一併設置導水溝，但是導水溝不但很容易阻塞，而且也無法應付颱風期間或熱帶雷雨時，大量雨水傾洩的速度：針對這點，伯斯與辛普森很用心地設計了斷斷續續、有規則的大量開口，稱為滲洞，如此將使水很容易就能通過女兒牆下流出〔見圖 6-3〕.[26]

其他值得注意的施工細節是關於天花板與屋谷〔roof valleys，譯注：即屋頂兩片斜面交接處的Y型結構〕的部份。雖然赫斯特早在1895年就力陳必須使用瀝青塗料來代替具危險性的灰泥，不過工部仍堅持使用灰泥塗在天花板，不顧其重量問題與臺灣地區不間斷的颱風地震侵襲。同時，在迴廊、走廊與浴室將使用格子狀結構的天花板，以確保屋頂部份的木材能有適當的通風，降低其腐朽之可能性。屋谷，形成於屋頂兩片斜面的相接處，很顯然地已證實是領事官邸屋頂強固性的弱點，於是乎這份施工細節又再次精確地說明這兩片屋頂斜面要如何銜接才穩固〔見圖 6-3〕。[27]

打狗領事官邸的新迴廊與屋頂重造工程於1900年11月16日完工。雖然這足足比合約上規定的日期晚了六個月，辛普森考慮到這延誤是源自於包商方面無法掌控的狀況所導致，例如抗白蟻的香坡疊木太慢運到，以及颱風季節的開始，因此英國政府沒有對俊司要求罰金賠償。[28]

到了1901年，外國人在福爾摩沙南部的影響力與重要性正漸漸消失，本區的助理領事官被調離，以及最能融入適應打狗生活的外國住民之一，買醫師的離開，就是此事的

The top of the parapet wall must be of selected hard-burned jiss bricks or tiles, and must be covered with a double slope in cement mortar thus—

rising about 1° in centre.

The parapet wall is <u>not</u> to be built on the roof tiles, but is to be a proper continuation of the main walls and the roof tiles are to abut against the parapet wall. The base of the parapet wall next roof must have a cement mortar skirting 6" high thus,

Face　　　　　Section

and the toe of this skirting must be shaped on plan so as to throw the water into the weep holes thus

Plan of Parapet Wall

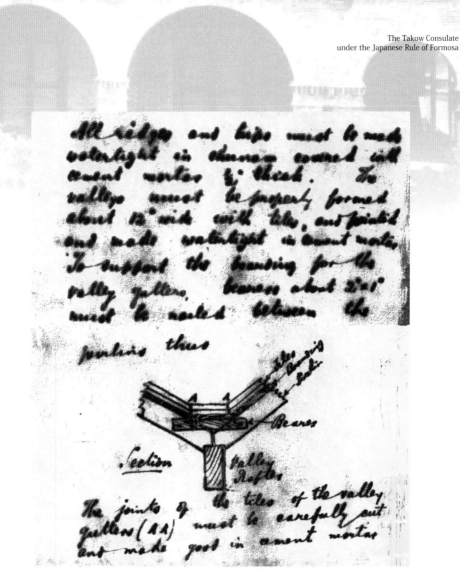

圖 6-3：1900年整修的施工細節。
伯斯的矮垣牆設計與屋頂相接處凹溝設計之素描。
〔圖像版權屬於英國政府，FO 678/3158，非經授權，不得翻印〕

Image 6-3：Details from Specifications for 1900 restoration
Cecil Simpson's sketches for the Parapet Wall design and and Roof Valley design from the 1900 Office of Works, Shanghai, Specifications given to Robert Hastings for the restoration of the Takow Consular Residence.

例證。獨自被留在福爾摩沙南部的領事肯尼，不得不延攬邊阿蘭〔Allan Weatherhead Bain，又譯艾倫‧威勒赫‧班〕為臨時領事〔Pro-Consul〕，幫他管理安平與打狗兩個港口的事務，邊阿蘭是一位在福爾摩沙南部有35年經驗的商人，曾長期擔任荷蘭的領事代理人〔Consular Agent〕。除了助理領事官被調離打狗之外，買醫師，這位已經在與領事官邸隔著打狗港入口遙遙相望的薩拉森山頭住了20年的人，並且一直以來都是打狗最堅定、最熱心的支持者與熱愛者之一，但是他卻離開此地到了福州的羅星塔島，並在那兒成為領事代理人。[29]

1901年6月，工部為辦理山下領事辦公處的整修工程，與鄭桂記〔Tēng Kùi-kì〕這個人（登記的行號是桂記）簽了一個合約，工程的範圍包括辦公室的區域與牢房。這個整修工程的規模包括更新屋頂、船隻停靠處的整頓，還有各式各樣的修理與裝潢工作：合約上要求桂記在1901年9月10前履約，然後可領取2035銀元。再一次，監督工程的合約發包給海斯汀，這次的服務價金則降到450銀元。用來停放領事坐船的船隻停靠處雖然在合約上有被提及，但是在1879馬歇爾所畫的領事館平面配置圖〔見圖 4-4〕與1899年拍的打狗領事辦公處照片〔見圖 5-8〕中，都沒有出現船隻停靠處的模樣。不過，在1905年有一位後來才上任的領事曾提到打狗的吊艇柱〔boat davits，譯注：一種設於水岸邊的兩根柱狀結構，上有機關可將小艇從水面吊起置放於陸地上〕是由岩石、磚塊與水泥所砌成，是一巨大而穩重的結構，就設置在已經蓋好很多年的領事辦公處大門前。[30]

§

In February 1897, the new Consul, William Joseph Kenny, arrived to take over charge of South Formosa from Griffiths. Advised that the Consul could easily manage South Formosa from Anping, upon arrival Kenny immediately proceeded with Griffiths down to Takow, where they spent three days making a thorough inventory of everything on the Consular premises and returned to Anping with the Consular Archives. It appeared to the foreign merchants that the British government was withdrawing from Takow, as Tait & Co [德記洋行] promptly offered

$6,000 for the perpetual lease on the Consular Offices and land. However, Kenny advised Tokyo both that the offer was very low and that the prospects for Takow harbour under the Japanese were good. [12]

In January 1897, William Cowan, who had taken charge as Acting Surveyor at the Office of Works in Shanghai from Marshall, was immediately authorised by Boyce in London to reconstruct the Consul's Residence at Takow and instructed to begin work before the end of the 1896/97 financial year. Unfortunately, Cowan was in Japan on duty when the authorisation was received. By the time Cowan returned to Shanghai, there was insufficient time to begin the work before the end of the financial year on 31 March, and Cowan was forced to delay the reconstruction until he had made his own survey of the building. [13]

By June 1897, Cowan had duly surveyed the Takow Consular Residence, and proposed that changes be made to the verandah and roof. With regard to the verandah, it was proposed that the wooden verandah be replaced by a brick one with parapet, which would solve the problem of white ants, and also protect the roof from typhoons. With regard to the roof itself, Cowan proposed that the wood framing of the roof should be of white ant-resisting Yacul wood [香坡疊], covered with a double thickness of Amoy tiles. The remainder of the building Cowan deemed to be sound. [14]

The Board of Works in London approved of Cowan's plans for rebuilding the verandah and making a new roof for the Takow Consular Residence and authorised the work for 1897/8, subject to Boyce's comments on the design. Boyce, being familiar with the torrential downpours at Takow, cautioned Cowan against relying on a parapet gutter to carry away rainwater, but rather to use small openings holes in the parapet wall to allow the rainwater to flow directly off the tiles and beneath the parapet. This point is more fully examined in the discussion of the specifications below. [15]

Despite the work on the Takow Consular Residence verandah and roof having been authorised 1897/98, it was not carried out due to problems with the tenders, nor did Cowan submit any further request for the work to be authorised for 1898/99. Taiwan was in a very disturbed state at this time, culminating in the repressive rule of the third Governor-General, Nogi Maresuke [乃木希典], and a great many Chinese Formosans chose to flee across the Taiwan Strait to avoid the disorder, which might explain Cowan's difficulties. [16]

In fact, quotes for carrying out the work at the Takow Consular Residence in Spring 1898 had been successfully obtained by Acting Consul Griffiths and given to Cowan. However, it appears that Cowan took no further action and Boyce ordered him to put the request for 1899/1900. The work would now be carried out by Cecil John William Simpson, Cowan's Assistant Surveyor. [17]

In February 1899, Boyce retired from the Office of Works in London as Principal Surveyor for Foreign Work. He was promptly sent out by H.M. Treasury on a tour of inspection of Consular buildings in the Far East, including Takow and Anping which he probably visited in late 1899. Boyce estimated the value of the Takow Consular Buildings at £5000. At Takow he found all the Consular buildings to be unoccupied save for a native caretaker, as were all the merchants' houses: the merchants preferring to reside up at Anping, except during the months of July to October when sugar is loaded at Takow. Boyce was pessimistic about the prospects for trade at Takow, yet advised that the Consular buildings be retained for a few years to determine whether the Japanese would improve the harbour and build the southern railway terminus there as they apparently intended. The only permanent resident at Takow was Dr. Myers, who was now a Political Adviser to the Formosan Government, as well as being Surgeon and Instructor at the David Manson Memorial Hospital and Medical School. [18]

A massive typhoon that swept over the southern areas of Formosa in August 1899 ensured that action would be taken. At Hengch'un [恆春] the atmospheric pressure fell to 714.6 mm and the wind velocity blew away the wind cups used for its measurement; such an intense typhoon would not recur in South Formosa until the devastating August 1911 storm. [19]

In October 1899, the roof of the Takow Consular Residence was showing still further typhoon damage, but the materials for the reconstruction work were beginning to be assembled. The Office of Works arranged for the purchase of some 40 casks, each containing 400 lbs, of cement, manufactured by the Green Island Cement Company [青洲英坭公司], from

Shewan, Tomes & Co [新旗昌洋行] in Hongkong, and confirmed that work would begin in the Spring of 1900. Meanwhile, Acting Consul Griffiths reported that the Takow Consular Residence had suffered badly in the recent storms, with the rafters of the roof of the verandah being bare in parts as the tiles had been blown away, making the work ever more urgent (see Image 6-1). [20]

On 16 January 1900, a contract was finally signed between the Office of Works and Chun Sai [俊司] for the renewal of the roof, the rebuilding of the Verandah, and sundry repairs and renovations at the Consul's House at Takow. The work, to be completed within four months for the sum of 6,208 Gold Yen, was to begin immediately. Chun Sai also separately agreed to maintain the work performed by him under the contract in good order and condition for a period of two years after final completion. [21]

The work at the Takow Consular Residence was to be supervised by Robert John Hastings [希士頓], who is described as 'a man of some standing, [who] possesses local knowledge and speaks the native dialect; his services are therefore invaluable'. Hastings was to be paid 564 yen (equivalent to 600 Mexican dollars) for his supervisory services. [22]

Robert John Hastings (see Image 6-2), whose father was a Tea Merchant in England, is believed to have come out to China in the 1860s and to have fought under General Charles George Gordon [戈登] in the Ever-Victorious Army [常勝軍] in the vicinity of Shanghai during the Taiping Rebellion [太平天國之亂]. Hastings joined the Imperial Maritime Customs at Shanghai in December 1868 and was sent to Anping, Formosa, as a Tidewaiter [鈐字手] in 1869. In 1871 Hastings married Huang Yün-kuan [黃允官] of Hai-tou-she [海頭社], Anping. In 1882, after becoming an Assistant Examiner [三等驗貨] in the Imperial Maritime Customs, Hastings left the Customs service and joined Russell & Co [旗昌洋行] at Anping, and subsequently Wright & Co [喚記洋行]. Hastings died at Anping on 11 December 1912, having spent over 40 years on Formosa. [23]

The specifications for the 1900 restoration of the Takow Consular Residence not only detail most of the materials to be used, but also offer some clues about the problems discovered with the original building. [24]

With regard to the materials, the specifications stipulate that the bricks and roofing tiles are to be the very best, hard-burned ones from Amoy. The roofing timbers are specified as being of Yacal [香坡壘], an ant-resistant hardwood; while most of the other timber to be used should be Foochow Shamok. While the lime to be used for general construction is to be the best stone lime, that used for interior plastering and ceilings should be the best shell lime. The specifications also refer to a highly-durable soil/cement/lime mixture, known as Chunam [朱南], that was to be used to make the surface to the yard and to finish the side walls of the entrance steps. [25]

In the specifications, as in Boyce's original 1897 instructions, much attention is paid to the construction of the parapet wall that should stand above the new brick pillars. The brick pillars were to be built to avoid any risk of white ants infesting and weakening the Verandah structure. It is believed that the parapet wall was added above the brick columns to lessen the chance of the typhoon winds getting under the tiles and stripping them from the roof, as had apparently occurred in the August 1899 typhoon. However, parapet walls were usually used in conjunction with parapet gutters, which would not only block easily but also be unable to cope with the immense amount of rainwater run-off during a typhoon or tropical storm: Boyce and Simpson were therefore very specific in designing intermittent openings, known as weep holes, that would allow the water to pass easily under the parapet walling (see Image 6-3). [26]

Other noteworthy specifications concern the ceilings and the roof valleys. Despite Hurst's urgings in 1895 that painted boarding be used instead of the perilous plaster, the Office of Works persisted in the use of plaster for the room ceilings, despite its weight and susceptibility to the incessant typhoons and earthquakes. Meanwhile, trellis ceilings were to be used for the Verandahs, the corridor and the bathrooms to ensure the adequate ventilation of the roof timbers to diminish the possibility of rot. The roof valleys, formed at the meeting point of two roof sections, had clearly proven a weak point in the integrity of the Consular Residence roof, and the specifications are again meticulous in stating how the two roof planes should be joined (see Image 6-3). [27]

The new Verandah and re-roofing work at the Takow Consular Residence was completed on 16 November 1900. Although this was 6 months later than the stipulated date, Simpson considered the delay to be due to circumstances beyond the contracted party's control, such as the late delivery of the ant-resistant Yacal and the onset of the typhoon season, and no penalty was incurred by Chun Sai. [28]

The diminishing presence of foreigners in South Formosa by 1901 is exemplified by the withdrawal of the Consular Assistant for the district and the departure of one of Takow's most resilient residents, Dr. Myers. Left alone in South Formosa, Consul Kenny was obliged to appoint Allan Weatherhead Bain [邊阿蘭], a merchant with 35 years' experience of South Formosa and the long-standing Consular Agent [領事代理人] for the Netherlands, as Pro-Consul [臨時領事] to help him handle the two ports of Anping and Takow. In addition, Dr. Myers, who had spent over 20 years living on Saracen's Head on the opposite side of the harbour mouth from the Consular Residence at Takow, and who had been one of Takow's greatest promoters and enthusiasts, departed for Pagoda Island at Foochow, where he subsequently became Consular Agent. [29]

In June 1901, another contract was signed between the Office of Works and Tēng Kùi-kì [鄭桂記] trading as Kwai Kee for work at the Takow Consular Offices, comprising the Office Block and Gaol. The scope of the work included renewing the roof, putting the boat slip in order, and various repairs and decoration work: Kwai Kee was to be paid 2,035 Silver Yen for carrying out the contract by 10 September 1901. Once again, Hastings was contracted to superintend the work, this time for a reduced fee of 450 Silver Yen. The boat slip, which would be used for the Consular Gig, mentioned in the contract does not appear in either Marshall's 1879 plans (Image 4-4) nor in the 1899 photograph of the Takow Consular Offices (Image 5-8). However, a later Consul recorded in 1905 that the boat davits at Takow were built of stone, brick and cement and were large and cumbersome structures situated in front of the Consulate Offices gate that had been in place for many years. [30]

Takow Consulate falls into Disuse
棄置荒廢的打狗領事館

　　日本官方於1899年開始建造一條從南方的打狗到北方的臺北，貫穿南北的鐵路，它的工程是同時在每個車站一起動工。打狗到臺南的這段鐵路在1900年11月28日正式開通，兩地旅程所費時間爲1小時20分鐘，每天往返各兩班次。這樣的交通建設讓領事雖坐鎮在安平，但卻能輕易地管理打狗的事務。[31]

　　實際上，福爾摩沙南部的最後一任領事是阿佛列‧恩尼斯特‧威勒曼〔Alfred Ernest Wileman〕，他由葛里菲斯手中接任後，從1903至1909年擔任英國駐臺南領事。沒有證據顯示他曾在打狗住過，雖然人住在安平，他似乎很成功地執行領事的工作。在安平，除了他之外，還有一小群外商與人數眾多的傳教士居住在那裡。[32]

　　1904年8月，威勒曼倒是親自到打狗領事官邸作了一次勘查。他在報告中說，少了木製的迴廊柱子之後，白蟻現在轉而啃食地板與門框；此外，鋪瓦屋頂又開始漏水漏得很厲害。繼胡力檔之後，威勒曼再一次呼籲在打狗領事館鋪設專利型的瀝青屋頂毛氈，因爲這種材料已經被用在安平領事館，而且證明了效果令人滿意。兩年之後，在1906年，威勒曼再一次到打狗勘查領事官邸。之前的建議一點動靜也沒有。白蟻現在也蹂躪到窗框了，漏水的屋頂又使牆壁開始褪色，並且浸濕了地板。[33]

　　工部在接到威勒曼的第二次報告後，很迅速地採取行動，於是西索‧約翰‧威廉‧辛普森〔Cecil John William Simpson〕找到了渡邊金平〔或錦平〕先生〔Mr. Kimpei Watanabe〕來執行整修的工作，他是安平領事館內一位令人信任的日文書辦，被找來監督打狗領事館建築物的屋頂重鋪與各式各樣的雜項修理工作。[34]

§

The Japanese authorities began construction of a through railway from Takow in the South to Taipei in the North in 1899, with construction commencing at each terminus simultaneously. The section between Takow and Tainan was officially opened for traffic on 28 November 1900, with the journey time being about 1 hour and 20 minutes and two trains running each way daily, which allowed the Consul to manage affairs at Takow easily from Anping. [31]

Effectively, the last Consul for South Formosa was Alfred Ernest Wileman, who, after taking over from Griffiths, was the British Consul at Tainan from 1903 until 1909. There is no evidence that Wileman lived down at Takow and he seems to have performed his service successfully from Anping, where he and the small number of foreign merchants lived with a rather larger number of missionaries living on the east side of Tainan. [32]

In August 1904, Wileman did make an inspection of the Consul's Residence at Takow. He reported that the white ants, deprived of the wooden Verandah pillars, were now devouring the floorboards and door frames; moreover, the tiled roof was once again leaking very badly. Wileman yet again urged that patent roofing felt be used at Takow as it had already proven so satisfactory up at the Anping Consulate. Two years later, in 1906, Wileman inspected the Consul's House at Takow again. No action had been taken. The white ants now also infested the window frames, and the leaking roof was once again discolouring the walls and soaking the floorboards. [33]

The Office of Works was prompt to take action upon Wileman's second report, and Cecil John William Simpson obtained the services of Mr Kimpei Watanabe, the trusted Japanese Writer at the Anping Consulate, to supervise the reroofing and sundry repairs at the Takow Consular buildings. [34]

Re-registration
of the Consular properties
領事館財產重新註冊

　　臺灣歷史上的動盪不安產生了複雜的土地所有權形態，所有權不只是分為三種基本類型，而且每筆土地的範圍如果不是從未，也很少有機會被測量。這種情勢使得要公平地為土地課徵任何的稅都是問題重重。 劉銘傳曾嘗試推動激進的改革，並於1886年提出新的土地測量計畫，但是遭遇的抵抗之大，可以說導致了他在1891年的辭職。一般常見的土地所有權結構是土地的名義擁有者，或稱大租主，必須向政府繳納定額的地稅，不過他們名下有很多其他的土地是沒有向政府報備的；另一種常見的土地所有權人是佃戶，或稱小租主，他們經常要負擔大租主所要求的嚴苛的租金。因為如此，在農業地帶，大租通常都是有錢有勢的豪門大族。日本人於1898年開始準備另一次福爾摩沙的土地測量，不過，這次的測量足足費了十年才完成。[35]

　　1904年5月25日，日本政府頒布律令第6號，取消了大租的權利，於是佃戶成為土地的真正所有權人。但是，相較之下，外國永久租約所有權人的地位卻變得模糊了。1904年時，威廉·高凡曾提醒領事威勒曼，打狗領事館的兩塊地號，1號與4號，在當年馬歇爾取得永久租約時，其登記資料有些許的出入:1號地登記的是由盧天送永久租給英國工部委員會，而4號地則是登記為由盧大度永久租給工部首席委員。高凡於是敦請威勒曼將這兩塊土地的登記轉移到大英工部與公共建築委員〔the Commissioners of His Majesty's Works and Public Buildings〕的名下。雖然日本政府在1904年頒布的第6號律令並沒有明文規範永久租約地的權責移轉，不過，在1905年時威勒曼認為此事需謹慎對待，雖無明文要求但應該預先向當局申請將兩塊地的登記轉移。於是在1905年11月20日〔明治38年11月20日〕，領事威勒曼向鳳山廳〔Hōzan Chō〕申請，請求將上述的兩塊土地以及外國人墓園土地的永久租約登記在大英工部與公共建築委員名下。1905年11月23日〔明治38年11月23日〕，這些物業的權利很順利地被轉移到上述的工部與公共建築委員名下，並登記於外國人持有永久租約的檔案中，由廳長橫山虎次〔Yokoyama Toraji〕署名〔見圖6-4〕。[36]

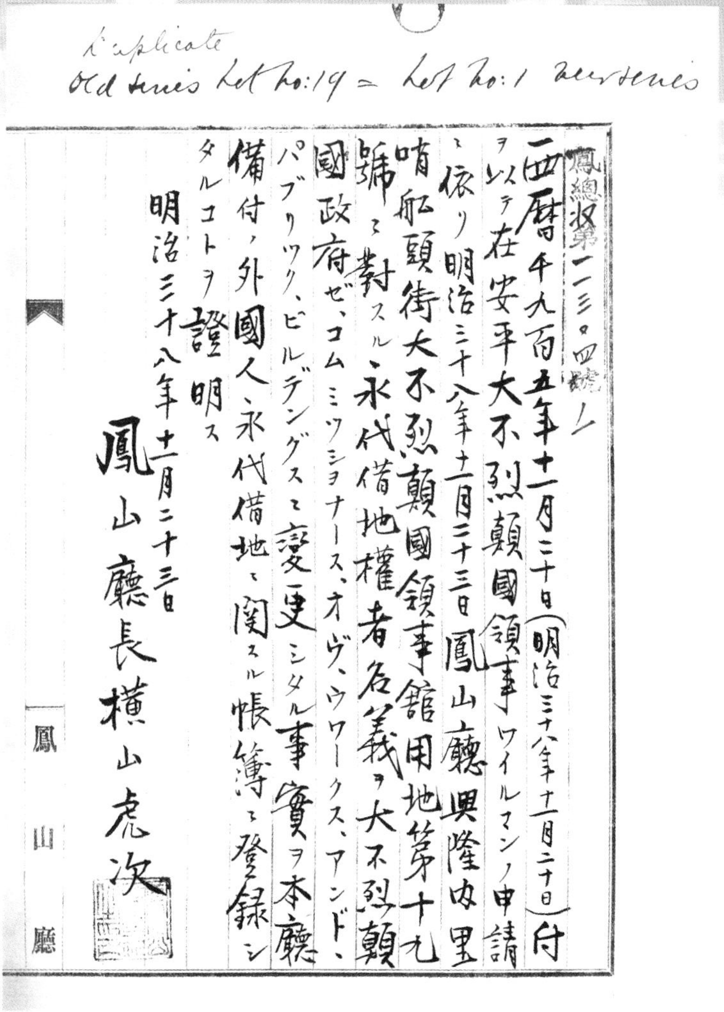
Duplicate
Old series Lot No: 19 = Lot No: 1 new series

鳳總收第一一三〇四號

西暦千九百五年十一月二十日（明治三十八年十一月二十日）付ヲ以テ在安平大不列顛國領事ワイルマンノ申請ニ依リ明治三十八年十一月二十三日鳳山廳興隆内里哨船頭街大不列顛國領事館用地第十九號ニ對スル永代借地權者名義ヲ大不列顛國政府ゼ、コムミツシヨナース、オヴ、ウワークス、アンド、パブリツク、ビルデングスニ變更シタル事實ヲ本廳備付ノ外國人永代借地ニ関スル帳簿ニ登録シタルコトヲ證明ス

明治三十八年十一月二十三日

鳳山廳長横山虎次

鳳山廳

圖 6-4：1905年將領事官邸的土地之永久租約轉移到大英國工部與公共建築委員名下之檔案文書。
〔版權屬於英國政府，WORK 10/33/10，版權所有，翻印必究〕

Image 6-4：1905 Transfer of Perpetual Lease of part of the Consular Residence Lot to H.B.M.'s Commissioners of Works & Public Buildings
Certificate, dated 23 November 1905, issued by Yokoyama Toraji the Hozan Chōchō, confirming the transfer of the Perpetual Lease on part of the Consular Residence lot, to H.B.M.'s Commissioners of Works and Public Buildings, in Japanese with English translation.
(Images are Crown Copyright. WORK 10/210. All rights reserved)

Translation

Hozan Chō neral office
No. 4

Certificate.

Hozan November 23, 1905.

I hereby certify that the rights
of perpetual lease lot No: 19, being
the lot of land, situated at Shaou
Chun Tau, (Tacow), in the district
of Hozan Chō, and owned by His
Britannic Majesty's Consulate,
have been transferred on this, the
23rd day of November, (38th year of
Meiji) to His Britannic Majesty's
Commissioners of Works and
Public Buildings and that the
transfer has, in accordance with
the request preferred by His
Britannic Majesty's Consul at
Anping on the 20th November, 1905,
(38th Year of Meiji), been duly
entered in the register appertaining to
perpetual leases of foreigners kept at
the Hozan Chō.

(Sd) Yokoyama Toraji
Hozan Chōchō
(Seal)

True Translation:
A. Wileman
HBM's Consul

Tainan
November 24. 1905

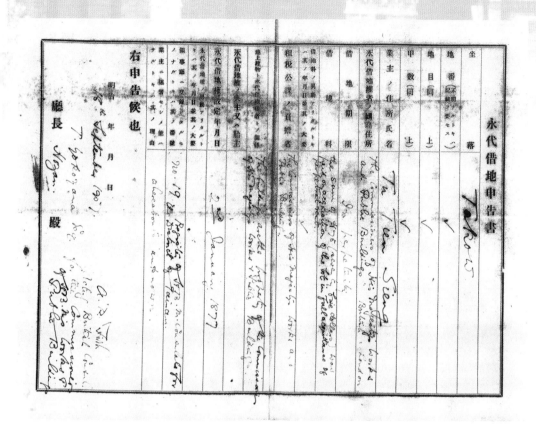

到了1907年7月12日，日本官方頒布律令，規範福爾摩沙（臺灣）地區永久租賃的物業之調查、註冊以及改正，此律令於1907年8月1日起生效，要求永久租約所有人必須在6個月內向各地方的廳提出上述事項之申請。英國代理領事官阿弗列・李察・佛斯〔Alfred Richard Firth〕遵照規定，以大英工部與公共建築委員的名義，於1907年9月18日向鳳山廳長橫山虎次提出要登記領事館務業的申請〔見圖6-5〕。1909年9月1日，日本官方確認了所有以大英工部與公共建築委員之名義登記持有的領事館及外國人墓園土地，其相關的中文名稱是有效的，於是這些地的永久租約乃順理成章地被臺灣政府承認。[37]

§

The turbulence of Formosa's history had produced land ownership holdings that were not only divided into three basic classes, but where the area of each holding had seldom, if ever, been measured. The situation made an equitable collection of any land tax problematic. Liu Ming-ch'uan attempted a radical reform of the situation and a new land survey in 1886, but met with such strong resistance that it can be said to have led to his resignation in 1891. The typical structure of land ownership was the patent-holders, or Ta-tsu [大租], who paid a nominal rent to the government on their land holdings, many of which were not reported; and the tenants, or Hsiao-tsu [小租], who paid often exorbitant rents to the Ta-tsu. Thus in the agricultural area the Ta-tsu were often families of great power. The Japanese started preparations for another survey of the land holdings in Formosa in 1898, though this would not be completed for ten years. [35]

IOn 25 May 1904 the Japanese promulgated Ordinance No. 6 which abolished the rights of the Taiso (Ta-tsu), and the tenant became the owner of the land. However the position of the foreign Perpetual Lease holder became less clear. In 1904 William Cowan had informed Consul Wileman that two lots at Takow, Nos. 1 and 4, had been registered inconsistently by Francis Julian Marshall: Lot No. 1 had been leased in perpetuity by Lu T'ien-sung [盧天送] to H.M. Board of Works, and Lot No. 4 had been leased by Lu Ta-tu [盧大度] to H.M.'s First

Commissioners of Works. Cowan had requested Wileman to transfer these two lots to the Commissioners of His Majesty's Works and Public Buildings. Despite the 1904 Ordinance No. 6 making no overt provision covering the transfer of Perpetual Leases, in 1905 Wileman considered it prudent to make a provisional application to transfer the two Lots. Consul Wileman accordingly requested the Hōzan Chō (Fengshan Prefecture) [鳳山廳] to transfer the rights of both these Perpetual Leases and also that of the Foreign Cemetery into the name of the His Britannic Majesty's Commissioners of Works and Public Buildings on 20 November 1905 [明治38年11月20日]. The rights to these properties were duly transferred to H.B.M. Commissioners of Works and Public Buildings and entered into the Register of perpetual leases held by foreigners by Yokoyama Toraji [橫山 虎次], the Hozan Chōchō (Prefect), on 23 November 1905 [明治38年11月23日] (see Image 6-4). [36]

On 12 July 1907, the Japanese authorities promulgated Ordinances regarding the Investigation, Registration and Adjustment of Perpetual Leasehold Property in Formosa, effective 1 August 1907, requiring applications to be made within 6 months at the Government District Office (Chō). Alfred Richard Firth, the Acting British Consul, duly made an application, on behalf of the Commissioners of H.B.M.'s Works and Public Buildings, to register the Consular Properties on 18 September 1907 to Prefect Yokoyama at the Hōzan Chō (Fengshan Prefecture) (see Image 6-5). On 1 September 1909, the Japanese authorities confirmed the validities of the relevant Chinese titles to the Consulate lots and the Foreign Cemetery, all held in the name of the Commissioners of H.B.M. Works and Public Buildings, which were duly recognized by the Formosa Government as Perpetual Leases. [37]

Closure of the Consular Buildings in South Formosa

南臺灣領事館之落幕

　　現實是如此地諷刺，就在日本官方開始著手要改善長久以來一直被忽視的打狗港設施時，英國政府正好決定要撤離南臺灣。

　　自1897年以來，打狗的領事官邸實際上就處於一種封藏不用的狀態，而到1908年之後，英國政府發現連打狗的領事辦公處現在對政府的空間需求而言，也形同多餘，因此從1908年7月1日開始，英國政府正式地將它們租給怡記洋行〔Bain & Co〕。[38]

　　雖然比較起來德記洋行〔Tait & Co〕在安平多苟延殘喘了2年，但怡記洋行卻是在南臺灣存活到最後的主要英國公司。外國貿易一點一滴衰退的理由可歸因於日本對製糖廠、銀行設施與船運路線不斷加緊的控制與強化所有權。到了1908年時，怡記洋行主要的股東是阿圖〔Harry Walter Arthur，又譯哈利・瓦特勒・亞瑟〕與邊阿蘭。由於邊阿蘭在1906年終於返回英格蘭，同時他也交出了領事代理人的職位，怡記洋行留下來的資深股東阿圖於是被指定為新的臨時領事。[39]

　　1909年日本官方開始在打狗港進行一連串主要的港口改善措施。這些措施包括：疏濬與挖深內外港口、拓寬打狗港入口、在哈瑪星〔Hamasen〕鄰接新完成的鐵道轉運車站旁地區興建碼頭。[40]

　　在1909年的同一時間，威廉・梅西・洛伊德〔William Massy Royds〕，在5月1日接過威勒曼領事的工作後，馬上開始準備將英國領事館撤出南臺灣的相關事宜。隨著1908年從北到南貫通福爾摩沙島的國營鐵路終於完成，在南部保留一個獨立運作的領事館顯得並非必要，尤其是擔任臨時領事的阿圖本人也不再願意擔任領事代理人。1909年11月，英國駐日本大使竇納樂爵士〔Sir Claude Maxwell MacDonald，又譯竇納樂克勞德・馬克士威爾・麥克當勞〕試圖延攬臨時領事阿圖來擔任臺南的無給職副領事或領事代理人，阿圖有條件地答應了這項新職位。然而，在1910年3月1日時，他卻取消了擔任無給職副領事或領事代理人的承諾，所持的原因是他的公司怡記洋行事務繁忙；基於這個理由，他同時辭去了臨時領事一職。洛伊德於是建議安平領事館，因為它偏離重要的國營鐵路幹道，應該要想辦法賣掉，而打狗領事館建築則應該被保留，等待1912-13年預期中的港口改善工程完成，這個工程將讓打狗轉變為南臺灣最優良的港口。洛伊德更進一步指出，有一家英國公司已經出價30,000日元要購買打狗領事官邸，他預期這價格非常可能在打狗港改善完後增加。[41]

關於駐臺領事的問題，駐東京大使竇納樂爵士的結論是現在島上只需要一個領事就好，而且他應該進駐於北臺灣；安平領事館應該賣掉；至於打狗領事館建築則暫時保留，辦公處建築繼續租給怡記洋行，而領事官邸則找人看守管理。雖然打狗的領事一直都負責全臺的領事業務，但從1877年11月起，臺灣被畫分成兩個領事區：南部領事區由一位坐鎮於打狗語臺灣府的領事管轄；而北部則有另一位領事（之前為副領事）駐在淡水。[42]

於是，在1911年的4月，南臺灣的領事辦公重心遂被移到北臺灣的淡水，然後以每月7元日幣的薪酬，僱用一個管理人看管打狗領事官邸。圖6-6是一系列於1911年2月拍攝的領事館物業的照片。[43]

§

It is ironic that, in the very year that the Japanese authorities commenced work on improving the long-neglected harbour facilities at Takow, the British government decided to withdraw from South Formosa.

With the Consular Residence at Takow effectively mothballed since 1897, it was found by 1908 that the Consular Offices at Takow were now also surplus to the British government's requirements and these were officially rented out to Bain & Co [怡記洋行] from 1 July 1908. [38]

圖 6-6：1911年拍攝的領事官邸與領事辦公處照片。
1911年2月打狗領事公館照片，顯示西側與南側；以及打狗領事辦公室，顯示南側。
〔版權屬於英國政府，WORK 55/1 版權所有，翻印必究〕

Image 6-6：1911 Photographs of Consular Residence & Consular Offices
February 1911 photographs of Takow Consular Residence,
showing West Elevation and South Elevation; & Takow Consular Offices, showing South Elevation.
(All images Crown Copyright. WORK 55/1. All rights reserved)

Although Tait & Co [德記洋行] continued on for two more years at Anping, Bain & Co was the last major British company to survive in South Formosa. The reasons for the erosion of foreign trade can be attributed to the ever-tightening Japanese control and ownership of the sugar mills, banking facilities and shipping routes. By 1908, the major partners in Bain & Co were Harry Walter Arthur [阿圖] and Allan Weatherhead Bain. With the final departure to England of Allan Bain and the relinquishment of his Consular posts in 1906, the remaining senior partner in Bain & Co, Harry Arthur, had been appointed as the new Pro-Consul. [39]

In 1909 the Japanese authorities began carrying out a series of major improvements at Takow harbour. These included: the dredging and deepening of the inner and outer harbours, the widening of the harbour entrance, and the construction of the wharfs at Hamasen [哈瑪星] adjacent to the new railway terminal. [40]

Equally in 1909, Acting Consul William Massy Royds, who took over from Consul Alfred Ernest Wileman on 1 May, was soon preparing for the withdrawal of the British Consulate from South Formosa. With the completion of the Government railway from the north to the south of the island of Formosa in 1908, it was considered unnecessary to maintain a separate Consulate in the south, especially as Pro-Consul Harry Arthur was no longer willing to act as Consular Agent. The British Ambassador to Japan, Sir Claude Maxwell MacDonald [竇納樂], had sought to appoint Pro-Consul Harry Walter Arthur as the unpaid Vice-Consul or Consular Agent at Tainan in November 1909, Arthur conditionally accepted the new position. However on 1 March 1910 Pro-Consul Harry Arthur withdrew his acceptance of the position as the unpaid Vice-Consul or Consular Agent, citing the demands of his company, Bain & Co; for the same reason, Arthur also resigned his post of Pro-Consul. Royds accordingly advised that the Anping Consulate, being off the main Government railway line, should be sold and that the Takow Consular buildings should be kept pending the expected completion in 1912-13 of the harbour works, which would transform Takow into the premier port of South Formosa. Royds further noted that a British firm had already offered ¥30,000 for the Takow Consular Residence, an amount he considered likely to increase as Takow is improved. [41]

Sir Claude Maxwell MacDonald, the British Ambassador at Tokyo, concluded that there should now be only one Consul on the island and that he should reside in North Formosa; that the Anping Consulate should be sold; and that the Takow Consular buildings kept for the time being, with the Consular Offices to continue to be occupied by Bain & Co and the Consular Residence to be in the charge of a caretaker. Although the Consul at Takow once served all of Formosa, in November 1877 the island had been divided into two Consular Districts: South Formosa, with one Consul residing at Takow and Taiwan; and North Formosa, with one Consul, previously a Vice-Consul, residing at Tamsui.[42]

Accordingly in April 1911, the South Formosa Consular Chest was removed up to Tamsui Consulate in North Formosa, and a caretaker employed at Takow at ¥7 per month. A series of photographs of the Consular properties taken in February 1911 are shown in Image 6-6. [43]

Sale of Consular Properties at Takow
打狗領事館物業的出售

1917年1月英國駐東京大使，威廉‧康寧漢‧格林爵士〔Sir William Conyngham Greene〕送給淡水的領事湯瑪斯‧哈林頓〔Thomas Harrington〕一份來自工部的文件副本，文中建議放棄安平與打狗的領事館物業。[44]

哈林頓雖然同意現在已經沒有英國貿易商留在南臺灣，以及英國可能永遠不再需要安平領事館這兩點，但是他也提出以下的意見：

比較起來，放棄打狗不像放棄安平那麼理所當然，因為它（打狗）是南臺灣唯一一個條件良好而且重要的海港，境內有鐵路可以貫通到北部，而英國籍的船有時還會進港來⋯。兩個港口的領事館建築狀況都很差，特別是打狗的辦公室與官邸。甚至於在1913年底，我上一次在那兒時，這些剛在1912年進行整修的建築就已經開始產生損毀了，此外，從拜訪打狗港而順道檢視這物業的北臺灣外國居民所帶來的報告中，也證實了裡面許多木製結構已經被白蟻蛀食，部份的邊界圍牆已經崩毀，灰泥與裝飾板條已經脫落，屋頂也不再能防水，只有堅硬的磚造結構沒有受損⋯。兩個港口自1912年後都完完全全沒有受過毀滅性颱風的侵襲⋯。[45]

哈林頓領事無法估算出打狗領事館物業的價格，因為他說到：「我找不到工部近幾年來有針對這物業的價值進行精算的紀錄（雖然最近他們曾估計安平領事館物業約值31,300日圓或3,060英鎊）。不過，即使工部（最近）真的有精算過，這些建築的破敗毀損也將大大地降低其價格。山腳下辦公室的地點已不再像以前一樣優越，城鎮、港口與鐵路已經在有一小段距離之外的地區發展 。此外，建築已經老舊腐朽，似乎比較適合整個拆除再重新改建，而非修繕復舊。至於領事官邸，位於陞岹山丘，受限於沒有辦法能讓有輪子的交通工具到達，它唯一的優點是風景優美。」[46]

　　數年後，在1917年時，由於湯瑪斯‧哈林頓已經四年沒探訪過打狗的領事館了，他安排一次旅行到此處檢視，之後他對東京的格林大使與上海工部辦事處呈上的報告如下：

　　在打狗，官邸的修復情況良好，如果我們只看磚造部分的話確實是如此。然而，白蟻已經在木製結構內，似乎還有一處或兩處會輕微漏水的地方。走進其中一個後排房間後，我所站的一小片地板開始慢慢下陷，不過下陷的速度很慢，所以我還能趕緊跑出來；不過，有四或五片瓦掉入下面的地窖。檢查之後發現那個房間底下的所有木樑都因為受潮而變成黑色，可能已經腐朽不堪了。其他地方的有些樑木仍然是白色的，可能還安全。這種木結構的潮濕受損可能是因為一個破掉的窗戶使得地板持續潮濕。有一處或兩處的木地板似乎很軟、很有彈性，視察時可得謹慎小心。…假如這些產業在未來的六個月左右還在我們手中未曾脫手，我想，我們有必要花一小筆費用來修理牆壁與屋頂，防止損害擴大的速度過快。[47]

　　1919年2月，臺灣政府中最高階的海軍官員的其中兩位，擔任海軍參謀長的益田上校〔Captain T. Masuda〕與擔任上尉指揮官的井上男爵〔Lieutenant Commander Baron K. Inoue〕，他也是總督明石元二郎的侍從副官〔Aide-de-camp to Governor General Motojiro〕，聯袂拜訪在淡水的哈林頓領事，出價38,584日圓想要購買南臺灣的英國領事館物業：依據日本海軍當局的估算，安平物業價值14,488日圓；而打狗官邸與辦公室價值24,096日圓。[48]

　　拜比‧亞斯頓〔Beilby Alston〕，他是1919年與1920年駐東京的英國大使，在1919年

11月曾建議在淡水的代理領事保羅‧達林波‧巴特勒〔Paul Dalrymple Butler〕，關於雙方洽談中的土地買賣，應該只能包含實際上的領事館房地，打狗外國人墓園那塊地絕對不應該包括在買賣中，不然這看起來會很像死要錢的行為。[49]

1919年10月，山下汽船株式會社〔Yamashita Steamship Company〕的米滿先生〔Mr. Yonemitsu〕正式向巴特勒出價100,000日元，要購買打狗領事館建築，也就是辦公處與官邸兩處。然而，代理領事巴特勒沒有答應，他相信以打狗領事館而言，即使這價錢也還太低，因為同樣的這位米滿先生才剛要完成購買位於打狗港入口另一頭屬於買醫師的物業，總價落於22,000 至25,000英鎊間〔相當於 195,000與220,000日元之間〕，依照這個價位標準，以總價150,000日元來談打狗領事館物業的買賣是有可能的。然而，實情是買醫師位於打狗的物業從沒有賣給山下汽船株式會社，而是於1920年，由上述的井上男爵與代理領事巴特勒雙方合意，以100,000日元的價格賣給海軍，相當於16,000英鎊。1920年3月買醫師正計畫要由他在羅星塔島的領事代理人職位上退休，以便再回英格蘭居住，所以他必須趕在離開中國前解決這個問題。然而令人難過的是，在解決物業問題不久後，買醫師於1920年3月20日在羅星塔島的職位上逝世。[50]

由於巴特勒的催促，工部針對打狗的物業安排了一次視察，之後就同意可以向井上男爵提出150,000日元的報價，若要出售打狗領事館物業這是一個適當的價碼。在收到工部的建議後，巴特勒於是回絕了山下汽船株式會社提出的購買打狗領事館物業的價碼，這是因為他知道日本海軍當局已經準備好要提出一個比山下汽船更高的價格。接著，巴特勒對井上男爵提出150,000日元的開價，當時井上已是在臺灣的資深海軍官員，他答應把此價格報到東京。在一週內，井上男爵回報說東京海軍軍部「原則上答應」以180,000日元〔相當於26,000英鎊〕購買英國在打狗與安平的物業，這個比較高的回覆價格據說是因為臺灣新任總督，田健治郎男爵〔Baron Den Kenjirō〕本人出面干預所致。[51]

田健治郎男爵為第八任的臺灣總督，也是第一位日本文官總督。1919年10月走馬上任後，他集中精力進行對臺灣人的同化政策，這個同化政策是建立在一個健全的教育體系。然而，在他的任內，總督的人事任命權力，還有特別是對軍務事宜的控制，很明顯地在消退。缺乏對臺灣地區內海軍事務的控制或許可以解釋為何直到1923年9月他任期結束的這段時間，購買打狗領事物業這件事再也沒有進一步的行動。[52]

　　1923年的夏天，英國再次地考慮他們是否選擇放棄南臺灣的領事館物業。最後的決定是，安平與打狗的領事館物業應該要直接地賣給出價最高者，包括墓園那塊土地裡沒有真正用於埋葬的部份。換句話說，南臺灣的英國領事館物業，除了在打狗的外國人墓園外，都要被出售。[53]

　　在1919年與1920年間，針對這些土地的歷次開價，其後續的效力都被撤消，然後在1924年7月，臺灣總督府針對購買南臺灣的英國領事館物業，開出一個不願接受加價的價錢，78,511.89日圓，而且取得國會〔Diet〕的同意。不過打狗的外國人墓園在此次交易之外，它將永久租給英國政府，免除稅捐及其他一切費用。[54]

　　領事傑拉德・海斯汀・菲普斯〔Gerald Hastings Phipps〕對於安平與打狗這兩個領事館曾有以下讓人宛如歷歷在目的描述。他描述安平是「在暮氣沉沉的窮鄉僻壤中，孤立著一棟半傾頹房子」。至於打狗，菲普斯認為「這些處於極度腐朽失修狀態的大房子，無法讓人一望而心生瞻仰大英帝國威望之感，特別是在一個像打狗這般如此繁忙的船泊港口，一眼望去就認出這破敗的建築居然是屬於英王陛下政府的物業，實在無法讓人有景仰之感。」[55]

　　既然海軍軍部很清楚地對購買這些地點不再有興趣，外交部並不難建議英國財政部接受臺灣總督府所開的價錢。臺灣總督府隨即把此筆預定開支編入1925/6年度的預算，以便於送到1925年9月即將開議的國會會期中去審查。[56]

　　在這件事尚未塵埃落定之前，菲普斯就被轉調到檀香山，而由艾力克・亨利・狄邦森〔Eric Henry de Bunsen〕接任淡水的英國代理領事一職。這使得工部須要在1925年5月7日草擬一份新的委任書，授權艾力克・亨利・狄邦森先生，如此一來他才能夠代表英國政府完成財產轉移。[57]

　　經過一些對合約草稿字斟句酌的小協商後，日本帝國政府與英國政府終於在1925年12月4日針對打狗與安平領事館物業之買賣達成協議，排除了外國人墓園後，其餘物業總額

Valuation of Land and Buildings on the former British Consulates at ANPING
and TAKAO and of that portion of the "Cemetery
"Let at TAKAO outside the walls of the
Takao Foreign Cemetery.

Locality.	Class of land.	Number of "ko" S.	Land Tax	Land. Value per "ko" Yen	Land. Value of lot. Yen	Valuation. Buildings. Number of tsubo.	Buildings. Valuation. Yen	TOTAL VALUATION. Yen
			Yen					
1. ANPING: British Consulate	Building	.7986	15.97	733.50 x	565.77	160.35	21,061.37	21,647.14
2. TAKAO: British Consulate Offices	Building	.2746	46.66	58,680 x 16,113.53		151.78)		
do. Consul's residence	Building	.1398	1.82)			)	44,511.14	
			)	8,502 x 11,895.02		174.12)	16,502.59)	
do. Garden etc.	Forest	1.2116	- -)					
3. do. : Land outside wall of foreign cemetery	Cemetery	.8421	- -	14,670 x 12,383.61		-	12,383.61	
					40,947.93		37,563.96	78,511.89

N.B. 1 "ko" equals 2934 tsubo, and the valuation given are accordingly equivalent to Yen 0.25, Yen 20, Yen 3 and Yen 5 per tsubo respectively. 1 "ko" equals 2.3967 acres. 1 tsubo equals 3.95353 square yards.

164

Schedule

No.2 of 176 Aza Shaemento Takao, Takao City, Takao Province Building Land			2 Bu	7 Rin	4 Mo	6 Shi
No. 1 of 176 the same Building Land			1 Bu	3 Rin	9 Mo	8 Shi
No.176 the same Hill and Forest Land	1 Ko		2 Bu	1 Rin	1 Mo	6 Shi
No.127 the same From out of the Cemetery Lot 1 Ko 2 Mo 7 Shi			3 Bu	4 Rin	2 Mo	1 Shi
No.949 Anping Tainan City, Tainan Province Building Land			7 Bu	9 Rin	8 Mo	6 Shi
In all	3 Ko		2 Bu	6 Rin	6 Mo	7 Shi

The Perpetual Lease Rights in respect of the Lands hereinabove specified and the Buildings Trees and all and sundry other things that are situate on such Perpetual Lease Lands.

圖 6-7：南臺灣（英國領事館）物業之估價、買賣合約與轉移物業一覽表。
〔版權屬於英國政府，WORK 10/33/10 版權所有，翻印必究〕

Image 6-7 : Valuation, Agreement of Sale and Schedule of South Formosa Properties.
(All Images are Crown Copyright. WORK 10/33/10. All rights reserved)

Takao and Amping.   Agreement of Sale.   Translation.

CONTRACT IN RESPECT OF THE SALE OF PERPETUAL LEASE RIGHTS
TO LANDS AND THINGS THEREON.

An agreement as follows is hereby made in respect of the
transfer by sale to the Imperial Japanese Government of the
Rights to certain Lands held on perpetual lease by the
British Government and of the Buildings Trees and all and
sundry other things that are on such Perpetual Lease Lands.

1.   The British Government agrees to sell to the Imperial
Japanese Government the Perpetual Lease Rights now held by
it in the name of the Commissioner of His Britannic Majesty's
Works and Public Buildings and specified in the schedule
hereto and the Buildings Trees and All and Sundry Things
that are on such Perpetual Lease Lands.

2.   The Imperial Japanese Government shall after the
execution of this agreement and simultaneously with registration or with the transfer of the objects concerned pay
Yen 78,511.89 as the Purchase Price of the Perpetual Lease
Rights in question and of the Buildings Trees and all and
sundry things that are on such Perpetual Lease Lands.

3.   The British Government shall as required by the Imperial
Japanese Government perform the duties relating to the
registration of the conveyance of the Perpetual Lease Rights
in question and to the transfer of the objects concerned and
all other obligations incidental thereto.

4.   With regard to the existing Joint Foreign Cemetery
(enclose area 1 Bu 6 Rin 0 Mo 6 Shi) situated within the
Cemetery at No. 127 Aza Shosento Takao, Takao City, Takao
Province, the Imperial Japanese Government agrees to
construct a road nine shaku in width in a straight line
from the front of the entrance gate of the cemetery to a
point on the public road on the South (Minato-Cho Gochome
Main Road), to establish a Right of Way and to assume the
responsibility

183

responsibility, as long as the need exists, of providing
construction works for the purpose of giving effect to such
servitude, and of repairing such construction works. Be
it provided that the creation of such servitude shall be
free of cost.

5.   The representatives of the two parties hereinafter
written shall be empowered to settle matters of detail
incidental to this agreement.

6.   This agreement shall be drawn in duplicate and each party
shall retain a copy.

IN CONFIRMATION OF THE EXECUTION OF THIS AGREEMENT the
Representatives of both Governments have set their names
and Seals hereunder.

This fourth day of December, 1925.

The VENDOR: The COMMISSIONER OF HIS BRITANNIC MAJESTY'S

WORKS AND PUBLIC BUILDINGS

Representative of the Foregoing

ERIC HENRY de BUNSEN

ACTING BRITISH CONSUL IN TAMSUI

The PURCHASER: The IMPERIAL JAPANESE GOVERNMENT

Representative of the Foregoing

TAKIO ISAWA

THE GOVERNOR GENERAL OF FORMOSA

SEAL OF THE
GOVERNMENT
GENERAL OF
FORMOSA

190

275

為78,511.89日圓；買家日本帝國政府是由臺灣總督伊澤多喜男〔Takio Izawa〕代表；賣方，大英工部與公共建築物委員，由英國駐淡水代理領事艾力克‧亨利‧狄邦森代表〔見圖6-7〕。[58]

1926年1月6日，上海工部辦公處的建築師朱立阿斯‧布雷德利〔Julius Bradley〕，終於可以拍電報給倫敦的工部，通知打狗與安平領事館物業買賣程序已經完成，而且價款已經被存入橫濱〔Yokohama〕的香港上海匯豐銀行。稍晚的一份工部文件紀錄顯示，換算成英國貨幣，78,511.89日圓約等於為6,974英鎊14先令0便士【〔譯注：1970年之前，每一英鎊等於20先令〔shillings（s.）〕，每一先令又可分成12便士〔pennies（d.）〕】。[59]

1925年12月4日，原先以大英工部與公共建築物委員名義持有的英國打狗與安平領事館物業，除了打狗外國人墓園實際用於埋葬的部份之外，在這一天賣給了日本政府，並隨即在臺南的地方法院註冊。[60]

§

In January 1917 Sir William Conyngham Greene, the British Ambassador at Tokyo, sent Consul Thomas Harrington at Tamsui a copy of an Office of Works recommendation for the disposal of the Consular properties at Anping and Takow. [44]

Harrington, while conceding that there were now no British traders in South Formosa and that the Anping Consulate would probably never be required, commented as follows:

The case for giving up Takow is not quite so evident as that of Anping, as it is the only good and important port in South Formosa, with through railway connection to the North, while British ships enter occasionally. … The buildings at both ports are in poor condition especially the Office and Residence at Takow. Even at the end of 1913 when I was last

*there they had deteriorated since the repairs of 1912, while reports from Foreign residents
of North Formosa who have looked over the property when on a visit to the port confirm
the facts that much of the woodwork is rotten with white ants, part of the boundary wall
has collapsed, plaster and mouldings have fallen and the roof is no longer watertight, while
only the solid brick work remains undamaged. ... Both ports have been singularly free
from disastrous typhoons since 1912 ... .* [45]

Consul Harrington was unable to estimate the value of the Takow property as "I can find
no definite valuation of the property by the Office of Works in recent years [though they had
recently estimated the Anping property at ¥31,300 or £3,060]. Even if there were any [recent
valuation] the serious deterioration of the buildings would greatly reduce the value. The
office which is at the foot of the hill is no longer in a very good position, the town, harbour
and railway having developed at some distance. Moreover the building is old and dilapidated,
and seems more suitable for demolition and replacement than for repair. The residence, on a
steep hill, suffers from having no approach available for wheeled traffic, its only asset being a
beautiful view." [46]

Later in 1917, as Consul Thomas Harrington had not visited the Consular buildings at
Takow for four years, he made a tour of inspection of the site and reported to Ambassador
Greene at Tokyo and the Office of Works at Shanghai as follows:

*At Takow the ... Residence seems in good repair so far as the brickwork is concerned.
White ants are in the woodwork, however, and there seem to be one or two small leaks. On
entering one of the back rooms the patch on which I stood began to give way beneath my
feet, slowly, however, so that I was able to scramble out; four or five tiles, however, went
down into the cellar below. Examination showed that all the wooden beams under that
room are black with moisture and probably quite rotten. Other beams elsewhere were still*

white and are probably safe. Probably continued wetting of the floor through a broken window has caused the damage. One or two wooden floors seemed rather springy, and would probably have to be explored with caution. .... Should these properties not pass out of our possession in the next six months or so I think it will be necessary to expend a small sum of money to repair walls and roofs to prevent damage from spreading too rapidly. [47]

In February 1919, two of the highest-ranking Japanese Naval officers in the Formosan government, Captain T. Masuda (the Chief of Navy Staff), and Lieutenant Commander Baron K. Inoue (Aide-de-camp to Governor General Motojiro Akashi [明石元二郎]), visited Consul Harrington at Tamsui and offered ¥38,584 for the British Consular properties in South Formosa: the Japanese Naval Authorities valued the Anping property at ¥14,488; and the Takow Residence and Office properties at ¥24,096. [48]

Beilby Alston, the British Minister at Tokyo in 1919 and 1920, advised Acting Consul Paul Dalrymple Butler at Tamsui in November 1919 that the proposed sale should cover the actual Consular lots only, and that the Foreign Cemetery at Takow should not be included in any sale, as this would appear ghoulish. [49]

In October 1919, a Mr. Yonemitsu of Yamashita Steamship Company [Yamashita Kisen K.K., 山下汽船株式会社] had made a formal offer to Butler of Yen 100,000 for the Takow Consular buildings, that is, the Offices and Residence. Yet Acting Consul Butler believed that even this offer was low, as the same Mr. Yonemitsu was just completeing the purchase of Dr. Myers' property on the opposite side of the harbour entrance at Takow for a sum between £22,000 and £25,000 [equivalent to between ¥195,000 and ¥220,000], and that a sum of ¥150,000 for the Takow Consular properties was possible. However, it appears that Dr. Myers' property at Takow was never bought by Yamashita and that the actual sale price of the Myers property to the Navy Department in 1920, that had been arranged between Baron Inoue and Acting Consul Butler, was ¥100,000, then equivalent to some £16,000. Myers was retiring from his position as Consular Agent at Pagoda Island in March 1920 in order live again in England and needed the issue resolved before his departure from China. Yet, sadly, Myers was to die at his post on Pagoda Island shortly thereafter on 20 March 1920. [50]

As a result of Butler's urgings, the Office of Works made an inspection of the properties at Takow and agreed that ¥150,000 would be a suitable counter-offer to Baron Inoue for the Takow Consular properties. Upon the advice of the Office of Works, Butler then rejected the Yamashita offer for the Takow properties on the understanding that the Japanese Naval Authorities were prepared to make a higher offer than that of Yamashita. Whereupon, Butler put the counter-offer of ¥150,000 to Baron Inoue, now the senior Naval Officer in Formosa, who agreed to put the offer to Tokyo. Within a week Baron Inoue returned to say that the Navy Department in Tokyo 'had practically agreed' to purchase the British properties at Takow and Anping for ¥180,000 [equivalent to about £26,000], the higher figure allegedly being due to the personal intervention of Baron Den Kenjirō [田健治郎], the newly-appointed Governor-General of Formosa. [51]

Baron Den, the 8th Governor-General of Formosa, was also the first Japanese civilian to hold that post. Appointed in October 1919, Den concentrated his energies on an assimilation policy towards the Taiwanese that centred on the provision of a sound education system. However, during Den's tenure, the power of the Governor-General over appointments and, particularly, military matters ebbed away. This lack of local control over naval matters may well explain the fact that no further action was taken on purchasing the Takow Consular properties during Den's term in office which lasted until September 1923. [52]

In the summer of 1923, the British again considered their options regarding the disposal of the Consular properties in South Formosa. It was resolved that the Anping and Takow Consular sites should simply be offered for sale to the highest bidder, together with that portion of the Cemetery Plot that was not used for actual interments. In other words, all the British Consular properties in South Formosa exclusive of the Foreign Cemetery at Takow were to be sold forthwith. [53]

Any continued validity of the 1919 and 1920 offers for the sites was disregarded, and in

July 1924 the Japanese Government of Formosa made a definite offer ¥78,511.89, subject to Diet [國會] approval, for the British Consular properties in South Formosa, with the exception of the Foreign Cemetery, which would remain leased to the British government in perpetuity free of all taxes or other charges. [54]

Tamsui Consul Gerald Hastings Phipps had some telling words to say about the two Consulates at Anping and Takow. Anping he described as "a half-ruined house in a dead-alive backwater". As for Takow, Phipps considered that "it adds little to British prestige to see large buildings in a state of extreme dilapidation and disrepair, particularly in a busy shipping port such as Takao, pointed out as being the property of His Majesty's Government." [55]

As the Navy Department clearly had no further interest in buying the sites, the Foreign Office had no difficulty in recommending acceptance of the offer made by the Government of Formosa to the British Treasury. The Formosan Government thereupon included the proposed expenditure in the 1925/6 budget to be laid before the forthcoming session of the Diet to be held in September 1925. [56]

Before any final decision was reached, Gerald Phipps was transferred to Honolulu and Eric Henry de Bunsen took over at Tamsui as the Acting British Consul. This necessitated the Office of Works drawing up a new Power of Attorney in favour of Mr. Eric Henry de Bunsen on 7 May 1925, to enable him to complete the transaction on behalf of the British government. [57]

After some minor negotiation over the precise wording of the draft agreement, the Imperial Japanese Government and the British Government reached agreement on 4 December 1925 regarding the sale of the Takow and Anping Consular properties, excluding the Foreign Cemetery, for the sum of ¥78,511.89: the purchaser, the Imperial Japanese Government was represented by Takio Izawa [伊澤 多喜男], the Governor General of Formosa; the vendor, the Commissioner of His Britannic Majesty's Works and Public Buildings, was represented by Eric Henry de Bunsen, the Acting British Consul in Tamsui (see Image 6-7). [58]

On 6 January 1926, Julius Bradley, the Architect at the Office of Works in Shanghai was able to cable the Office of Works in London to advise of the completion of the sale of the Consular properties at Takow and Anping, and that the purchase money had been paid into the Hong Kong and Shanghai Bank in Yokohama. A later note at the Office of Works records that the British pound sterling equivalent of the sum paid, ¥78,511.89, was £6,974:14s:0d. [59]

The sale on 4 December 1925 to the Japanese Government of the British Consular Properties at Anping and Takow formerly held in the name of the Commissioners of His Britannic Majesty's Works and Public Buildings, with the exception of that portion of the Foreign Cemetery Lot at Takow which is actually used for internments, was duly registered at the Local Court of Tainan. [60]

In Remembrance
後記

　　這場買賣成立之後，在南臺灣屬於英國政府的物業只剩下老外國人墓園，它被一座牆所圍起，裡面長眠著傳教士、海關職員、商人、海員水手，以及瑪麗·唐納桑，領事霍必瀾的夫人。只有這塊墓園還註冊在大英工部與公共建築物委員的名下。[61]

　　蒲特尼·畢格婁〔Poultney Bigelow〕，一位美國記者與作家〔譯注：其父為紐約時報創辦人〕，寫了一篇他在1920年代造訪南臺灣的文章，或許為英國領事館在福爾摩沙南部的歲月，提供了最能喚起回憶的墓誌銘：

　　在安平，當我們凝視著被遺忘在時光之流裡的大英帝國領事館，訝異著門廊的石獅與獨角獸怎麼沒有被正統的觀光客偷走。還有另一個被遺棄的領事館在打狗，這兩處地方分別訴說著當商賈也身兼探險家的昔時美好歲月，或者當約翰牛〔John Bull，譯注：代表擬人化的英國或英格蘭，有如山姆大叔代表美國〕的影響力甚至深入福爾摩沙叢林時。從東方的眼光來看，石獅與獨角獸不應有損尊嚴地被棄置在那裡，因為這些有趣與手法巧妙的紋章，具體表現了一個偉大政府的高貴威嚴；因為如此，這些紋章值得每天的照顧。謹向日本警察，尤其要向福爾摩沙島上的華人致上敬意，他們小心看護，不讓這些外國人的物業受破壞損傷。時至如今，它們應該已經被日本政府買下，飄揚著旭日高升的大日本〔Dai Nippon〕國旗。[62]

§

All that now remained of the British properties in South Formosa was the old Foreign Cemetery, enclosed by a wall and containing the remains of missionaries, customs officers, traders, seafarers, and Mary Donnithorne Warren, the wife of Consul Warren. This cemetery alone remained registered in the name of the Commissioners of His Majesty's Office of Works and Public Buildings. [61]

Poultney Bigelow, the American journalist and author, writing of a visit he made to South Formosa in the 1920s, provides perhaps the most evocative epitaph to the days of the British consulate in South Formosa:

At Amping we gazed on the neglected Consulate of Great Britain and marvelled that no orthodox tourist had stolen the lion and unicorn from over the doorway. There's another abandonned Consulate in Takao, each speaking of the good old days when merchants were adventurers and when the long arm of John Bull reached even into the Formosan jungle. From the Oriental point of view, the lion and unicorn should not remain exposed to indignity, for these interesting and acrobatic bits of heraldry embody the majesty of a great government; and, as such, deserve daily care. All honour, therefore, to the Japanese police and above all to the Chinese Formosans who see that no harm come to these alien properties. By this time they have probably been purchased and fly the sun-burst of Dai Nippon. [62]

Notes to Chapter Six
第六章註解

1. Ruxton, Ian (Ed), The Correspondence of
   Sir Ernest Satow, British Minister in Japan,
   1895-1900, Lulu Press Inc., 2005, Vol. 1, p. 4,
   Kimberley to Satow, 25 June 1895; Ruxton, Vol.
   1, p. 301, Satow to Enslie, 16 March 1896.

2. WORK 10/33/10, Satow to Kimberley, 25
   March 1896; WORK 10/33/10, Marshall
   to O.W.L., 8 April 1896; Ruxton, Vol. 1, p.
   301, Satow to Enslie, 16 March 1896.

3. FO 262/735, Longford to Satow, 30 April 1896.

4. FO 262/735, Hurst to Satow, 28
   April 1896, Enclosures 1 & 2.

5. FO 262/735, Hurst to Satow, 28 April 1896,
   Encl. Hurst to Marshall, 7 February 1895.

6. FO 262/735, Longford to Marshall, 9 June 1896.

7. WORK 10/33/10, Satow to Kimberley,
   25 March 1896; WORK 10/33/10,
   Marshall to O.W.L., 8 April 1896.

8. WORK 10/33/10, F.O. to O.W.L., 7 May 1896;
   WORK 10/33/10, Boyce Memo at O.W.L., 8 May
   1896; WORK 10/33/10, Boyce to F.O., 26 May 1896;
   Ruxton, p. 37, Marshall to Satow, 22 July 1896;
   Ruxton, p. 484, Longford to Satow, 2 January 1897.

9. The modified Decauville tramways used in Taiwan,
   known as daisha in Japanese, were pushed along
   the light railway by labourers and thus also known
   as push-car railways; see Knapp, Ronald G., Push
   Car Railways and Taiwan's Development, Chapter
   10 in China's Island Frontier, SMC Publishing Inc,
   Taipei, 1980; Hurst, R. W., Report for the Year 1895
   on the Trade of Tainan, H.M.S.O., London, p. 8.

10. WORK 10/33/10, Marshall to O.W.L.,
    30 November 1896; Ruxton, pp.250-

11. Will of Francis Julian Marshall; 1861 England
    Census returns, RG 9/788, Folio 54, Page 47; G.R.O.
    Deaths, Margaret Marshall died aged 49, registered
    4th Quarter 1881 at Camberwell Volume 1d, page
    477; 1915 National Probate Calendar, p. 152, Francis
    Julian Marshall died at The Bolton Mansions
    Hotel, South Kensington, on 16 December 1914.

12. Ruxton, pp.484-486 (Longford to Satow, 2 January
    1897); FO 262/773, Kenny to Satow, 6 February
    1897; FO 262/773, Kenny to Satow, 9 February 1897.

13. William Cowan, born c1855 in Scotland, for title
    see Post Office Directory for London, 1899; WORK
    10/33/10, Boyce to Cowan, 8 January 1897; WORK
    10/33/10, Cowan to O.W.L., 23 February 1897.

14. Yacul, also known as Yakal or Yacal, is a termite-
    resistant wood from South East Asia, Shorea obtusa;
    WORK 10/33/10, Cowan to O.W.L., 25 June 1897.

15. WORK 10/33/10, Boyce to Cowan, 13 August 1897.

16. WORK 10/33/10, Cowan to O.W.L., 22 April
    1898; WORK 10/33/10, Boyce to Cowan, 21 June
    1898; Griffiths E. A., Report on the Trade of the
    Consular District of Tainan (South Formosa) for
    the Year 1898, H.M.S.O., London, pp. 11-12; Hayase,
    Yukiko, The Career of Goto Shinpei, Japan's
    Statesman of Research, 1857-1929, Dissertation
    for PhD, Florida State University, 1974, pp. 40-41.

17. FO 262/794, Griffiths to Satow, 10 September 1898;
    FO 678/3157, Simpson to Griffiths, 14 October 1899.

18. WORK 10/56/6, Reports on Legation and Consular
    buildings in China, Korea, Japan and Siam by R. H.
    Boyce, CB, 1899-1900; and China Directory, 1899.

19. The Government-General of Formosa

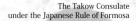
Bureau of Communications, The Climate, Typhoons, and Earthquakes of the Island of Formosa (Taiwan), Taihoku Meteorological Observatory, Taihoku, 1914, p. 65.

20. FO 678/3157, Simpson to Griffiths, 14 October 1899; FO 678/3157, Griffiths to Simpson, 23 October 1899.

21. FO 678/3157, Contract between Office of Works and Chun Sai, 16 January 1900; The amount of 6,208 Gold Yen was then equivalent to about 6,600 Mexican dollars, or £635; FO 678/3157, Contract between Office of Works and Chun Sai, 16 January 1900; FO 678/3157, Memo by Kenny, 16 January 1900.

22. WORK 10/33/10, Cowan to O.W.L., 8 February 1900; FO 678/3157, Contract for Services of Mr R. J. Hastings, 7 January 1900.

23. 1842 Birth Certificate, Lincoln No. 107, for Robert John Hastings; G.R.O. 1840 Marriage Certificate, Southwell, Nottinghamshire, No. 62, Hastings – Wadeson (parents), gives father's profession as 'Tea Dealer'; 1841 England Census returns for St. Martin's Parish, Lincoln, shows John Hastings as a Tea Dealer from Scotland, HO 107/651, Book 9, Folio 55, Page 14; Hastings' I.M.C. Records; Davidson, James W., The Island of Formosa Past and Present, Kelly & Walsh, Hong Kong, 1903 (Repr. by SMC Publishing Inc., 1992), p. 177; FO 678/3024; FO 763/5; 1895 Marriage Certificate, Anping Office of Tainan Consulate, Robert John Hastings and Huang Yün-kuan, annotated 'a previous marriage lex loci alleged to have taken place in 1871'; 1912 Death Certificate for Robert John Hastings (registered at Tamsui Consulate No. 35), died 11 December 1912, Anping.

24. FO 678/3158.

25. Shorea obtusa, also known as Yacul or Yakal; see also WORK 10/33/10, Memo, Simpson, 12 February 1901; FO 678/3158.

26. WORK 10/33/10, Boyce to Cowan, 13 August 1897; FO 678/3157, Griffiths to Simpson, 23 October 1899; FO 678/3158.

27. FO 262/735, Hurst to Marshall, 7 February 1895; FO 678/3158.

28. WORK 10/33/10, Simpson to O.W.L., 12 February 1901; see also Contract of Chun Sai in FO 678/3157.

29. FO 262/856, Kenny to MacDonald, 21 February 1901; Ruxton, pp. 250-252 (Bonar to Satow, 8 October 1896); FO 262/856, Kenny to MacDonald, 1 April 1901; Lo & Bryant, pp. 322-23.

30. FO 678/3160; In 1901 the value of the Japanese Silver Yen and the Gold Yen were the same, thus the amount was equivalent to about 2,165 Mexican dollars or £210; FO 262/939, Wileman to MacDonald, Tainan 24, 10 November 1905.

31. Kenny, W. J., Report on the Trade of the Consular District of Tainan (South Formosa) for the Year 1899, H.M.S.O., London, pp. 17-18; Griffiths E. A., Report on the Trade of the Consular District of Tainan (South Formosa) for the Years 1900-01, H.M.S.O., London; and Griffiths E. A., Supplementary Report on the Trade of the Consular District of Tainan (South Formosa) for the Year 1901, H.M.S.O., London, p. 9. See also FO 262/919, Wileman to MacDonald, Tainan 29, 2 November 1904, which details Consul Wileman's trips and rail fares from Anping to Takow.

32. Alfred Ernest Wileman, born 1860, Uttoxeter, Staffordshire; From 1900 to 1910, the number of foreign firms remained fairly constant at 4 companies, employing a total of about

8 foreign merchants; however, there were usually about 16 members of the Presbyterian Mission in the district for each year.

33. FO 262/919, Wileman to MacDonald, 13 August 1904; FO 262/958, Wileman to MacDonald, 5 September 1906.

34. Cecil John William Simpson, born 1867. In 1897 he was appointed as assistant in the Office of Works, and in 1906 he was posted to Shanghai as Architect to H. M. Office of Works Far Eastern Division. While based there he was admitted LRIBA on 20 March 1911 his proposer being the Chief Architect Sir Henry Tanner. He had returned to the Westminster Office of Works by 1914 when he replaced William Thomas Oldrieve as architect in the charge at the Edinburgh office, remaining there until 1922 when he was succeeded by John Wilson Paterson. [Source: Dictionary of Scottish Architects; 1881 UK Census]. China Directory 1907 gives "K. Watanabe" as Writer.

35. Takekoshi, Yosaburo, Japanese Rule in Formosa, Longmans, Green & Co., London, 1907 (Reprinted by SMC Publishing Inc., Taipei, 1996), pp. 117-132; Davidson, p. 253; Takekoshi, pp. 125-132; Hayase, pp. 75-78; see also FO 678/3156.

36. Hayase, pp. 75-78; FO 262/939, Wileman to MacDonald, Tainan 22, 26 October 1905; WORK 10/210, FO 678/3184.

37. FO 678/3113, Firth to Foreign Residents, 18 July 1907; Alfred Richard Firth, b.1875, Norfolk, England; FO 678/3156; WORK 10/210, Royds to Ashmead, 2 September 1909.

38. FO 262/773, Kenny to Satow, 6 February 1897; WORK 10/210, Wileman to Bain & Co, 25 June 1908; Bain & Co to Wileman, 26 June 1908.

39. China Directories, 1900 to 1914; FO 262/958, Wileman to MacDonald, 25 April 1906.

40. Wileman, A. E., Report on the Trade of the Consular District of Tainan (South Formosa) for the Year 1908, H.M.S.O., London, pp. 13-15.

41. FO 262/1041, Royds to MacDonald, 1 May 1909; Royds, W. M., Report on the Trade of the Consular District of Tainan (South Formosa) for the Year 1909, H.M.S.O., London, p. 10; FO 262/1041, Royds to MacDonald, 29 November 1909; FO 262/1041, Royds to MacDonald, 29 November 1909 (enclosure); FO 262/1041, Royds to MacDonald, 23 December 1909; FO 262/1059, Arthur to Royds, 1 March 1910.

42. FO 262/1059, MacDonald to Firth, 19 May 1910.

43. FO 262/1059, Firth to MacDonald, 11 April 1910.

44. FO 262/1293, Harrington to Greene, 14 February 1917.

45. FO 262/1293, Harrington to Greene, 14 February 1917.

46. FO 262/1293, Harrington to Greene, 14 February 1917.

47. FO 262/1293, Harrington to Greene, 10 May 1917; FO 262/1293, Harrington to Greene, 5 September 1917.

48. Akashi died on 26 October 1919 while still serving on Formosa and is buried at Fuyin Mountain Christian Cemetery in Sanchih Township, Taipei County [臺北縣三芝鄉福音山]; FO 262/1409, Harrington to Greene, 7 February 1919.

49. FO 262/1409, Alston to Butler, 29 November 1919.

50. FO 262/1409, Butler to Alston, 14 October 1919; WORK 10/33/10, FO to O.W.L., 6 December

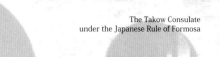

1923; WORK 10/33/10, Phipps to Eliot, 24 April 1924; WORK 10/33/10, O.W.L. to Treasury, 2 September 1924; see Bank of Japan, Statistics Department, Hundred-year Statistics of the Japanese Economy (Tokyo: Bank of Japan 1966), pp. 318-321; FO 262/1409, Butler to Alston, 20 October 1919; FO 262/1450, Butler to Alston, 21 February 1920; Lo & Bryant, pp. 322-323.

51. FO262/1450, Butler to Alston, 12 January 1920; FO 262/1409, Butler to Alston, 14 October 1919; FO262/1450, Butler to Alston, 12 January 1920; WORK 10/33/10, FO to O.W.L., 6 December 1923; WORK 10/33/10, Phipps to Eliot, 24 April 1924; WORK 10/33/10, O.W.L. to Treasury, 2 September 1924; FO 262/1450, Butler to Alston, 20 February 1920 (The equivalent figure of about £26,000 is given by Butler in his February 1920 despatch to Tokyo).

52. Lamley, Harry J., Taiwan Under Japanese Rule, 1895-1945: The Vicissitudes of Colonialism, in Rubinstein, Murray A.(Ed.), Taiwan a New History, M. E. Sharpe, New York, 1998, pp. 221-223.

53. WORK 10/33/10, Phipps to Pailaret, 24 July 1923; WORK 10/33/10, O.W.L. Minute of 26 October 1923; WORK 10/33/10, Phipps to Eliot, 9 July 1924.

54. WORK 10/33/10, O.W.L. Minute, 10 October 1923; WORK 10/33/10, Phipps to Eliot, 9 July 1924.

55. WORK 10/33/10, Phipps to Eliot, 9 July 1924.

56. WORK 10/33/10, FO to O.W.L., 25 August 1924; WORK 10/33/10, Treasury to O.W.L., 6 September 1924; WORKS 10-33/10, Phipps to Eliot, 3 November 1924.

57. WORKS 10-33/10, Roberts to O.W.L., Telegram, 15 April 1925; WORKS 10-33/10, FO to O.W.L.,

23 April 1925; WORKS 10-33/10, Treasury Solicitor to O.W.L., Minute, 8 May 1925.

58. WORKS 10/33-10, Translation of Agreement of Sale, 4 December 1925.

59. WORK 10/33/10, Bradley to O.W.L., Telegram, 6 January 1926; WORKS 10-33/10, Note in O.W.L. file, 4 June 1926; In 2013 sterling values, £6,974:14s:0d would be approximately equivalent to £365,000, according to the UK Office of National Statistics data.

60. WORKS 10-33/10, de Bunsen to Dormer, 4 February 1926.

61. WORKS 10-33/10, de Bunsen, Memorandum dated 5 February 1926.

62. Bigelow, Poultney, Japan and her Colonies, being extracts from a diary made whilst visiting Formosa, Manchuria, Shantung, Korea and Saghalin in the year 1921, E. Arnold & Co., London, 1923, p. 119.

重建補述

*Reconstruction
of British Consulate
at Takow*

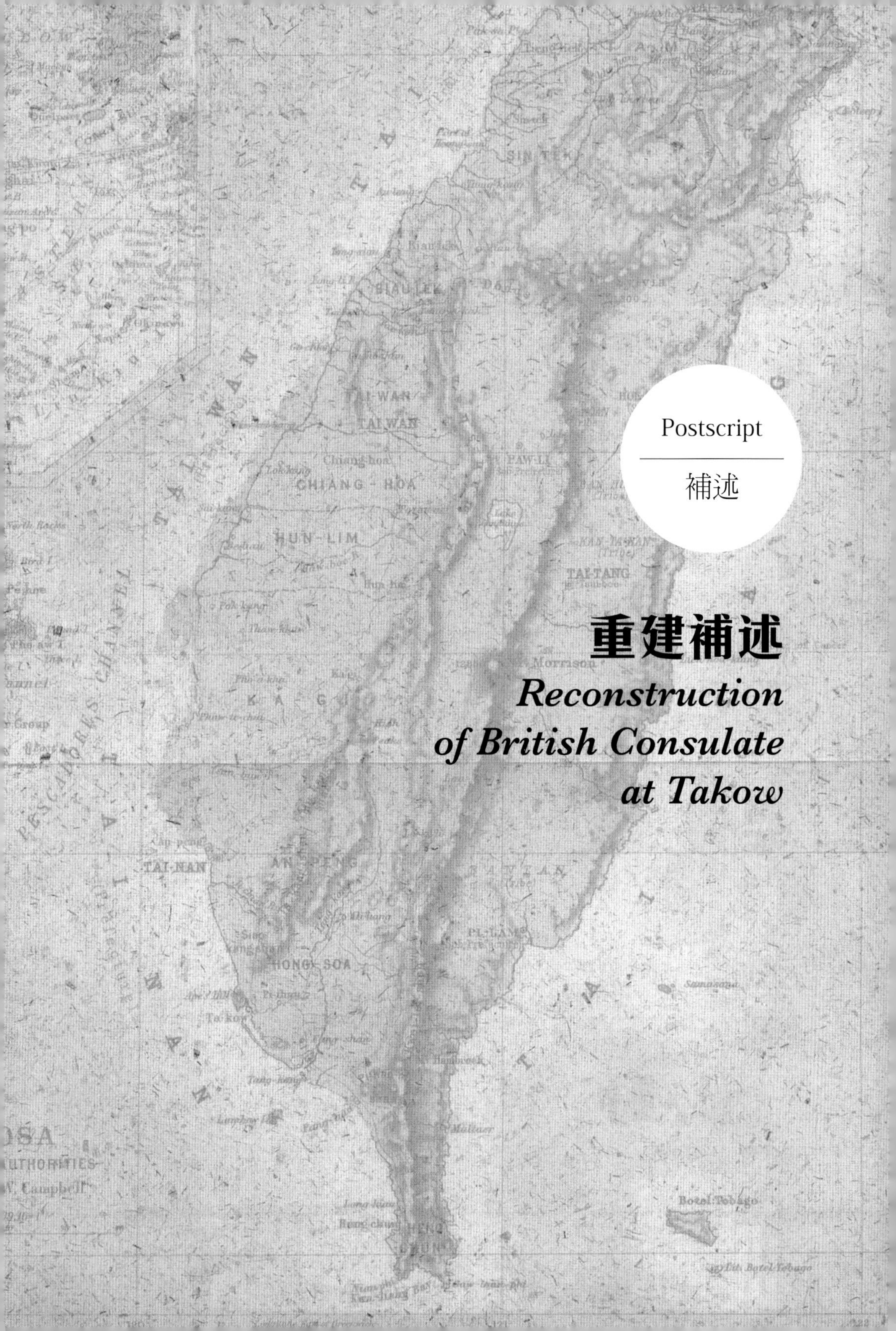

當然,在被日本收購之後,關於英國領事館的故事並未就此結束。

如前章所示,官邸、領事辦公處,以及部份尚未使用的墓園土地在1925年12月4日被賣給日本政府。1929年,日本政府將打狗英國領事館官邸改設爲臺灣總督府高雄海洋觀測所,二樓爲大辦公室、預報室、值班休息室、三間眷舍,底層爲氣壓室、地震室、庫房、廚房等。1946年國民政府接收,定名爲臺灣省氣象局高雄測候所,1973年5月,因地點位於山坡上,其觀測資料無法代表高雄氣候特性,遂遷移至前鎮而成閒置狀態。多年來因房舍老舊疏於維護,1977年賽洛瑪颱風後處處斷垣殘壁,直至1985年高雄市政府著手修復,完成後闢爲高雄史蹟文物陳列館,1987年4月由內政部公告爲二級古蹟。2003年起,透過民間企業共同參與維護,以文化資產活化再利用形

式展現,成爲民眾造訪休閒的文化歷史空間。

而山下的打狗英國領事館辦公室,則因日本治臺後開始注意水產開發的重要性,於1932年設立高雄州水產試驗場,主要從事罐頭製造的實驗,1939年改稱臺灣總督府水產試驗場高雄支場,增加水產皮革之試驗研究,以充實戰時之皮革資源。二戰後國民政府接收臺灣,1950年6月定名臺灣省水產試驗所高雄分所,主要任務爲研究水產加工,提高其經濟價值。直至1976年,因辦公空間不敷使用遷至前鎮,原址則成爲該所的員工宿舍,迄2004年員工全數搬離,於2005年高雄市政府公告爲市定古蹟。而連接山上官邸與山下辦公室的步道,多年來石階被次生植物淹沒封閉,也於同年公告爲市定古蹟。

修復前的打狗英國領事官邸

打狗英國領事館的發展歷程，因為政權及產權的多次轉移，加以史料的不足，長期以來多被曲解，近年經學界詳查英國國家檔案局資料，逐步梳理釐清全貌。2009年7月，高雄市政府文化局將哨船頭山上數十年來被誤認為「打狗英國領事館」的洋樓，正名為「打狗英國領事官邸」，山下原水產試驗所建築物，正名為「打狗英國領事館」，以還原史實，同時開始進行領事館及古道之修復，與山上官邸整合為文化園區，為臺灣唯一完整呈現英國領事館官邸、古道、辦公室之重要古蹟群落，深具文化意涵。

打狗英國領事館見證了打狗開港後世界海洋經貿發展歷程，不僅體現臺灣在19世紀末全球化時代躍上世界舞臺的過程，更歷經高雄開港深刻的洗禮，迄今成為高雄市知名文化觀光景點之一。在此重要歷史場域重現開放之際，回首來時路，臺灣第一個領事館屹立打狗港的文化故事，正以新生的姿態接續下去。

高雄市政府文化局

臺灣省水產試驗所高雄分所時期

水產試驗所修復前

登山古道修復前

打狗英國領事官邸修復後

Sources and Bibliography
參考資料

Primary Sources
主要資料來源

The National Archives, London
The Archives contain a vast collection of British Government documents. The following are referred to in the footnotes to the text by their department codes: FO refers to records created and inherited by the Foreign Office, 1567-2004; MPK refers to maps and plans extracted to flat storage from records of the Foreign Office, early 18th century-1966; and WORK refers to the records of the successive works departments, and of the Ancient Monuments Boards and Inspectorate 1609-2002.

Particular use has been made of the following FO series: FO 17 which contains General Correspondence between the Foreign Office and the Legation in China, 1815-1905; FO 228, containing General Correspondence between the Consulates and Legation in China, 1834-1930; FO 262, containing General Correspondence between the Embassy and Consulates in Japan, 1859-1972; and FO 678, containing Deeds from various Consulates in China, 1837-1959.

The China Directories
The China Directories, as available, have also provided much information. The Special Collections Library of the University of Hong Kong holds many of these annual directories, which vary in actual title. The directories provide listings of foreign companies and individuals for Takow/Takao and Taiwan/Tainan, covering most of the years from 1864 to 1926.

Annual Trade Returns and Reports
Maritime Customs Annual Returns and Reports of Taiwan, 1867 – 1895 [清末台灣海關歷年資料]. 2 vols. Institute of Taiwan History Preparatory Office, Academia Sinica, Taipei, 1997.

Annual Reports on the Trade of South Formosa, 1887-1909; Reprinted by Ch'eng Wen Publishing Company [成文出版社有限公司], Taipei, 1972.

Jardine Matheson Archives
Jardine Matheson Archives B8/6/12 & 14, reprinted in the Kaohsiung Historiographical Journal, Vol 6, Issue 3 [高市文獻第6卷第3期] pp. 17-21.

Ching Dynasty Official Titles
European and Chinese official titles from the late Ching period under study have been taken from W. F. Mayers' The Chinese Government: A Manual of Chinese Titles. The original edition was printed in 1877 and revised for an 1897 edition by G. M. H. Playfair (see full title below).

Sundry Data (Tertiary Source)
A resource that has proven extremely useful in researching this period has been Wikipedia, The Free Encyclopedia. However, Wikipedia has not been relied upon as a primary source but only used for background information, as a reference for correct terminology and search terms, and as a starting point for further research. That said, the author highly commends the use of Wikipedia as a major on-line aid to research. The English language site can be found at http://en.wikipedia.org/, and both Simplified and Traditional Chinese language versions can be found at http://zh.wikipedia.org/.

Bibliography and Other Sources
傳記與其他來源

Aalsvoort, Lambert van der [蘭伯特]; 風中之葉：福爾摩沙見聞錄 [Leaf in the Wind: A history of Taiwan through Western eyes]; 經典雜誌, 台北市, 民91 [Tzu Chi Culture and Communications Foundation, Taipei, 2002]

Anderson, Lindsay (Capt.); A Cruise in an Opium Clipper; T F Unwin, London, 1891. [Reprinted by Ibex, Melbourne, 1989]

Bard, Solomon; Traders of Hong Kong: Some Foreign Merchant Houses, 1841-1899; Urban Council, Hong Kong, 1993.

Beazeley, Michael; Notes of an Overland Journey through the southern part of Formosa, from Takow to the South Cape, in 1875, with an Introductory Sketch of the Island; Proceedings of the Royal Geographical Society and Monthly Record of Geography, New Series 7; January 1885: pp. 1-23.

Bigelow, Poultney; Japan and her Colonies, being extracts from a diary made whilst visiting Formosa, Manchuria, Shantung, Korea and Saghalin in the year 1921; E. Arnold & Co., London, 1923.

Campbell, Rev. William; Handbook of South Formosa Mission [台南教士會議事錄]; Taiwan Church Press [台灣教會公報社], 2004.

Carrington, George W.; Foreigners in Formosa 1841-1874; Chinese Materials Center Inc., San Francisco, 1977.

Coates, Patrick D.; The China Consuls: British consular officers, 1843-1943; Oxford University Press, Hong Kong, 1988.

Collingwood, Cuthbert.; Rambles of a naturalist on the shores and waters of the China Sea: Being observations in natural history during a voyage to China, Formosa, Borneo, Singapore, etc., made in Her Majesty's vessels in 1866 and 1867; John Murray, London, 1868.

Crisswell, Colin N.; The Taipans: Hong Kong's Merchant Princes; Oxford University Press, Hong Kong, 1981.
Davidson, James W.; The Island of Formosa Past and Present; Kelly & Walsh Ltd, Hong Kong, 1903. Reprinted by SMC Publishing Inc., Taipei, 1988.

Darwent, Rev. C. E.; Shanghai: A Handbook for Travellers and Residents to the Chief Objects of Interest in and around the Foreign Settlements and Native City; Kelly & Walsh Ltd., Shanghai, 1920.

Dodd, John; Journal of a Blockaded Resident in North Formosa 1884-1885; Daily Press Office, Hongkong, 1888. [Reprinted by Ch'eng Wen Publishing, Taipei, 1972].

Dudbridge, Glen [ed.]; Aborigines of South Taiwan in the 1880s: Papers by the South Cape Lightkeeper George Taylor; SMC Publishing Inc., Taipei, 1999.

Eskildsen, Robert [ed.]; Foreign Adventurers and the Aborigines of Southern Taiwan, 1867-1874; Academia Sinica, Taipei, 2005.

Fairbank, John K., and Reischauer, Edwin O.; China: Tradition & Transformation; Houghton Mifflin Company, Boston, 1989.

Fernandez, Fr. Pablo; One Hundred Years of Dominican Apostolate in Formosa 1859-1958; University of Santo Tomas, Manila, 1959. Reprinted by SMC Publishing Inc., Taipei, 1994.

Gratton, F. M.; Freeemasonry in Shanghai and Northern China; Shanghai, 1900 (Reprinted by Ch'eng Wen Publishing Co, Taipei, 1971).

Griffin, Eldon; Clippers and Consuls, American Consular and Commercial Relations with Eastern Asia, 1845 – 1860; Edwards Brothers Inc., Ann Arbor, Michigan, 1938. Republished by Ch'eng Wen Publishing Co., Taipei, 1972.

Hall, Peter; 150 Years of Cricket in Hong Kong; The Book Guild Ltd, Lewes, Sussex; 1999.

Hayase, Yukiko; The Career of Goto Shinpei, Japan's Statesman of Research, 1857-1929; Dissertation for PhD; Florida State University, 1974.

Hibbert, Christopher; The Dragon Wakes: China and the West, 1793-1911; Longman Group Ltd., London, 1970.

Hoe, Susannah; Women at the Siege, Peking 1900; The Women's History Press, Oxford, 2000.

Hughes, Mrs Thomas Francis [Julia]; Among the Sons of Han, Notes of a Six Years' Residence in Various Parts of China and Formosa; Tinsley Bros., London, 1881.

Huang Hsiao-ping [黃小平]; The Conflict between Liu Ao & Liu Ming-ch'uan and the Sino-French War in Taiwan; pp.288-276 in the Bulletin of Historical Research, No1. January, 1973 [師大歷史學報：第一期 中華民國62年元月出版].

Hung, Chien-chao; A History of Taiwan; Il Cerchio Iniziative Editoriali,Rimini, 2000.

Izumida, H., British Consular and Legation Buildings in East Asia Part I, Journal of the Society of Architectural Historians of Japan, Vol. 15, pp.93-104, 1990.

Izumida, H., British Consular and Legation Buildings in East Asia Part II, Journal of the Society of Architectural Historians of Japan, Vol. 16, pp.78-91, 1991.

King, Anthony D., The Bungalow: The Production of a Global Culture; Routledge & Kegan Paul; London, 1984.

Knapp, Ronald G.[Ed.]; China's Island Frontier; SMC Publishing Inc, Taipei, 1980.

Lamley, Harry J.; Taiwan Under Japanese Rule, 1895-1945: The Vicissitudes of Colonialism; in Rubinstein, Murray A.(Ed.); Taiwan a New History; M. E. Sharpe, New York, 1998. Pp.201-260.

Lamley, Harry J.; The 1895 Taiwan Republic: A Significant Episode in Modern Chinese History; Journal of Asian Studies, 27:4(Aug. 1968), pp.739-762.

Landsborough, David; The Development of Scientific Medicine and its Impact on Society in Taiwan, 1865 to 1945; unpublished paper.

Lo Hui-min [ed.], The Correspondence of G. E. Morrison, Vol. 2, 1912-1920, Cambridge University Press, Cambridge, England, 1978.

Lo Hui-min and Bryant H., British Diplomatic and Consular Establishments in China: 1793-1949, SMC Publishing Inc., Taipei, 1988, Vol.2.

Manson-Bahr, Philip; Patrick Manson; Thomas Nelson, Edinburgh, 1962.

Mayers, William Frederick; The Chinese Government: A Manual of Chinese Titles, Categorically Arranged and Explained, with an Appendix; Kelly & Walsh, Shanghai 1897. (Reprinted by Ch'eng-Wen Publishing C., Taipei, 1970).

Morse, Hosea B.; The Trade and Administration of the Chinese Empire; Kelly & Walsh, Shanghai, 1908.

Oakley, David [李夢哲]; The Foreign Cemetery at Kaohsiung [座落於高雄的外國墓園]; Taiwan Historica, Vol. 5, Issue 3, September 2005, pp.265-295 [臺灣文獻 卷期56:3 民94.09頁265-295].

Otness, Harold M.; One Thousand Westerners in Taiwan, to 1945; A Biographical and Bibliographical Dictionary; Academia Sinica, Taipei, 1999.

Pelcovits, Nathan A.; Old China Hands and the Foreign Office; Octagon Books, New York, 1969.

Pickering, William A.; Pioneering in Formosa: Recollections of Adventures among Mandarins, Wreckers & Head-hunting Savages; Hurst & Brackett Ltd, London, 1898. Reprinted by SMC Publishing Inc., Taipei, 1993.

Rouil, Christophe; Formose, Des Batailles Presque Oubliees …; Les Editions du Pigeonnier, Taiwan, 2001.

Ruxton, Ian (Ed); The Correspondence of Sir Ernest Satow, British Minister in Japan, 1895-1900; Lulu Press Inc., 2005.

Smithers, A. J., Honourable Conquests: An account of the enduring work of the Royal Engineers throughout the Empire, Leo Cooper, London, 1991.

Takekoshi, Yosaburo; Japanese Rule in Formosa; Longmans, Green & Co., London, 1907. Reprinted by SMC Publishing Inc., Taipei, 1996.

Yeh, Chen-hui [葉振輝]; The opening of Formosa to foreign commerce [清季臺灣開埠之 究]; Taipei, 1985.

Yen, Sophia Su-fei; Taiwan in China's Foreign Relations 1836-1874; Hamden, Connecticut: The Shoe String Press, Inc., (1965).

Glossary of Names
中英譯名對照

[H] signals Hokkien pronunciation using Campbell.
[J] signals Japanese pronunciation using modified Hepburn.

English & Japanese Terms 英日文原名	Traditional Rendering 古譯	Modern Rendering 今譯
Adkins, Thomas	雅公瑪	艾勒勤，湯瑪斯
Akitsushima (I.J.N.)	秋津州	秋津州
Alabaster, Chaloner	阿查利	阿拉巴士德，歐隆那
Alborado, Antonio	阿不拉多	阿不拉多，安東尼歐
Alcock, Sir Rutherford	阿禮國	阿禮國，拉塞福爵士
Allen, Herbert James	阿赫伯	艾倫，赫伯特，詹姆斯
Alston, Beilby		亞斯頓，拜比
Anderson, Lindsay		安德森，林賽
Amoy	廈門	廈門
An-hai Street	安海街	
Anglo-Japanese Treaty of Amity and Commerce	日英修好通商条約	日英修好通商條約
Anping	安平	
Anping Fort [Eternal Golden Castle]	億載金城	安平礮堡或億載金城
Ape's Hill	猴山	壽山、柴山
Arthur, Harry Walter	阿圖	亞瑟，亨利·瓦特
Assistant Chinese Secretary	漢文副使	助理中文秘書
Assistant Examiner	三等驗貨	助理檢察員
Bain, Allan Weatherhead	邊阿蘭	班，艾倫·威勒赫
Bain & Co	怡記洋行	
Basilica of the Immaculate Conception	聖母無原罪聖殿	
Beauclerk, William Nelthorpe	寶克樂	寶克樂，威廉·尼爾頌
Benares	貝拿勒斯	（鴉片名）
Bigelow, Poultney		畢格婁，蒲特尼
Black Flag Militia	黑旗軍	
Board of Ordnance	軍械部	
Board of Works	大英工部	
Bourne, Frederick Samuel Augustus	班德瑞	班德瑞，斐德烈·撒姆爾·奧古斯都
Boyce, Robert Henry	伯斯	伯斯，羅伯·亨利
Brown & Co	水陸洋行	
Bradley, Julius		布雷德利，朱立阿斯
Braune, George Compigné Parker	布老雲	布勞，喬治·康皮內，帕克
British Consulate	大英國領事館	
British Vice-Consulate	大英國副領事館	
British Minister at Peking (full title)	大英欽差駐劄中華便宜行事大臣	英國駐北京大臣、公使
British Minister at Peking (ordinary title)	駐京大臣	英國駐北京公使
British Legation (at Peking)	大英國公使館	北京英國公使館
British Treasury	大英度支部	英國財政部
Bund	外灘	

Paul Dalrymple Butler		保羅・達林波・巴特勒
Canton	廣東	
Carroll, Charles	賈祿	凱洛，查爾斯
Chabo	蔡查某	
Chang Meng-yuan	張夢元,道臺	張夢元，道台
Chaochow	潮州	
Chargé d'Affaires	署欽差大臣	代理公使
Chefoo (Yentai)	芝罘（煙臺）	
Chefoo Convention	煙臺條約	
Chen Shun-ho	陳順和	
Cheng-kim [H] (Chien-chin)	前金	
Chihou [H: Kī u]	旗後	
Ching dynasty	清朝	
Chinkiang	京江	鎮江
Chō (Prefecture)	廳	
Chōch （Sub-Prefect）	廳長	
Chun Sai	俊司	
Chunam	朱南	
Clarendon, Earl of		克拉林登，伯爵（外相）
Colonial Office (Brit)	藩政院	
Commanding in Chief (British)	總司令	
Commissioner of Customs	稅務司	
Companion of the Order of the Bath (CB)	巴斯勳章	
Consul	領事官	
Consul's Office	領事辦公室	
Consul, Acting	代理領事官	
Consular Agent	代理領事	領事代理人
Consular Assistant	副繙譯官	副翻譯官
Consular Court	領事法庭	
Consular Gaol	領事牢房	
Consular Offices	領事處	
Consular Residence	領事官邸	
Consular Shipping Office	領事船務辦公室	
Cooper, William Marsh	固威林	庫柏，威廉・馬許
Courbet, Amédée Anatole Prosper	孤拔	孤拔，安慕第
Crossman, Major William		克里斯曼，威廉少校
Cuthbert,Collingwood		庫斯伯特，考林伍德
Decauville tramway	臺車	臺車道
Den Kenjiro	田健治郎	
Dent & Co	寶順洋行	顛地洋行
Diet (Japanese Assembly)	國會	
Disraeli, Benjamin		狄士芮利，班傑明（首相）
Donaldson, Charles Melville	唐納森 (ph)	唐納森，查爾斯・梅維爾
Donaldson, Charles Peter McArthur		唐納森，查爾斯・彼得・麥克阿瑟
Dutch Fort at Tamsui	紅毛城	淡水紅毛城
East India Company	東印度公司	
Eighteen Nobles Temple	十八王公廟	
Elles & Co	怡記洋行	

Elles, Jamieson		傑美笙・艾里士
Ever-Victorious Army	常勝軍	
Fengshan (J:Hozan)	鳳山	
Fengshan Magistrate	鳳山縣令	
Fengshan Prefecture	鳳山廳	
Field-Marshal [UK]	元帥	
Foochow	福州	
Foreign Office (British)	外政衙門	
Formosa (Foreigners' name for Taiwan.)	臺灣	
Fraser, Hugh	傅磊斯	傅磊斯・修
Fraser, Michie Forbes Anderson		傅磊斯・米其・富比士・安德森
Frater, Alexander	費里德	費里德・亞歷山大
Freshwater Creek	打水灣	
Firth, Alfred Richard		佛斯・阿佛列・理察
Fuchien (Province)	福建(省)	
Futai (Governor)	撫台（巡撫）	
Gibson, John	吉必勳	吉必勳・約翰
Gordon, Charles George	戈登	戈登・查爾斯・喬治將軍
Granville, Earl		格蘭維爾・伯爵（外相）
Green Island Cement	青洲英泥公司	青州水泥公司
Greene, William Conyngham		格林・威廉・康尼罕
Gregory, William	額勒格里	格里哥利・威廉
Griffiths, Ernest Alfred		格里菲斯・恩尼斯特・阿佛列
Grosvenor, Thomas George	格維納	葛羅斯維爾・湯瑪斯・喬治
Haikuan	閩海關	海關（台語發音）
Hai-tou-she	海頭社	
Hamasen	哈瑪星	
Hankow	漢口	
Harbour, Inner	內港	
Harbour, Outer	外港	
Hastings, Robert John	希士頓	海斯汀・羅伯・約翰
Hausser, Pierre Frederick	赫思義	赫思義・皮耶・斐德烈
Heilungkiang	黑龍江	
Hengch'un (J: Koshun)	恆春	
Hewlett, Archer Rotch	有雅芝	修雷特・亞契・羅區
Hobson, Herbert Edgar	好博遜	霍布森・赫伯特・艾德加
Holland, William	何藍田	賀蘭・威廉
Holt, Henry Frederic William	何爲霖	赫特・亨利・斐德烈・威廉
Holy Rosary Cathedral	玫瑰聖母聖殿主教座堂	
Howard, Captain H F		霍華・船長
Hozan [J]	鳳山	
Hsia Hsien-lun	夏獻綸	
Hsiung-chen North Gate	雄鎮北門	
Hsu Chien-hsun, [H] Kho Kiàn-hun	許建勳	
Huang Yun-kuan	黃允官	
Hughes, Thomas Francis	許妥瑪	休斯・湯瑪斯・法蘭西斯
Hunan	湖南	
Hurst, Richard Willett	胡力樹	赫斯特・理察・威勒特

Imperial Maritime Customs (I.M.C.)	海關	大清海關
Inoue	井上	
Interpreter	繙譯官	翻譯官
Jardine Matheson & Co (Jardine Matheson)	怡和洋行	
Kabayama Sukenori	樺山資紀	
Kamsuikiang	鹽水港	
Kaohsiung City	高雄市	
Keelung	基隆	
Kiāu [H] (Chihou)	旗後	
King, Walter Edward	京華坨	金・瓦特・愛德華
Kiukiang	九江	
Kiungchow	瓊州	
Koshun [J]	恆春	
Kwai Kee (the firm of [H] T ng Kúi-ki)	桂記（鄭桂記）	
Lespes, Sébastien Nicolas Joachim	李士卑斯	李士卑斯・塞巴斯丁
Liang Yuan-kuei	梁元桂	
Liangkiau Bay	琅喬灣	
Li Chai	李察	
Li Chao-tang [Tao-t'ai Li]	黎兆棠	（黎道台）
Li Hung-chang	李鴻章	
Ling-a-liau [H]	笭仔寮	笭雅區
Ling Ju-tseng	凌汝曾	
Liu Ao	劉璈	（劉道台）
Liu Cheng-liang	劉成良	
Liu Ming-ch'uan	劉銘傳	（巡撫）
Liu Yung-fu	劉永福	
Longford, Joseph Henry		
Lo Tung-chih	羅東芝	
Lu Fen-lai	盧分來	
Lu Jan-lao	盧然老	
Lu Ta-tu	盧大度	
Lu T'ien-sung	盧天送	
MacDonald, Claude Maxwell	竇納樂	麥克當勞・克勞德・麥斯威爾（大使）
Mannich & Co	東興洋行	
Mannich, Julius		曼尼克・朱立阿斯
Manson, Dr David	萬大衛	梅森醫師・大衛
Manson (David) Memorial Hospital	萬大衛紀念醫院	
Manson, Dr Patrick	萬巴德	梅森醫師・派崔克（爵士）
Marshall, Francis Julian (Officer Ma)	（馬委員）	馬歇爾・法蘭西斯・朱立安
Matsu [Goddess]	媽祖	
Matsushima (I.J.N.)	松島	
Maxwell, Dr James Laidlaw	馬雅各	麥斯威爾醫師，詹姆斯・雷德勞；馬雅各醫師
Maxwell, Dr James Laidlaw (Junior)	馬雅各二世	
McPhail & Co	天利行	天利洋行
Meiji Emperor	明治天皇	
Mexican Silver Dollar (Foreign Eagle)	墨西哥銀元（鷹洋）	
Motojiro Akashi	明石元二郎	（總督）
Myers, Dr William Wykeham	買威令醫生	梅爾醫師・威廉・威克翰

Nagasaki	長崎市	
Newchwang	牛莊	
Ningpo	寧波	
Nogi Maresuke	乃木希典	
O'Brien-Butler, Pierre Essex		歐布萊恩—巴特勒，皮耶‧艾塞克斯
O'Conor, Nicholas Roderick	歐格訥	歐格訥‧尼可拉斯‧羅德瑞克
Office of Works for the Treaty Ports of China & Japan (H.B.M.) Shanghai	大英工部總署	
Oluanpi [H]	鵝鑾鼻	
Opium	鴉片	
Pagoda Island	羅星塔	
Pahsienjao Cemetery	八仙橋公墓	
Parkes, Sir Harry Smith	巴夏禮	派克斯爵士‧亨利‧史密斯（大使）
Patna	巴特那	（鴉片名）
Pedder, William Henry	柏威林	佩德‧威廉‧亨利
Peninsular & Orient Steam Navigation Company	半島東方汽船公司	
Perkins, Bertram Mark Nevill		柏金斯‧柏權‧馬克‧那維爾
Permanent Lease	永久租賃權	
Pescadores	澎湖群島	
Phillips, George	費笠士	費笠士‧喬治
Phipps, Gerald Hastings		菲普斯‧傑拉德‧海斯汀
Pickering, William Alexander	必麒麟	畢格林‧威廉‧亞歷山大
Pidgin English	洋涇濱英語	
Pingtung County	屏東縣	
Playfair, George Macdonald Home	佩福來	佩福來‧喬治‧麥克當勞‧洪
Pro-Consul	代理領事	
Robinet & Co	羅賓奈洋行	
Rooney, Matthew	魯尼	魯尼‧馬修
Rooney, Matthew [alt]	莫澐如（另譯）	魯尼‧馬修
Royds,William Massy		洛伊德‧威廉‧梅西
Russell & Co	旗昌洋行	盧梭洋行
Sainz, Fr. Fernando	郭德剛	聖茨‧佛南度神父
Sand Island (Pescadores)	沙島（澎湖群島）	
Saracen's Head	薩拉森頭	薩拉森山頭
Satow, Sir Ernest Mason	薩道義	薩道義爵士‧恩尼斯特‧馬森
Sea Beach Regulations	海埔海灘章程	
Secretary of State for War [British]	陸軍大臣	英國軍政大臣
Shanghai	上海	
Shao Yu-lien	邵友濂	
Shao-chuan-tou	哨船頭	
Shewan, Tomes & Co	旗昌洋行	
Silva, Polydoro Francisco da	達錫華	錫華‧玻里多羅‧法蘭西斯科‧達；達錫華
Simpson, Cecil John William		辛浦森‧西索‧約翰‧威廉
Sinclair, Charles Anthony	星察理	辛克萊‧查爾斯‧安東尼
South Cape (Oluanpi)	南岬（鵝鑾鼻）	
Spence, William Donald	施本施	史賓賽‧威廉‧唐納德
Spinney, William Franklin	司必立	史賓尼‧威廉‧富蘭克林
Student Interpreter	繙譯學生	學生翻譯官

Sullivan, Thomas	沙利文	蘇利文，湯瑪斯
Sun Kho-kwan	孫可觀	
Sundius, Ambrose John	孫德雅	孫德雅，安布洛斯．約翰
Surveyor-General (HK)	量地官	
Swatow	汕頭	
Swinhoe, Robert	郇和	史溫侯，羅伯
Tainan	臺南（台南）	
Tainan-fu	臺南府	
Taipei	臺北（台北）	
Taiping Rebellion	太平天國之亂	
Tait & Co	德記洋行	
Taiwan	臺灣	臺灣《通用》
Taiwan-foo	臺灣府	
Taiwan Pioneer Land God Temple	開臺福德宮	
Takau-kon	打狗港	
Takio Izawa	伊澤 多喜男	（總督）
Takow	打狗	
Takow Trade Commissioner	旗後通商分局委員	打狗通商分局委員
Tamsui	淡水	
Tao-t'ai (Circuit Intendant)	道臺（巡撫）	
Taylor, William Henry	泰勒	泰勒，威廉，亨利
Tek-pai (Formosan catamaran)	竹排仔	竹筏（閩南語發音）
Tengchow	登州	
Tidewaiter	鈐字手	海關驗貨員
Tien-hou Temple, Chi-hou	天后宮	旗後天后宮
Tientsin	天津	
Tientsin, Treaty of	天津條約	
Tingchai	聽差	
Ting Jih-chang	丁日昌	
Ting Pao	定保	
Tongking	東京	
Treaty of Nanking	南京條約	
Treaty of Shimonoseki [in Chinese: Maguan]	馬關條約	
Treaty of Tientsin	天津條約	
Treaty Port	商埠	
Tso Tsung-t'ang	左宗棠	
Unequal Treaties	不平等條約	
Vice-Consul	副 事官	
Vietnam	越南	
Wade, Thomas Francis	威妥瑪	威德，湯瑪斯，法蘭西斯
Walsham, Sir John	華爾身	華爾深爵士，約翰
Walsham, Percy Romilly	華普	華爾深，柏西．羅密立
Wan, Commandant	萬	萬司令
Wanchin	萬金	
Warren, Pelham Laird	霍必瀾	華倫，佩翰．萊爾德
Warren, Richard Laird	霍李家	華倫，理察．萊爾德
Watters, Thomas	倭安瑪	瓦特士，湯瑪斯
Weiyuan (International Affairs Officer)	委員	國際《外交》事務委員

Wenchow	溫州	
Wileman, Alfred Ernest		威勒曼·阿佛列·恩尼斯特
Woosung Railway	吳淞鐵路	
Wright & Co	喇記洋行	萊特洋行
Writer (Consular)	官方的鈔寫員	書辦·文書
Wuchow		烏圻
Yacal (Yakal, Yacul) [Shorea obtusa]	菲律賓 [南洋櫸木]	
Yamashita Steamship Company	山下汽船株式会社	山下汽船株式會社
Yenshui	鹽水港	
Yokoyama Toraji	橫山 虎次	
Yoshino (I.J.N.)	吉野	
Yuen-ming-yuen Road, Shanghai	圓明園路·上海	
Zelandia (Fort)	熱蘭遮城	
Abbreviations and Acronyms		
Co	Company	
Fr.	Father (priest)	
H.B.M.	Her/His Britannic Majesty	
H.M.S.	Her/His Majesty's Ship (British Royal Navy)	
I.J.N.	Imperial Japanese Navy [大日本帝國海軍]	
£: s: d.	Pounds sterling : shillings : pennies. (pre-decimal)	
O.W.L.	Office of Works, London	
R.E.	Royal Engineers	

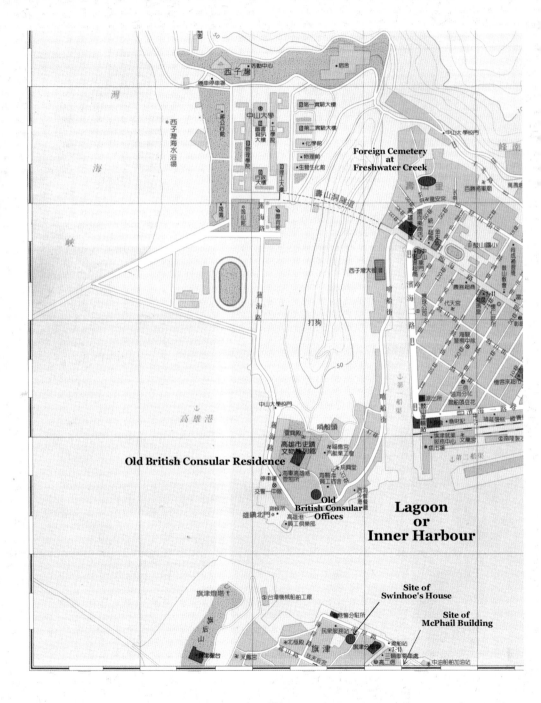

哨船頭與旗後地區現代地圖：
哨船頭與旗後地區現代地圖，顯示書中內文提到的主要地點。
〔地圖來自戶外生活圖書股份有限公司之慷慨授權，版權所有，翻印必究。〕

Modern Map of Shao-chuan-tou and Chihou Area :
Modern Map of Shao-chuan-tou and Chihou Area, showing key sites mentioned in text.
(Map by kind permission of Outdoor Life Books Co Ltd [戶外生活圖書股份有限公司]. All rights reserved)

臺灣第一領事館

洋人、打狗、英國領事館

The Story of the British Consulate at Takow, Formosa

作　　　者｜龔李夢哲（David Charles Oakley）
編　　　譯｜高雄市政府文化局
審　　　訂｜吳密察
出　版　者｜高雄市政府文化局
發　行　人｜史哲
諮 詢 委 員｜吳密察、張守真、謝榮祥、李文環、謝貴文、陳計堯
企 劃 督 導｜劉秀梅、郭添貴、潘政儀、林尚瑛
行 政 企 劃｜蔡潔妞、李旭騏
地　　　址｜802 高雄市苓雅區五福一路67號
電　　　話｜07-2225136　傳　　真｜07-2288814
網　　　址｜www.khcc.gov.tw

編 輯 承 製｜印刻文學生活雜誌出版有限公司
總 編 輯｜初安民
編 輯 企 劃｜田運良、林瑩華
視 覺 設 計｜黃裴文
地　　　址｜235 新北市中和區中正路800號13樓之3
電　　　話｜02-22281626　傳　　真｜02-22281598
網　　　站｜www.sudu.cc

總 經 銷｜成陽出版股份有限公司
電　　　話｜03-3589000　傳　　真｜03-3556521
郵 政 劃 撥｜19000691 成陽出版股份有限公司

國家圖書館出版品預行編目(CIP)資料

臺灣第一領事館：洋人、打狗、英國領事館 /
David Charles Oakley著；高雄市政府文化局編譯.
-- 初版. -- 高雄市：高市文化局, 2013.11
304面；17×23公分
中英對照
ISBN 978-986-03-8525-0（精裝）. --
ISBN 978-986-03-8526-7（平裝）

1.名勝古蹟 2.打狗英國領事館文化園區 3.高雄市

733.9/131.6　　　　　　　　　　102021480

共同出版　高雄市政府文化局　Bureau of Cultural Affairs Kaohsiung City Government　INK 印刻文學生活誌

初版一刷 2013年11月
精裝本 定價800元　ISBN 978-986-03-8525-0　GPN 1010202309
平裝本 定價350元　ISBN 978-986-03-8526-7　GPN 1010202310